Learn Chinese and Realize Your Chinese Dream!

Mandarin Conversation
for
English Speakers

Mingde & Cinanheim Shi

日用汉语短篇会话

明　德
　　　　编
施 辛 安 海

AuthorHouse™
1663 Liberty Drive
Bloomington, IN 47403
www.authorhouse.com
Phone: 1-800-839-8640

First published by AuthorHouse 5/5/2010

ISBN: 978-1-4490-1393-6 (sc)

Printed in the United States of America
Bloomington, Indiana

This book is printed on acid-free paper.

authorHOUSE®

PREFACE

This book is compiled for English speaking people who want to study Mandarin, the modern standard Chinese spoken language. It consists of fifty short passages arranged from easy and simple ones to more difficult ones. It suits elementary to intermediate students. The contents of the passages cover all activities of life, including food, clothing, shelter, transportation, work, and entertainment. According to recent studies, the minimum vocabulary a learner must possess in order to communicate in Chinese is about 1000 words (characters). Altogether this book contains 1096 of the most commonly used words and phrases. If a student learns one passage every week, the book can be finished in a year. After finishing the whole course, the student will possess a firm foundation of Mandarin and be able to communicate with Chinese speaking people on daily topics.

The book is divided into four parts:
1. The Chinese text: The characters used are those currently used in China and are adopted by the Secretariat of the United Nations as the official version of the Chinese language.
2. The phonetic transcripts of the text: The phonetic system used is the Scheme for the Chinese Phonetic Alphabet, adopted by the People's Congress in 1958. As the four tones of Chinese characters are a very important feature in Chinese speech, every sound in the text is marked with a tone number. The number 1, 2, 3, or 4 put after each syllable as a superscript indicates the tone. The phonetic transcripts indicate the real pronunciation after the shift of tones and the modification of sounds in the language environment.
3. The English translation of the text
4. Notes on grammar and usage of the key words and expressions in the text: In addition to comments, many examples are given in this section to help students understand the structures and patterns of the Chinese speech.

The four parts are arranged in side by side columns so that it is easy to refer to each other.

Following each text there is a vocabulary and exercises. The book has five appendixes, Chinese pronunciation, measure words, numerals, time words, and frequently used slang in Beijing dialect, which will help students further grasp the characteristics that distinguish Chinese from other languages.

Our greatest debt of gratitude is to Professor Chin-I Tu, Chairman of Confucius Institute and Chairman of Department of Asian Languages and Cultures, Rutgers University, NJ. and Professor Dietrich Tschanz, Rutgers University, NJ. They carefully reviewed the manuscript and made numerous valuable suggestions for revising and improving the book.

The authors

Abbreviations used in this book:

a., *adj.*	adjective
adv.	adverb
cf.	confer
colloq.	colloquial
conj.	conjunction
eg.	for example
int.	interjection
lit.	literally
meas.	measure word
n.	noun
num.	numeral
opp.	opposite
part.	particle
pl.	plural
pref.	prefix
prep.	preposition
pron.	pronoun
pstp.	postposition
sing.	singular
sb.	somebody
sth.	something
suff.	suffix
v.	verb

目 录 Contents

Text in Chinese Characters	Phonetic Transcripts

一. 你好[1]!

A: 你好!

B: 你好!

A: 请进! 请坐!

B: 谢谢!

A: 喝点儿[2] 什么[3] 吧? 茶、咖啡、

    还是[4] 橙汁儿[5]?

B: 喝杯水[6] 吧.

    ......

    谢谢!

    ......

    我该走了. 再见!

A: 再见!

1. Ni²hao³!

A: Ni²hao³!

B: Ni²hao³!

A: Qing³ jin⁴! Qing³ zuo⁴!

B: Xie⁴xie!

A: He¹ diar³ shen²me ba? Cha², ka¹fei¹,

    hai²shi cheng²zhər¹?

B: He¹ bei¹ shui³ ba.
    ......
    Xie⁴xie!
    ......
    Wo³ gai¹ zou³ le. Zai⁴jian⁴!

A: Zai⁴jian⁴

English Translation

1. Hello!

A: Hello!

B: Hello!

A: Come in, please! Please, sit down!

B: Thank you!

A: Would you like anything to drink?

    Tea, coffee, or orange juice?

B: Just a cup of water, please.

  ……

  Thank you.

  ......

  I need to go now. Bye!

A: See you!

Notes on Grammar and Usage

1. Notes

1. 你 好! (Ni^{2}hao^3!): Hcllo! Hi! The 3rd tone 你 (ni^3) is turned to the 2nd tone, as it is followed by another 3rd tone. (See Appendix 1, C.)

2. 点 儿 (diar^3): short for 一 点 儿 (yi^4 diar^3) a little, some In R suffixation, dian^3 + r becomes diar^3. Thc n sound is dropped. (See Appendix 1, E.) Retroflexion is very typical in Beijing dialect, but generally it does not occur in formal speech. Thus some people prefer not to use it.

3. 什 么 (shen^{2}me): what This is usually a question word, but here it means *anything* or *something*. 我 饿 了, 想 吃 点 儿 **什 么**. (Wo^3 e^4 le, xiang^3 chi^1 diar^3 **shen^{2}me**.) I'm hungry. I'd like to have something to eat.

4. 还 是 (hai^{2}shi): or 你 来 **还 是** 不 来? (Ni^3 lai^2 **hai^{2}shi** bu^4 lai^2?) Are you coming or not? (The syllable that bears no tone number is neutral. Cf. Appendix 1, D.)

5. 橙 汁 儿 (cheng^{2}zhər^1): orange juice When 儿 (er) is added to the zhi sound, the i becomes ər. The thus formed ər is a retroflexed central vowel. (See Appendix 1, E.)

6. 喝 杯 水 (he^1 bei^1 shui^3) = 喝 一 杯 水 (he^1 yi^4 bei^1 shui^3): drink a cup of water When the *num.* 一 (yi^1: one) follows a *v.* and precedes a *meas*, it is usually omitted. 吃 个 苹 果 = 吃 一 个 苹 果 (chi^1 [yi^2] ge ping^{2}guo^3) eat an apple, 买 本 书 = 买 一 本 书 (mai^3 [yi^4] ben^3 shu^1) buy a book But when it is emphasized, it is not omitted. 美 国 队 进 了 两 个 球, 中 国 队 只 进 了 一 个 球. (Mei^{3}guo^2 dui^4 jin^4 le liang^3 ge qiu^2, zhong^{1}guo^2 dui^1 zhi^3 jin^4 le **yi^2** ge qiu^2.) The American team scored two goals; the Chinese team scored only one.

1. Vocabulary

一 yi¹   *num.* one
a. each; all, whole
conj. once, as soon as

你 ni³   *pron.* you (sing.)

好 hao³   *a.* good, well (opp. 坏 huai⁴)
adv. well; how;
after *v.* to indicate completion of action;
before *adj.* or *adv.* to indicate high degree
part. (used independently) OK, It's settled.

你 好! Ni²hao³!   Hello! Hi!

请 qing³   *part.* please
v. invite; send for; request, ask

进 jin⁴   enter, come in (opp. 出 chu¹)

坐 zuo⁴   *v.* sit, sit down (opp. 站 zhan⁴)

谢 谢! Xie⁴xie!   Thanks!

喝 he¹   *v.* drink

点 dian³   *a.* a little, a bit, some
v. order (dishes in a restaurant)
n. dot, point
part. o'clock

儿 er²   *n.* child; son
part. used in retroflexion

什 么 shen²me   *a.* what
pron. what; something, anything

吧 ba   *part.* used at the end of a sentence to show suggestion, request, doubt, approval, etc.

茶 cha²   *n.* tea

咖 啡 ka¹fei¹   *n.* coffee

还 hai²   *adv.* yet, still; in addition; even more

是 shi⁴   *v.* be
part. yes

还 是 hai²shi   *conj.* or
adv. still; had better; it is…that

橙 cheng²   *n.* orange

汁 zhi¹   *n.* juice

杯 bei¹   *n., meas.* cup, glass

水 shui³   *n.* water

我 wo³   *pron.* I, me

该 gai¹   *v.* should, have to

走 zou³   *v.* leave; walk

了 le   *part.* to denote completion of an action or an event

我 该 走 了. Wo³ gai¹ zou³ le.   Time for me to go.

再 zai⁴   *adv.* again

见 jian⁴   *v.* see

再 见! Zai⁴jian⁴!   Bye-bye! See you!

Supplementary Vocabulary and Expressions

Coke	可 乐 (ke³le⁴)
cold water	冷 水 (leng²shui³)
mineral water	矿 泉 水 (kuang⁴quan²shui³)
warm water	温 水 (wen¹shui³)
Glad to meet you.	见 到 你 很 高 兴. (Jian⁴ dao⁴ ni³ hen³ gao¹xin⁴.) (Ni³ keeps its 3ʳᵈ tone, as it is not closely linked with the following word.)
Good evening!	晚 上 好! (Wan³shang hao³!)
Good morning.	早! (zao³.), 您 早! (Nin²zao³.)
Haven't seen you for a long time.	好 久 没 见 了. (Hao²jiu³ mei² jian⁴ le.)

EXERCISES

1. Exercises

I. Read aloud the following sounds:

a^1 a^2 a^3 a^4 a (weak)
yi^1 yi^2 yi^3 yi^4
o^1 o^2 o^3 o^4

II. Give the phonetic spellings (including tones) of the following words:

1. 进   2. 坐   3. 谢谢   4. 再见   5. 喝

6. 吧   7. 请   8. 什么   9. 你好   10. 橙汁儿

III. Pattern Drill:

请	进！
	坐！
	喝水.
	喝茶.
	喝咖啡.
	喝点儿橙汁儿.

IV. Choose the right expressions for the dialogs:

1. A: 你好！

   B: _____ （a. 你好！ b. 我好！ c. 再见!）

2. A: 请坐！

   B: _____ （a. 再见！ b. 喝点儿咖啡吧？ c. 谢谢!）

3. A: 喝点儿什么吧?

   B: _____ (a. 我该走了. b. 喝点儿茶吧. c. 你好!)

4. A: 我该走了.

   B: _____ (a. 再见! b. 走吧! c.请进!)

二．家庭人口

A: 你家[1]有几口人?

B: 有八口人: 爸爸、妈妈、一[2]
个[3]哥哥、一个姐姐、一个弟
弟、两[4]个妹妹和我.

A: 喔，是个大家庭!

B: 是啊. 所以[5]我家总是很热闹
的[6].

2. Jia[1]ting[2] Ren[2]kou[3]

A: Ni[3] jia[1] you[2] ji[2] kou[3] ren[2]?

B: You[3] ba[1] kou[3] ren[2]: ba[4]ba, ma[1]ma, yi[2]
ge ge[1]ge, yi[2] ge jie[3]jie, yi[2] ge di[4]di,
liang[3] ge mei[4]mei he[2] wo[3].

A: O[1], shi[4] ge da[4] jia[1]ting[2]!

B: Shi[4] a. Suo[2]yi[3] wo[3] jia[1] zong[3]shi[4]
hen[3] re[4]nao de.

2. Family Members

A: How many people are there in your family?

B: Eight people: dad, mom, elder brother, elder sister, younger brother, two younger sisters and me.

A: Wow, you have a big family!

B: Yes, indeed. That's why there's always so much excitement in my house!

2. Notes

1. 你家 (ni^3 jia^1): your family Between 你 (ni^3) and 家 (jia^1) the word 的 (de) is omitted. So the nominative is used as possessive. Eg. 你太太 (ni^3 tai^{4}tai) your wife, 他爸爸 (ta^1 ba^{4}ba) his dad

2. 一 (yi^1): one Note its different tones:
   a. 1st tone: when used independently or at the end of a word or sentence Eg. 十一 (shi^{2}yi^1) eleven, 统一 (tong^{3}yi^1) unify
   b. 2nd tone: when followed by a word with a 4th tone Eg. 一半 (yi^{2}ban^4) half, 一定 (yi^{2}ding^4) definitely
   c. 4th tone: when followed by a word of 1st, 2nd, or 3rd tone Eg. 一天 (yi^4 tian^1) one day, 一年 (yi^{4}nian^2) one year, 一本书 (yi^4 ben^3 shu^1) one book

3. 个 (ge^4): most commonly used *meas.* usually unstressed after a numeral or the pronouns 这 (zhe^4) *this* or 那 *that* (na^4)

4. 两 (liang^3) vs. 二 (er^4): Both mean *two.* 二 (er^4) is used: a. in counting 一, 二, 三 (yi^1, er^4, san^1) one, two, three b. in fractions 零点二 (ling^2 dian^3 er^2) 0.2 c. as an ordinal 二哥 (er^{4}ge^1) second brother, 二楼 (er^4 lou^2) second floor d. in unit's and ten's places 二十二 (er^4 shi^2 er^4) 22; 两 (liang^3) is used: a. before a *meas.* 两杯茶 (liang^3 bei^1 cha^2) two cups of tea b. before common nouns 三天两夜 (san^1 tian^1 liang^3 ye^4) 3 days and 2 nights Before 千 (qian^1 thousand) and 万 (wan^4 ten thousand) either 两 (liang^3) or 二 (er^4) can be used, depending on context.

5. 所以 (suo^{2}yi^3): therefore *conj.* to express relation of cause and effect 我家只有两口人, **所以**家里总是冷冷清清. (Wo^3 jia^1 zhi^2 you^3 liang^2 kou^3 ren^2, **suo^{2}yi^3** jia^1 li zong^{3}shi^4 leng^{2}leng^3 qing^{1}qing^1.) There are only two people in my family. Therefore, it is always cold and cheerless in my house.

6. 的 (de): used at the end of declarative sentences to produce an assertive tone 橙汁儿是甜**的**. (Zheng^{2}zhər^1 shi^4 tian^2 **de**.) Orange juice is sweet. 牛奶是白**的**. (Niu^{2}nai^3 shi^4 bai^2 **de**.) Milk is white.

2. Vocabulary

二 er^4 — *num.* two

家 jia^1 — *n.* family; home, house
meas. used with enterprises

家 庭 jia^{1}ting^2 — *n.* family

人 ren^2 — *n.* person, people

口 kou^3 — *n.* mouth, mouthful
meas. used in counting people in families, etc.

人 口 ren^{2}kou^3 — *n.* population, number of people in a family, city, or country, etc.

有 you^3 — *n.* there be; have (opp. 没 有 mei^{2}you^3, or 无 wu^2)

几 ji^3 — *pron.* how many; several

八 ba^1 — *num.* eight (pronounced with a 2nd tone before a 4th tone sound)

爸 爸 ba^{4}ba — *n.* dad

妈 妈 ma^{1}ma — *n.* mom

个 ge^4 — *meas.* a most frequently used measure word

哥 哥 ge^{1}ge — *n.* elder brother

姐 姐 jie^{3}jie — *n.* elder sister

弟 弟 di^{4}di — *n.* younger brother

两 liang^3 — *num.* two

妹 妹 mei^{4}mei — *n.* younger sister

和 he^2 — *conj.* and

喔 o^1 — *int.* expressing understanding or surprise

大 da^4 — *a.* big, great; old; eldest
adv. fully, to a big extent (opp. 小 xiao^3)

啊 a^1 or a — *int.& part.* expressing surprise or admiration

所 以 suo^{2}yi^3 — *conj.* so, therefore

总 zong^3 — *adv.* always
a. general; chief

总 是 zong^{3}shi — *adv.* always (opp. 难 得 nan^{2}de^2)

很 hen^3 — *adv.* very

热 re^4 — *a.* hot, warm (opp. 冷 leng^3)

闹 nao^4 — *a.* noisy (opp. 静 jing^4)

热 闹 re^{4}nao — *a.* lively, joyful, busy (opp. 冷 静 leng^{3}jing^4 or 冷 清 leng^{3}qing^1)

的 de — *part.* a. to form an attribute b. after a noun or pronoun to form a possessive c. to make an assertion

Supplementary Vocabulary and Expressions

aunt	姑 妈 (gu^{1}ma^1):	father's sister
	姨 妈 (yi^{2}ma^1):	mother's sister
granddaughter	孙 女 (sun^{1}nü^3):	son's daughter
	外 孙 女 (wai^4 sun^{1}nü^3):	daughter's daughter
grandson	孙 子 (sun^{1}zi):	son's son
	外 孙 (wai^{4}sun^1):	daughter's son
nephew	侄 子 (zhi^{2}zi):	brother's son
	外 甥 (wai^{4}sheng):	sister's son
niece	侄 女 (zhi^{2}nü^3):	brother's daughter
	外 甥 女 (wai^{4}shengnü^3):	sister's daughter
uncle	伯 伯 (bo^{1}bo):	father's elder brother
	叔 叔 (shu^{1}shu):	father's younger brother
	舅 舅 (jiu^{4}jiu):	mother's brother

Everything will prosper in a harmonious family.
家 和 万 事 兴. (Jia^1 he^1 wan^4 shi^4 xing^1.)

2. Exercises

I. Give the Chinese words the following spellings represent:

yi^1 diar^3 shen^{2}me   hai^{2}shi   wo^3

II. Choose the best expressions for the dialogs:

1. A: 你家有几口人?
    B: _____ (a. 一个爸爸, 一个妈妈. b. 两口人. c. 是个大家庭.)

2. A: 你妈妈好吧?
    B: _____ (a. 你妈妈好! b. 是啊! c. 她很好, 谢谢你!)

3. A: 请进!
    B: _____ (a. 我该走了. b. 谢谢! c.请坐!)

4. A: 我家有八口人.
    B: _____ (a. 喔, 是个大家庭! b. 所以我家总是很热闹的. c. 好啊!)

III. Translate the following into Chinese:

1. a cup of water

2. two cups of coffee

3. eight cups of orange juice

4. mom and dad

5. elder brother and younger sister

6. elder sister and younger brother

7. her mom

8. his family

9. I have a younger brother and a younger sister.

10. There are four people in my family.

三. 请[1]吃饭[2]

A: 星期六我想请你[3]和你太太来我家吃饭,不知道你们[4]有没有[5]空儿?

B: 谢谢你.星期六中午还是晚上?

A: 晚上.

B: 我们有空儿,可以来.

A: 那[6]太好了.星期六晚上六点等你们.

B: 好, 我们一定来.

3. Qing[3] Chi[1]fan[4]

A: Xing[1]qi[1]liu[4] wo[2] xiang[2] qing[3] ni he[2] ni[3] tai[4]tai lai[2] wo[3] jia[1] chi[1]fan[4], bu[4] zhi[1]dao ni[3]men you[3]mei[2]you[3] kõr[4]?

B: Xie[4]xie ni. Xing[1]qi[1]liu[4] zhong[1]wu[3] hai[2]shi wan[3]shang?

A: Wan[3]shang.

B: Wo[3]men you[3] kõr[4], ke[2]yi[3] lai[2].

A: Na[4] tai[4] hao[3] le. Xing[1]qi[1]liu[4] wan[3]shang liu[4] dian[3] deng[2] ni[3]men.

B: Hao[3], wo[3]men yi[2]ding[4] lai[2].

3. Dinner Invitation

A: I'd like to invite you and your wife to eat with us on Saturday. I want to know if you are available.

B: Thank you. Lunch or dinner?

A: Dinner.

B: We are free. We can come.

A: Great. We will be waiting for you at six on Saturday evening.

B: Okay, we'll be there.

3. Notes

1. 请 (qing^3): *v.* invite It is different from the *part.* 请 (qing^3: please) in Passage 1.

2. 吃饭 (chi^{1}fan^4): have a meal 饭 (fan^4) is *cooked rice.* In old times Chinese people only had rice for their meals. That is why the word 饭 stands for meal. 饭 was so important in old times that a set form of greeting "你吃过 **饭** 了吗?" (Ni^3 chi^1 guo **fan^4** le ma?) "Have you eaten (rice) yet?" was formed and is still frequently used today.

3. 你 (ni): you (sing.) When personal pronouns are in the objective position, they may become neutral in rapid speech.

4. 你们 (ni^{3}men): you (pl.) The word 们 (men, unstressed) is added to personal pronouns or nouns denoting people to make them plural.

我 (wo^3) I	我们 (wo^{3}men) we	
你 (ni^3) you	你们 (ni^{3}men) you	
他 (ta^1) he	他们 (ta^{1}men) they	
她 (ta^1) she	她们 (ta^{1}men) they	
它 (ta^1) it	它们 (ta^{1}men) they	

女士们, 先生们! (Nü^{3}shi^4 men, xian^{1}sheng men!) Ladies and gentlemen!

5. 有没有... (you^{3}mei^{2}you^3)?: Do you have ... (or not)? 有 (you^3) is *have*; 没有 (mei^{2}you^3) is *not have.* 有 and 没有 put together become a question word. 你 **有没有** 零钱? (Ni^2 **you^{3}mei^{2}you^3** ling^{2}qian^2?) Do you have any small change?

6 那 (na^4): *pron.* Here it refers to the fact that the invitation was accepted. 那不难. (**Na^4** bu^4 nan^2.) That is not difficult. See 那 in Vocabulary, Passage 23 for its different pronunciations.

3. Vocabulary

三 san[1] *num.* three

星 期 xing[1]qi[1] *n.* week

星 期 六 xing[1]qi[1]liu[4] *n.* Saturday

想 xiang[3] *v.* think, consider; would like to; miss (sb.), remember with longing

太 tai[4] *adv.* too; very

太 太 tai[4]tai *n.* wife (opp. 先 生 xian[1]sheng) In China wife or husband is sometimes also called 爱 人 ai[4]ren[2] (Lit. loved person); madam, Mrs.

来 lai[2] *v.* come (opp.去 qu[4]); do sth. (replacing a verb according to the context)

吃 chi[1] *v.* eat; (colloq.) get

饭 fan[4] *n.* cooked rice; meal

不 bu[4] *adv.* not
part. no

知 道 zhi[1]dao *v.* know

你 们 ni[3]men *pron.* you (pl.)

们 men *suff.* used to form plurals

没 有 mei[2]you[3] *v.* not have (opp. 有 you[3])
adv. not yet (opp. 已 经 yi[3]jing)

没 mei[2] *adv.* short for 没 有 (mei[2]you[3])

空 kong[4] *n.* spare time
When suffix r is added, kong becomes kõr. "~" indicates a nasal sound. See Appendix 1, E.

kong[1] *a.* empty; hollow
n. sky, space

中 zhong[1] *n., a.* middle
pstp. within (opp. 外 wai[4])
n. short for 中 国 (zhong[1]guo[2]) China

午 wu[3] *n.* noon, midday

中 午 zhong[1]wu[3] *n.* noon

晚 wan[3] *n.* evening, night;
a. late (opp. 早 zao[3])

晚 上 wan[3]shang *n.* evening, night (opp. 白 天 bai[2]tian[1])

上 shang[4] *adv.* up (opp. 下 xia[4]);
v. go to
a. previous (week, etc.);
(after *v.*, showing achievement of a goal or occurrence of some result) succeed in

shang (neutral) *pstp.* (after *n.*, indicating location) on, in, at

我 们 wo[3]men *pron.* we, us

可 以 ke[2]yi[3] *v.* may, can
a. passable, not bad

那 na[4] *pron.* that (opp. zhe[4])
conj. then

六 liu[4] *num.* six

等 deng[3] *v.* wait

一 定 yi[2]ding[4] *adv.* certainly, without fail (opp. 可 能 ke[3]neng[2])

Supplementary Vocabulary and Expressions

invite in advance 约 (yue[1])

attend a dinner party 参 加 宴 会 (can[1]jia[1] yan[4] hui[4])

Please come to visit us when you have time.
有 空 儿 请 常 来 玩.
(You[3] kõr[4] qing[3] chang[2] lai[2] wan[2].)

This is to be my treat. 我 请 客. (Wo[2] qing[3]ke[4].)

11

3. Exercises

I. Read aloud the following sounds to practice the tones:

ma¹ 妈 mom   ma² 麻 numb   ma³ 马 horse   ma⁴ 骂 swear at   ma 嘛 (a particle)

ba¹ 八 eight   ba² 拔 pull up   ba³ 把 handle   ba⁴ 爸 dad   ba 吧 (a particle)

II. Substitution Drills:

我		你	
你		他	喝茶.
她		我	
他	请	她	吃饭.
我们		他们	
你们		我们	喝咖啡.
他们		你们	

我		你	来不来.
她	想知道	他	喝不喝咖啡.
我们		你们	有没有空.
他太太		你太太	星期一还是星期六有空.

III. Make questions by using 有没有 for the following answers:

1. A: 星期六 _____?
   B: 我有空.

2. A: _____?
   B: 我有一个妹妹.

3. A: _____?
   B: 我没有弟弟.

4. A: _____?
   B: 我没有零钱.

IV. Read the following sentence:

妈妈骑马, 马慢嘛, 妈妈骂马. (骑 qi²: ride   慢 man⁴: slow)

12

四. 学中文

A: 您是中国人吗[1]?

B: 是, 是中国人.

A: 您说普通话, 还是广东话?

B: 说普通话.

A: 我想学普通话. 普通话难学[2]

吗?

B: 不[3]太容易. 但只要你肯下功

夫[4], 也就[5]不难了.

4. Xue[2] Zhong[1]wen[2]

A: Nin[2] shi[4] zhong[1]guo[2]ren[2] ma?

B: Shi[4], shi[4] zhong[1]guo[2]ren[2].

A: Nin[2] shuo[1] pu[3]tong[1]hua[4], hai[2]shi

Guang[3]dong[1]hua[4]?

B: Shuo[1] pu[3]tong[1]hua[4].

A: Wo[2] xiang[3] xue[2] pu[3]tong[1]hua[4].

Pu[3]tong[1]hua[4] nan[2] xue[2] ma?

B: Bu[2] tai[4] rong[2]yi[4]. Dan[4] zhi[3]yao[4] ni[2]

ken[3] xia[4] gong[1]fu, ye[3] jiu[4] bu[4] nan[2]

le.

4. Learning Chinese

A: Are you Chinese?

B: Yes, I am.

A: Do you speak Mandarin or Cantonese?

B: I speak Mandarin.

A: I'd like to learn Mandarin, but is it hard to learn?

B: It's not too easy. But if you focus your mind on learning it, it's not too hard.

4. Notes

1. 吗 (ma): used after declarative sentences to make them interrogative 你好吗? (Ni^2 hao^3 **ma**?) How are you doing? 您有空儿吗? (Nin^2 you^3 kõr^4 **ma**?) Do you have time?

2. 难学 (nan^2 xue^2): hard to learn As an *adv.* 难 is put before the verb it modifies. Eg. 难懂 (**nan**^{2} dong^3) hard to understand, 难说 (**nan**^{2}shuo^1) hard to say 明天会不会下雨还很难说. (Ming^{3}tian^1 hui^{4}buhui^4 xia^{4}yu^3 hai^2 hen^3 **nan**^{2} shuo^1.) It's hard to tell whether it will rain tomorrow.

3. 不 (bu^4): not 不 (bu^4) is used to negate the meaning of a *v.*, an *a.*, or an *adv.* that follows it. Eg. 难 (nan^2) *difficult*; 不难 (bu^4 nan^2) *not difficult* But the negative of 有(you^3: have) is 没有 (mei^{2}you^3), not 不有. Note the 4th tone 不 is pronounced with a 2nd tone when followed by a word with a 4th tone. Eg. 不用 (bu^2 yong^4) no need, 不客气 (bu^2 ke^{4}qi) you're welcome (a response to *thank you*)

4. 下功夫 (xia^4 gong^{1}fu): concentrate one's efforts 学好语言非下功夫不可. (Xue^2 hao^2 yu^{3}yan^2 fei^1 **xia**^{4} **gong**^{1}**fu** bu^4 ke^3.) The mastery of a language requires painstaking effort.

5. 只要… 就 (zhi^{3}yao^4…jiu^4): so long as 只要你同意, 我就干. (**Zhi**^{3}**yao**^{4} ni^3 tong^{2}yi^4, wo^3 **jiu**^{4} gan^4.) So long as you agree, I'll act at once. 就 (jiu^4) means *without delay*. The word 也 (ye^3) preceding 就 (jiu^4) is used to emphasize 就 (jiu^4).

4. Vocabulary

四 si[4]   *num.* four

学 xue[2]   *v.* study, learn (opp. 教 jiao[1])

中文 zhong[1]wen[2]   *n.* the Chinese language, same as 汉语 (han[4]yu[3]) (汉 han[4]: China's main nationality, 语 yu[3] language, speech)

文 wen[2]   *n.* language   *a.* civilian

您 nin[2]   *pron.* you (sing.) (polite form)

国 guo[2]   *n.* country, nation (same as 国家 guo[2]jia[1])

中国 zhong[1]guo[2]   *n.* China Lit. the Middle Kingdom (opp. 外国 wai[4]guo[2] Lit. outside country)

中国人 zhong[1]guo[2]ren[2]   *n.* Chinese people (opp. 外国人 wai[4]guo[2]ren[2])

吗 ma   *part.* used to form a general question

说 shuo[1]   *v.* speak, say

普通 pu[3]tong[1]   *a.* general, common (opp. 特别 te[4]bie[2])

话 hua[4]   *n.* speech, words, language, talks

普通话 pu[3]tong[1]hua[4]   *n.* standard Chinese speech, Mandarin

广东 Guang[3]dong[1]   *n.* a province in China

广东话 Guang[3]dong[1]hua[4]   *n.* Cantonese (a dialect spoken in Guangdong Province)

难 nan[2]   *a.* difficult (opp. 易 yi[4])   *adv.* with difficulty; unpleasantly

容易 rong[2]yi[4]   *a.* easy   *adv.* easily (opp. 困难 kun[4]nan

但 dan[4]   *conj.* but (same as 但是 dan[4]shi[4])

只要 zhi[3]yao[4]   *conj.* if, so long as

只 zhi[3]   *adv.* only

zhi[1]   *meas.* used with animal, box, boat, etc.

要 yao[4]   *v.* want, need; be going to;   *conj.* if (same as 要是 yao[4]shi)

肯 ken[3]   *v.* be willing to

下 xia[4]   *v.* use, apply, put in; (of rain, snow, etc.) fall; go to (restaurant, etc.); play (chess)   *adj.* lower; next (week, etc.)   *pstp., part., & adv.* down, below (opp. 上 shang[4])

功夫 gong[1]fu   *n.* time and energy; kungfu

也 ye[3]   *adv.* also, too; even (used to show emphasis)

就 jiu[4]   *adv.* at once; just, exactly (used to show an immediate result)

Supplementary Vocabulary and Expressions

American	美国人 (mei[3]guo[2] ren[2])
English	英国人 (ying[1]guo[2] ren[2])
	英语 (ying[1]yu[3])
Canadian	加拿大人 (jia[1]na[2]da[4] ren[2])
French	法语 (fa[2]yu[3]);
	法国人 (fa[2]guo[2] ren[2])
German	德语 (de[2]yu[3]);
	德国人 (de[2]guo[2] ren[2])
Japanese	日语 (ri[4] yu[3])
	日本人 (ri[4]ben[3]ren[2])
Russian	俄语 (e[2]yu[3])
	俄国人 (e[2]guo[2]ren[2])
Spanish	西班牙语 (xi[1]ban[1]ya[1]yu[3])
	西班牙人 (xi[1]ban[1]ya[1] ren[2])

Please speak slowly. 请说得慢一点儿.
(Qing[3] shuo[1] de man[4] yi[4]diar[3].)

15

4. Exercises

I. Give the phonetic spellings (including tones) of the following words:

    1. ·   2. 一定   3. 吃   4. 说   5. 晚上

    6. 和   7. 就   8. 功夫   9. 知道   10. 还是

II. Give the Chinese equivalents of the following days of the week: (Sunday is 星期天 xing^{1}qi^{1}tian^1 or 星期日 xing^{1}qi^{1}ri^4.)

Monday	Tuesday	Wednesday	Thursday
Friday	Saturday	Sunday	

III. Use 吗 to make the following declarative sentences interrogative, and then answer them in the negative:

    1. 我是中国人.

    2. 我说普通话.

    3. 我们星期六有空儿.

    4. 普通话难学.

    5. 我想喝水.

    6. 她星期六一定等我.

IV. Translate the following into Chinese:

    1. He is not Chinese.

    2. Is it hard to learn Cantonese?

    3. She will be waiting for me on Wednesday.

    4. Is she coming on Tuesday or Thursday?

五. 有几个[1]孩子?

A: 你有几个孩子?

B: 两个: 一个儿子, 一个女儿.

A: 一男一女, 不多不少[2], 最理想.

B: 你有几个孩子?

A: 一个也[3]没有.

B: 为什么[4]? 你不想生吗?

A: 我还没有[5]结婚哪!

5. You^2 Ji^3 ge Hai^{2}zi?

A: Ni^2 you^2 ji^3 ge hai^{2}zi?

B: Liang^3 ge: yi^2 ge er^{2}zi, yi^2 ge nü^{3}er^2.

A: Yi^4 nan^2 yi^4 nü^3, bu^4 duo^1 bu^4 shao^3, zui^4 li^{2}xiang^3.

B: Ni^2 you^2 ji^3 ge hai^{2}zi?

A: Yi^2 ge ye^3 mei^{2}you^3.

B: Wei^{4}shen^{2}me? Ni^3 bu^4 xiang^3 sheng^1 ma?

A: Wo^3 hai^2 mei^{2}you^3 jie^{2}hun^1 na!

5. How Many Children Do You Have?

A: How many children do you have?

B: Two: a son and a daughter.

A: Having a boy and a girl is perfect,

   neither too many, nor too few.

B: How many kids do you have?

A: None at all.

B: Why? Do you not want children?

A: I haven't gotten married yet!

5. Notes

1. 几个 (ji³ ge): how many, used for asking about quantities that are not very big. For bigger quantities use 多少 (duo¹shao). We cannot say: 中国有几个人口? (Zhong¹guo² you² **ji³ ge** ren²kou³?) The correct sentence is 中国有多少人口? (Zhong¹guo² you³ **duo¹shao** ren²kou³?). What's the population of China? If you ask: 你家有多少孩子? (Ni³ jia¹ you³ **duo¹shao** hai²zi? How many children do you really have?), it may imply that you already know that she has a lot of children and now you want to know the exact number. 几个 (ji³ ge) is usually not used with uncountable nouns.

2. 不多不少 (bu⁴ duo¹ bu⁴ shao³): neither too many, nor too few 不… 不 … (bu⁴ … bu⁴…) is *neither…nor…*. 不大不小 (bu²da⁴ bu⁴xiao³) neither too big nor too small, just right 不死不活 (bu⁴si¹ bu⁴huo²) lifeless (Lit. neither dead nor living) 电梯突然坏了, 不上不下, 卡在半空. (Dian⁴ti² tu¹ran² huai⁴le, **bu²**shang⁴ **bu²**xia⁴, ka³ zai⁴ ban⁴kong¹.) The elevator was suddenly broken. It was suspended in mid air. Note the shape of the character 卡 (ka³: block, check), which is half 上 (shang⁴ up) and half 下 (xia⁴ down). Another meaning of 不… 不 … (bu⁴ … bu⁴…) is *have got to…*. In this meaning the second 不 (bu⁴) is often followed by the word 行 (xing²: all right).

3. 一个也 (yi² ge ye³): not even one 他们 一个也 没有回来. (Ta¹men **yi² ge ye³** mei²you³ hui²lai.) None of them has come back. 也 is used for emphasis.

4. 为什么 (wei⁴shen²me): why (Lit: for what) 她 为什么 不来? (Ta¹ **wei⁴shen²me** bu⁴ lai²?) Why did she not come? The more colloquial form of 为什么 (wei⁴shen²me) is 为啥 (wei⁴sha³).

5. 还没有… (hai² mei²you³): not yet 她 还没 有来. (Ta¹ **hai² mei²you³** lai².) She has not come yet. Its opposite is 已经 (yi³jing…le). 她 已经 来了. (Ta¹ **yi³jing** lai² le) She has come.

5. Vocabulary

五 wu^3	*num.* five
孩子 hai^{2}zi	*n.* child (opp. 大人 da^{4}ren^2)
子 zi	suffix to nouns or other parts of speech to form different meanings
zi^3	*n.* son
儿子 er^{2}zi	*n.* son (opp. 女儿 nü^{3}er^2)
女 nü^3	*a.* female
	n. woman (opp. 男 nan^2)
女儿 nü^{3}er^2	*n.* daughter (opp. 儿子 er^{2}zi)
男 nan^2	*a.* male
	n. man
多 duo^1	*a., adv.* many, much, more
	adv. how
少 shao^3	*a., adv.* few, little, less
shao^4	*a.* young
最 zui^4	*adv.* most
理想 li^{2}xiang^3	*a.* ideal, perfect
为 wei^4	*prep.* for
wei^2	*part.* as
为什么 wei^{4}shen^{2}me	*adv.* why, what for
生 sheng^1	*v.* give birth to, be born; produce
	a. raw (opp. 熟 shu^2)
结 jie^2	*v.* form; tie; combine (opp. 解 jie^3)
婚 hun^1	*n.* marriage
结婚 jie^{2}hun^1	*v.* marry, get married; *n.* marriage
结婚 jie^{2}hun^1	*v.* marry, get married; *n.* marriage (opp. 离婚 li^{2}hun^1)
哪 na	*part.* same as 啊 (a^1), showing explanation, advice, or command, etc., used after words ending in *n* sound The *n* plus *a* (啊) becomes 哪 (na). Eg. 谢谢您哪! (Xie^{4}xie nin^2 na!)

adopt	领养 (ling^{2}yang^3)
adult	成人 (cheng^{2}ren^2)
birth control	计划生育 (ji^{4}hua^4 sheng^{1}yu^4)
born out of wed-lock	私生的 (si^{1}sheng^1 de)
family with a single parent	单亲家庭 (dan^{1}qin^1 jia^{1}ting^2)
only child	独生子 (du^{2}sheng^{1}zi^3)
	独生女 (du^{2}sheng^{1}nü^3),
parents	双亲 (shuang^{1}qin^1)
	父母 (fu^{4}mu^3)
pregnant	怀孕 (huai^{2}yun^4)
twins	双胞胎 (shuang^{1}bao^{1}tai^1)

Having a child changes everything.
有了个小孩儿,什么都变了.
(You^3 le ge xiao^{3}har^2, shen^{2}me dou^1 bian^4 le.)
She is still single.
她还是个单身.
(Ta^1 hai^2 shi^4 ge dan^{1}shen^1.

5. Exercises

I. Tone Practice:

po¹ 坡 slope   po² 婆 old woman   po³ 叵 impossible   po⁴ 破 broken
yu¹ 迂 winding   yu² 鱼 fish   yu³ 雨 rain   yu⁴ 玉 jade
    (Note: when there is no consonant before ü, it is written with *y* before it and the two dots are omitted.)

II. Choose 几个 or 多少 to fill into the following blanks:

　　1. 他有 ＿＿＿＿＿＿ 弟弟?

　　2. 你有 ＿＿＿＿＿＿ 零钱?

　　3. 那太难了. 要下 ＿＿＿＿＿＿ 功夫啊!

　　4. 她生了 ＿＿＿＿＿＿ 女儿?

III. Change the following sentences from affirmative to negative or from negative to
　　affirmative by changing 还没有 to 已经…了 or vice versa:

　　1. 他已经进来了.

　　2. 他们还没有吃饭.

　　3. 她还没有结婚, 但已经有孩子了.

　　4. 她已经结婚了, 已经有孩子了. (Insert 所以 in the new sentence.)

IV. Rewrite the following sentences by using the emphatic form 一 … 也:

　　1. 她没有孩子.

　　2. 我没喝一口茶.

　　3. 他没一点儿空.

V. Translate the following sentences into Chinese, by using 只要…就:

　　1. I'll come when I have time.
　　2. If you put a lot of effort into learning Mandarin, it will be very easy.
　　3. If he comes, I'll leave at once.
　　4. Come, whenever you want to.

六. 乌龙茶

A: 您在 [1] 喝咖啡吗?

B: 不 [2], 是茶.

A: 是什么茶?

B: 乌龙茶.

A: 好喝 [3] 吗?

B: 味道不错. 你要不要来一杯尝尝 [4]?

A: 好. ... 味道是不错.

B: 您知道经常喝茶可以预防癌症?

A: 是吗? 那 [5] 我也要开始喝茶了.

6. Wu[1]long[2] Cha[2]

A: Nin[2] zai[4] he[1] ka[1]fei[1] ma?

B: Bu[4], shi[4] cha[2].

A: Shi[4] shen[2]me cha[2]?

B: Wu[1]long[2] cha[2].

A: Hao[3] he[1] ma?

B: Wei[4]dao bu[2]cuo[4]. Ni[3] yao[4]buyao[4] lai[2] yi[4] bei[1] chang[2]chang?

A: Hao[3]. ... Wei[4]dao shi[4] bu[2]cuo[4].

B: Nin[2] zhi[1]dao jing[1]chang[2] he[1] cha[2] ke[2]yi[3] yu[4]fang[2] ai[2]zheng[4]?

A: Shi[4] ma? Na[4] wo[2] ye[3] yao[4] kai[1]shi[3] he[1] cha[2] le.

21

6. Oolong Tea

A: Are you drinking coffee?

B: No, it's tea.

A: What kind of tea?

B: *Oolong.*

A: Does it taste good?

B: Yes. Have a cup to try?

A: OK. … The taste *is* good.

B: Do you know frequently drinking tea

can help prevent cancer?

A: Really? Then I will start drinking tea.

6. Notes

1. 在 (zai⁴): used before verbs to denote an action is in progress 她 在 睡 觉. (Ta¹ **zai⁴** shui⁴jiao⁴.) She is sleeping. 我 在 看 书. (Wo³ **zai⁴** kan⁴shu¹.) I am reading.

2. 不 (bu⁴): No When 不 (bu⁴) is used independently at the beginning of a sentence, it is equivalent to *No*; when placed before a verb, adjective, or adverb, it is equivalent to *not*. Cf. Note 3, Passage 4.

3. 好 喝 (hao³ he¹): good to drink 好 (hao³) can be used before verbs. 好 听 (hao³ ting¹) pleasant to hear, 好 看 (hao³ kan⁴) good-looking, 好 吃 (hao³ chi¹) good to eat, 好 玩 (hao³ wan²) interesting (Lit. good to play) The opposite in this sense is 难 (nan²). 难 看 (nan² kan⁴) ugly, 难 听 (nan² ting¹) unpleasant to hear Here the meaning of 难 is not *hard*, as in 难 学 (nan² xue²) in Passage 4. The opposite of 难 学 (nan² xue²) is 好 学 (hao³ xue²) easy to learn.

4. 尝 尝 (chang²chang): have a taste Repeated verbs mean doing something for a short while. Eg. 让 我 看 看. (Rang⁴ wo³ **kan⁴kan**.) Let me have a look. 我 们 出 去 走 走! (Wo³men chu¹qu **zou³zou**!) Let's go out for a walk! The second verb is often unstressed.

5. 那 (na⁴): then, in that case 那 你 还 得 加 一 把 劲. (**Na⁴** ni³ hai² dei³ jia¹ yi⁴ ba³ jin⁴.) Then you'll have to work much harder. 这 样 不 行, 那 咱 们 怎 么 办? (Zhe⁴yang⁴ bu⁴xing², **na⁴** zan²men zen³me ban⁴?) Since that can't be done, what are we going to do?

6. Vocabulary

乌 龙 茶 wu^{1}long^2 cha^2 *n. Oolong* tea, a dark tea from Fujian and Taiwan that is partly fermented before being dried

乌 wu^1 *a.* black

龙 long^2 *n.* dragon

在 zai^4 *prep.* at, in
adv. showing an action in progress
v. be in, be at home; exist

味 道 wei^{4}dao   *n.* taste

错 cuo^4 *a.* wrong, mistaken (opp. 对 dui^4)
n. mistake

不 错 bu^{2}cuo^4 *a.* , not bad, pretty good; not wrong
adv. (indicating what has been said is right) yes, indeed, you are right

尝 chang^2 *v.* try the flavor

经 常 jing^{1}chang^2 *adv.* often (opp. 难 得 nan^{2}de^2)

预 防 yu^{4}fang^2 *v.* prevent.
n. prevention

癌 ai^2 *n.* cancer

症 zheng^4 *n.* disease; symptom

癌 症 ai^{2}zheng^4 *n.* disease of cancer

开 始 kai^{1}shi^3 *v.* begin (opp. 结 束 jie^{2}shu^4)

Biluochun   碧 螺 春 (bi^{4}luo^{2}chun^1) (a kind of green tea, produced in Suzhou)

black tea   红 茶 (hong^{2}cha^2)

Dragon Well tea   龙 井 茶 (long^{2}jing^3 cha^2) (a kind of green tea from Hangzhou)

green tea   绿 茶 (lü^{4}cha^2)

jasmine tea   茉 莉 花 茶 (mo^{4}li^4 hua^1 cha^2)

savor the tea   品 茗 (pin^{2}ming^3)

teahouse   茶 馆 (cha^{2}guan^3)

tieguanyin   铁 观 音 (tie^{3}guan^{1}yin^1) (a kind of *oolong* tea)

way of making tea   茶 道 (cha^{2}dao^4)

It is a Chinese custom to serve tea to visiting Guests.
客来送茶是中国人的习惯.
(Ke^4 lai^2 song^4 cha^1 shi^4 zhong^{1}guo^{2}ren^2 de xi^{2}guan^4.)

6. Exercises

I. Tone Practice:

shen[1] 身 body	shen[2] 神 spirit	shen[3] 审 trial	shen[4] 肾 kidney
sheng[1] 生 give birth	sheng[2] 绳 rope	sheng[3] 省 save	sheng[4] 胜 victory

II. Use 不 or 没 to make the following sentences negative:

1. 他是中国人.
2. 他有儿子.
3. 那是乌龙茶.
4. 她一定来.
5. 你有女儿吗?
6. 普通话很难学.
7. 他爸爸有癌症.
8. 他爸爸知道喝茶可以预防癌症.

III. Complete the following sentences after the example:

Example: 你喝什么, <u>茶还是咖啡</u>? (茶…)

1. 你说什么话, _____? (普通话…)

2. 我要请你吃饭, 星期五中午你 _____? (有空…)

3. 她有一个孩子, 但我不知道是 _____. (儿子…)

4. 我想学普通话, 但不知道普通话 _____. (好学…)

5. 他们什么时候 (时候 shi[2]hou: time) 来, _____? (星期 六…)

IV. Answer the following questions:

1. 喝点儿茶, 好吗?

2. 这咖啡味道好吗?

3. 你为什么经常喝茶?

4. 生几个孩子最理想?

七. 姓名、地址、电话号码

A: 您叫什么名字?

B: 我叫李爱国[1].

A: 您住在[2]哪儿[3]?

B: 中央南大道二零七号[4].

A: 电话号码儿是多少?

B: 家里的[5]电话是一二三 - 四五
六 - 七八九零. 办公室的电话
是九八七 - 六五四 - 三二一零.
手机是一[6]三五 - 七九零 - 八八
八八[7].

7. Xing⁴ming², Di⁴zhi³, Dian⁴hua⁴ Hao⁴ma³

A: Nin² jiao⁴ shen²me ming²zi?

B: Wo³ jiao⁴ Li³ Ai⁴guo².

A: Nin² zhu⁴ zai⁴ nar³?

B: Zhong¹ Yang¹ Nan² Da⁴ Dao⁴ er⁴ ling² qi¹ hao⁴.

A: Dian⁴hua⁴ hao⁴mar³ shi⁴ duo¹shao?

B: Jia¹ li de dian⁴hua⁴ shi⁴ yi¹ er⁴ san¹ – si⁴ wu³ liu⁴ – qi¹ ba¹ jiu³ ling². Ban⁴gong¹shi⁴ de dian⁴hua⁴ shi⁴ jiu³ ba¹ qi¹ - liu⁴ wu³ si⁴ – san¹ er⁴ yi¹ ling². Shou³ji¹ shi⁴ yao¹ san¹ wu³ - qi¹ jiu³ ling² - ba¹ ba¹ ba¹ ba¹.

7. Name, Address, and Phone Number

A: What's your name?

B: My name is Li Aiguo.

A: Your address?

B: 207 South Central Avenue.

A: And phone number?

B: My home phone is (123) 456 – 7890,
and my work phone is (987) 654 –
3210. My cell phone is (135) 790 –
8888.

7. Notes

1. 李爱国 (Li^3 ai^{4}guo^2) In Chinese the family name goes first, followed by the given name. Here 李 (li^3) is the family name.

2. 住在… (zhu^4 zai^4): This 在 is a *prep.* of place. It is different from the 在 in 在 喝咖啡 (zai^4 he^1 ka^{1}fei^1) *drinking coffee* in Passage 6, where it is an *adv.*, showing an action is in progress.

3. 哪儿 (nar^3): where 她上哪儿去啦? (Ta^1 shang^4 **nar^3** qu^4 la?) Where has she gone? Less colloquial is 哪里 (na^{3}li).

4. 中央南大道 207 号 (zhong^1 yang^1 nan^2 da^4 dao^4 er^4 ling^2 qi^1 hao^4): In Chinese the street name always goes before the number, and the word 号 (hao^4), meaning *number* …, follows the numeral.

5. 的 (de): 的 (de) is used after a *n*, an *adj.*, an *adv*, a phrase, or a clause to form an attribute. 茶的香味 (cha^2 **de** xiang^1 wei^4) the aroma of tea, 用功的学生 (yong^{4}gong^1 **de** xue^{2}sheng) a hard working student, 没妈妈的孩子 (mei^2 ma^{1}ma **de** hai^{2}zi) a child without a mother 我要找的人就是你. (Wo^3 yao^4 zhao^3 **de** ren^2 jiu^4 shi ni^3.) It's you that I want to look for.

The possessive case of pronouns is formed also by adding 的 (de) to the nominative case:
我的 (wo^{3}de) my   我们的 (wo^{3}mende) our
你的 (ni^{3}de) your   你们的 (ni^{3}mende) your
他的 (ta^{1}de) his   他们的 (ta^{1}mende) their
她的 (ta^{1}de) her   她们的 (ta^{1}mende) their
它的 (ta^{1}de) its   它们的 (ta^{1}mende) their

6. 一 (yi^1): one The number 一 (yi^1: one) can be pronounced as yao^1 in phone, room, and flight numbers, etc.

7. 八八八八 (ba^1 ba^1 ba^1 ba^1): The Chinese people like the number 八 (ba^1) as it is a homophone of 发 (fa^1), which means *make a fortune*. So license plates with the number 8 are very expensive. They hate the number 四 (si^4), as its pronunciation is close to 死 (si^3), meaning *death*.

7. Vocabulary

七 qi¹ — *num.* seven (pronounced with 2ⁿᵈ tone when followed by a 4ᵗʰ tone sound)

姓 xing⁴ — *n.* last name

名 ming² — *n.* first name

地址 di⁴zhi³ — *n.* address

电话 dian⁴hua⁴ — *n.* telephone

号 hao⁴ — *n.* number

号码 hao⁴ma³ — *n.* number

叫 jiao⁴ — *v.* call, be called; yell; tell (sb. to do sth.)

名字 ming²zi — *n.* name

李 Li³ — *n.* a last name

爱 ai⁴ — *v.* love, like (opp. 恨 hen⁴)

爱国 Ai⁴guo² — *n.* a first name (Lit. love country)

住 zhu⁴ — *v.* live

哪儿 nar³ — *adv.* where

哪 na³ — *pron.* which

As an interrogative *pron.* or *adv.*, 哪 is usually pronounced as nei³ or nai³ before measure words or numerals + measure words or in the following combinations: 哪个 (which one), 哪些 (which), 哪样 (which kind of), and (哪会儿 at what time).

中央 zhong¹yang¹ — *a.* central (opp. 四周 si⁴zhou¹`)

南 nan² — *n.* south (opp. 北 bei³)

大道 da⁴dao⁴ — *n.* big road, avenue

零 ling² — *num.* zero

多少 duo¹shao — *adv.* how many, how much

家里 jia¹li — at home

里 li — *pstp.* (after a *n.*) in, at (opp. 外 wai¹)

li³ — *n.* inside; Chinese unit of distance (= ½ kilometer)

九 jiu³ — *num.* nine

办 ban⁴ — *v.* do, handle

公 gong¹ — *n.* official business *a.* public (opp. 私 si¹)

办公 ban⁴gong¹ — *v.* work (in an office)

室 shi⁴ — *n.* room

办公室 ban⁴gong¹shi⁴ — *n.* office

手机 shou³ji¹ — *n.* cell phone

手 shou³ — *n.* hand (opp. 脚 jiao³)

机 ji¹ — *n.* machine, appliance

Supplementary Vocabulary and Expressions

DOB — 出生日期 (chu¹sheng¹ ri⁴qi¹)

domestic long distance — 国内长途 (guo²nei⁴ chang²tu²)

international long distance — 国际长途 (guo²ji⁴ chang²tu²)

cannot get through — 打不通 (da³ bu⁴tong¹)

zip number — 邮编 (you²bian¹)

A cell phone is something that you can't do without.
手机是个不可缺少的东西.
(Shou³ji¹ shi⁴ ge bu⁴ ke³ que¹shao³ de dong¹xi.)

27

7. Exercises

I. Tone Practice:

yi¹ 一 one   yi² 移 move   yi³ 已 already   yi⁴ 亿 hundred million
di¹ 低 low   di² 笛 flute   di³ 底 bottom   di⁴ 弟 younger brother
qi¹ 七 seven   qi² 骑 ride   qi³ 起 get up   qi⁴ 气 gas

II. Give your own answers to the following questions:

1. 您叫什么名字?

2. 您住在哪儿?

3. 您家的电话号码儿是多少?

4. 您结婚了吗?

5. 您有孩子吗? 几个儿子? 几个女儿?

III. Read aloud the following numbers in Chinese:

1. 一 三 五 七 九

2. 二 四 六 八 零

3. 七 九 四 零 二 二 六 八 · 五

IV. Write the following numbers in Chinese:

1. 1325

2. 7481

3. 9872

4. 168860

5. 98053085417

V. What is it?
一片 (pian⁴: thin slice) 两片, 三、四片, 五片, 六片, 七、八片,
落到 (luo⁴dao: fall into) 水里都 (dou¹: all) 不见.

八. 年龄

A: 黄小姐¹, 你爸爸、妈妈都

好²吗?

B: 谢谢, 他们都好.

A: 你爸爸多大岁数³了?

B: 五十六了.

A: 妈妈呢⁴?

B: 四十九.

A: 你小妹妹几岁了?

B: 才两岁半.

A: 你今年多大了?

B: 对不起, 我不能告诉你.

8. Nian²ling²

A. Huang² xiao³jie, ni³ ba⁴ba, ma¹ma dou¹

hao³ ma?

B: Xie⁴xie, ta¹men dou¹ hao³.

A: Ni³ ba⁴ba duo¹da⁴ sui⁴shu le?

B: Wu³ shi liu⁴ le.

A: Ma¹ma ne?

B: Si⁴ shi jiu³.

A: Ni² xiao³ mei⁴mei ji³ sui⁴ le?

B: Cai² liang³ sui⁴ ban⁴.

A: Ni³ jin¹nian² duo¹da⁴ le?

B: Dui⁴buqi³, wo³ bu⁴ neng² gao⁴su ni.

8. Age

A: Miss Huang, how are your parents doing?

B: They are both very well. Thank you!

A: How old is your father?

B: He's 56.

A: And your mom?

B: 49.

A: How old is your small sister?

B. Only two and half.

A: How old are you?

B: I'm sorry. I can't tell you.

8. Notes

1. 黄 小 姐 (Huang² xiao³jie): Miss Huang In Chinese, names go before salutations or titles. Eg. 吴 太 太 (Wu² tai⁴tai) Mrs. Wu, 杨 先 生 (Yang² xian¹sheng) Mr. Yang, 王 经 理 (Wang² jing¹li³) Mr. Wang, the manager, 李 大 夫 (Li³ dai⁴fu) Doctor Li, 张 主 任 (Zhang¹ zhu³ren⁴) Director Zhang

2. 都 好 (dou¹ hao³): both are well 都 is used with two or more things or persons, equivalent to *both* or *all*. The 好 (hao³) here means *be in good health*, same as the 好 (hao³) in 你 好! (Ni²hao³!)

3. 多 大 岁 数 (duo¹da⁴ sui⁴shu): how old The original meaning of 多 (duo¹) is *many* or *much*; it also means *how* when followed by an adj. or an *adv.* 大 (da⁴) usually means *big*; here it means *old*. 岁 数 (sui⁴shu) is *age*. Note the different question words used to ask the age of different people. 多 大 岁 数 (duo¹da⁴ sui⁴shu) is usually used to ask the age of elderly people. 多 大 (duo¹da⁴, without 岁 数 sui⁴shu) is used to ask the age of not too old people. 几 岁 (ji³sui⁴) is generally used to ask the age of children or teenagers. Eg. 你 小 儿 子 几 岁 了? (Ni² xiao³ er²zi **ji³sui⁴** le?) How old is your small son?

4. 呢 (ne): used to form a short question, following the preceding statement. It is also used at the end of a declarative sentence to show assertion or emphasis. 我 可 想 你 呢! (Wo² ke² xiang³ ni² **ne**!) I miss you very much!

8. Vocabulary

年龄 nian^{2}ling^2 *n.* age

黄 huang^2 *n.* a family name;
a. yellow

小 xiao^3 *a.* small (opp. 大 da^4)

小姐 xiao^{3}jie   *n.* miss, young lady
(Lit. small elder sister)

都 dou^1 *adv.* both, all; already

他 ta^1 *pron.* he, him

他们 ta^{1}men   *pron.* they, them

多大 duo^{1}da^4 *adv.* how big; how old

岁 sui^4 *n.* year (for age)

岁数 sui^{4}shu   *n.* age

十 shi^2 *num.* ten

呢 ne   *part.* to form a short
question or to
emphasize a statement

才 cai^2 *adv.* only; just; only
then (used before verbs
to show sth. takes place
late); used to
emphasize the
following word

半 ban^4 *n., a.* half

今年 jin^{1}nian^2 this year

对 dui^4 *part.* yes
prep. toward, to, for
adj. right, correct
adv. rightly, correctly
(opp. 错 cuo^4)

对不起 dui^{4}buqi^3 sorry; excuse me

能 neng^2 *v.* can, may

告诉 gao^{4}su   *v.* tell

Supplementary Vocabulary and Expressions

age discrimination	年龄歧视 (nian^{2}ling^2 qi^{2}shi^4)
aging	老化 (lao^{3}hua^4)
baby	婴儿 (ying^{1}er^2)
old age	老年 (lao^{3}nian^2)
old people	老人 (lao^{3}ren^2)
privacy	隐私 (yin^{3}si^1)
young people	年轻人 (nian^{2}qing^{1}ren^2)
youthfulness	青春 (qing^{1}chun^1)

He is young and vigorous.
他年轻力壮.
(Ta^1 nian^{2}qing^1 li^{4}zhuang^4.)

8. Exercises

I. Tone Practice:

bai¹ 掰 break off   bai² 白 white   bai³ 白 hundred   bai⁴ 败 defeat
cai¹ 猜 guess   cai² 才 just   cai³ 彩 colorful   cai⁴ 菜 dish

II. Write the following numerals in Chinese:

1. seventy   2. fifty   3. sixty four   4. forty two   5. eighty one

III. Ask appropriate questions to suit the following answers:

1. A: _____?
   B: 我爸爸七十八了.

2. A: _____?
   B: 我妹妹二十一岁.

3. A: _____?
   B: 他两岁半.

4. A: _____?
   B: 我不告诉你.

IV. Turn the following questions into shortened ones by using 呢:

Example: 我还没有吃饭, 你吃饭了吗? → 我还没有吃饭, 你呢?

1. 我妈妈很好, 你妈妈好吗?

2. 黄小姐在办公室, 李小姐在哪儿?

3. 你有三个男孩, 他有几个孩子?

4. 我没有现钱 (xian⁴qian²: cash), 你有没有现钱?

5. 你想吃好的, 你钱在哪儿?

6. 人都在哪儿啊? 我一个也没见!

九. 中国小说

A: 嚯! 这么些[1] 书哪能[2] 看得完[3] 啊!

B: 书总是不会嫌多的. 我喜欢文学, 我的书多半是文学书.

A: 有小说吗?

B: 有. 有《三国》、《红楼梦》和《水浒》[4], 你要看吗?

A: 我很喜欢中国小说. 可是我的中文还不太好, 我只能看英文的中国小说.

9. Zhong¹guo² Xiao³shuo¹

A: Huo⁴! Zhe⁴mexie¹ shu¹ na³neng² kan⁴ de wan² a!

B: Shu¹ zong³shi⁴ bu² hui⁴ xian² duo¹ de. Wo² xi³huan wen²xue², wo³de shu¹ duo¹ban⁴ shi wen² xue² shu¹.

A: You² xiao³shuo¹ ma?

B: You³. You³ 《San¹ Guo²》,《 Hong² Lou² Meng⁴》 he² 《Shui² Hu³》. Ni³ yao⁴ kan⁴ ma?

A: Wo² hen² xi³huan zhong¹guo² xiao³shuo¹, ke³shi⁴ wo³de zhong¹wen² hai² bu² tai⁴ hao³, wo² zhi³ neng² kan⁴ ying¹wen² de zhong¹guo² xiao³shuo¹.

9. Chinese Novels

A: Wow! Can you finish reading so many books?

B: You can never have too many books. I like literature and most of my books are literature.

A: Any novels?

B: Yes. I have *Three Kingdoms*, *Dream of the Red Chamber*, and *Water Margin*. Do you want to read them?

A: I like Chinese literature, but my Chinese is not very good. I can only read the English versions.

9. Notes

1. 这么些 (zhe⁴mexie¹): meaning *so many* (*much*) or *so few* (*little*), depending on the context 你有**这么些**中国朋友啊! (Ni² you³ **zhe⁴mexie¹** zhong¹guo² peng²you a!) You have so many Chinese friends! 就**这么些**钱, 哪够用啊! (Jiu⁴ **zhe⁴mexie¹** qian², na³ gou⁴yong⁴ a!) Will such little money be enough for it? In the second example above there is the word 就 (jiu⁴; only) before 这么些 (zhe⁴mexie¹); hence the meaning must be negative. Less colloquial for 这么些 (zhe⁴mexie¹) is 这么多 (zhe⁴me duo¹) or 这么一点 (zhe⁴me yi⁴dian³) .

2. 哪能 (na³neng²): how can 你如果不用功, **哪能**学好汉语呢? (Ni³ ru²guo³ bu² yong⁴gong¹, **na³neng²** xue²hao³ han⁴yu³ ne?) If you do not work hard, how can you learn Chinese?

3. 看得完 (kan⁴ de wan²) be able to finish reading ...得... (...de...) put between a verb and a complement expresses degree or result. 睡**得**晚 (shui⁴ **de** wan³) go to bed late, 唱**得**好 (chang⁴ **de** hao³) sing well, 跑**得**快 (pao³ **de** kuai⁴) run fast 现在雨下**得**很大. (Xian⁴zai⁴ yu³ xia⁴ **de** hen³ da⁴.) It is raining heavily.

4. 《三国》、《红楼梦》、《水浒》 (San¹ Guo², Hong² Lou² Meng⁴, Shui² Hu³): *Three Kingdoms, Dream of the Red Chamber, Water Margin* These three novels plus *A Journey to the West* (西游记 Xi¹ You² Ji⁴) are the four famous Chinese classic novels.

9. Vocabulary

小 说 xiao^{3}shuo^1 *n.* novel, fiction

嚯 huo^4 *int.* expressing surprise or praise

这 zhe^4, zhei^4 *pron.* this (opp. 那 na^4)

When 这 is used independently or is followed by a noun, it is pronounced as zhe^4; when it is followed by a measure word or a numeral + a measure word, it is usually pronounced as zhei^4. In 这 个(zhei^4 ge: this), 这 些 (zhei^{4}xie^1: these), 这 会 儿 (zhei^{4}huər^4: this time), and 这 样 (zhei^{4}yang^4: so, such, in this way), the 这 is also usually pronounced as zhei^4.

这 么 zhe^{4}me   *adv.* so, such

些 xie^1 *a., adv.* some

这 么 些 zhe^{4}mexie^1 so many, so much, these many, these much; so little, so few

书 shu^1 *n.* book

哪 能 na^{3}neng^2 how can

看 kan^4 *v.* read; look, watch; visit

得 de   *part.* to show degree or result

de^2 *v.* get

de^2 *part.* all right

dei^3 *v.* have to, need

完 wan^2 *v.* finish

会 hui^4 *v.* can; be likely to; learn, grasp
n. meeting; a short time (会 儿 huər^4)

嫌 xian^2 *v.* dislike

不 会 嫌 bu^2 hui^{4}xian^2 cannot be too …

喜 欢 hi^{3}huan   *v.* like, love

文 学 wen^{2}xue^2 *n.* literature

多 半 duo^{1}ban^4 *adv.* mostly (Lit. more than half)

红 hong^2 *a.* red

楼 lou^2 *n.* a storied building; floor

梦 meng^4 *n. & v.* dream

浒 hu^3 *n.* water margin

可 是 ke^{3}shi^4 *conj.* but

英 文 ying^{1}wen^2 *n.* the English language
a. English

Supplementary Vocabulary and Expressions

author	作 者 (zuo^{4}zhe^3)	
classic	古 典 的 (gu^{2}dian^3 de)	
modern	现 代 的 (xian^{4}dai^4 de)	
novelist	小 说 家 (xiao^{3}shuo^{1}jia^1)	
original version	原 文 (yuan^{2}wen^2)	
story	故 事 (gu^{4}shi^4)	
translation	翻 译 (fan^{1}yi^4)	
works	作 品 (zuo^{4}pin^3)	
writer	作 家 (zuo^{4}jia^1)	

Reading is always profitable.
开 卷 有 益.
(Kai^1 juan^4 you^3 yi^4.)

9. Exercises

I. Tone Practice:

wu¹ 屋 house   wu² 无 not have   wu³ 五 five   wu⁴ 雾 fog

tu¹ 秃 bald   tu² 图 map   tu³ 土 soil   tu⁴ 吐 vomit

II. Pattern Drill:

Subject	Verb intransitive	Particle	Adverb or Adjective Complement
我 你 他 她们	说	得	快.
	喝		多.
	学		好.
	来		晚.
	知道		不少.

III. Answer the following questions:

1. 你可以走快一点吗?

2. 你学了两年中文, 已经能看中文小说了吧?

3. 你可以告诉我你的年龄吗?

4. 喝咖啡能预防癌症吗?

IV. Rewrite the following sentences by using 哪能 to replace 一定, or vice versa without changing the meaning of the sentences:

Example: 学中国文学的人哪能不看《三国》和《红楼梦》? → 学中国文学的人一定要看《三国》和《红楼梦》.

1. 这么些书你哪能看得完!

2. 你家有八口人, 家里一定很热闹.

3. 他已经学了两年中文了, 中文一定说得好.

4. 黄小姐有空, 她哪能不来!

十．作息时间

A: 你每天几点钟[1]起床?

B: 七点一刻.

A: 几点上班儿?

B: 八点半.

A: 晚上什么时候睡觉?

B: 十点. 周末要[2]十二点.

A: 干什么[3]睡得这么晚哪?

B: 看电视呗[4].

A: 你太太也陪你看电视吗?

B: 那当然. 不过[5]她一看电视马

上[6]就 睡觉.

10. Zuo⁴xi¹ Shi²jian¹

A: Ni² mei³tian¹ ji² dian³zhong¹

qi³chuang²?

B: Qi¹ dian³ yi²ke⁴.

A: Ji² dian³ shang⁴bar¹?

B: Ba¹ dian³ ban⁴.

A: Wan³shang shen²me shi²hou shui⁴jiao⁴?

B: Shi² dian³. Zhou¹mo⁴ yao⁴ shi²er⁴ dian³.

A: Gan⁴shen²me shui⁴ de zhe⁴me wan³ na?

B: Kan⁴ dian⁴shi⁴ bei.

A: Ni³ tai⁴tai ye³ pei² ni³ kan⁴ dian⁴shi⁴ ma?

B: Na⁴ dang¹ran². Bu²guo⁴ ta¹ yi² kan⁴

dian⁴shi⁴ ma³shang⁴ jiu⁴ shui⁴jiao⁴.

10. Daily Schedule

A: What time do you get up every morning?

B: A quarter after seven.

A: What time do you go to work?

B: Eight thirty.

A: When do you go to bed in the evening?

B: Ten o'clock and on weekends, twelve.

A: Why so late?

B: Well, I just watch TV.

A: Does your wife always accompany you to watch TV?

B: Of course. But she cannot watch TV without going to sleep.

10. Notes

1. 几点钟 (ji^2 $dian^3$ $zhong^1$): what time The word 钟 ($zhong^1$) can be omitted. Another expression to ask about time is 什么时候 ($shen^2$me shi^2hou).

2. 要 (yao^4): need, desire; be going to Here it implies "not go to bed until as late as…"

3. 干什么 ($gan^4$$shen^2$me) = 干吗 ($gan^4$$ma^2$) or 为什么 ($wei^4$$shen^2$me): what for, used for asking purpose or intention 你**干什么**不早说呀? (Ni^3 **$gan^4$$shen^2$me** bu^4 zao^3 $shuo^1$ ya?) Why didn't you say it earlier? When the reason of objective things is asked, use only 为什么 ($wei^4$$shen^2$me).

4. 呗 (bei): *part.* used at the end of a sentence to denote sth. that is simple or easy to understand, or to indicate an agreement with reluctance 不懂, 就问**呗**! (Bu^4 $dong^3$, jiu^4 wen^4 **bei**!) If you don't understand, just ask!
   Wife: 亲爱的! 我要买这条珠项链. 我要买! ($Qin^1$$ai^4$de! wo^3 yao^4 mai^3 $zhei^4$ $tiao^2$ zhu^1 $xiang^4$$lian^4$. Wo^3 yao^4 mai^3!) I want to buy this pearl necklace! I want it, honey!
   Husband: 你一定要买, 就买**呗**. (Ni^3 $yi^2$$ding^4$ yao^4 mai^3, jiu^4 mai^3 **bei**!) Well, buy it, if you insist.

5. 不过 ($bu^2$$guo^4$): but, however This is the same as 但 (dan^4), 但是 ($dan^4$$shi^4$), or 可是 ($ke^3$$shi^4$). 他是个聪明的孩子, **不过**不太用功. (Ta^1 shi ge $cong^1$ming de hai^2zi, **$bu^2$$guo^4$** bu^2 tai^4 $yong^4$$gong^1$.) He's an intelligent but not very hardworking boy.

6. 一 … 马上 (yi^1… $ma^3$$shang^4$): as soon as 我一得到信息, **马上**告诉你. (Wo^3 **yi^4** $de^2$$dao^4$ $xin^4$$xi^1$ **$ma^3$$shang^4$** gao^4su ni.) I'll tell you the information the instant I get it. 天一亮我们得**马上**动身. ($Tian^1$ **yi^2** $liang^4$, wo^3men dei^3 **$ma^3$$shang^4$** $dong^4$$shen^1$.) We must start at dawn. The word 就 (jiu^4) following 马上 ($ma^3$$shang^4$) in the text is added for emphasis. The less colloquial for 马上 ($ma^3$$shang^4$) is 立刻 ($li^4$$ke^4$); the more colloquial is 立马儿.

10. Vocabulary

作 zuo^4	*n.* work (short for 工作 gong^{1}zuo^4)
息 xi^1	*n.* rest (short for 休息 xiu^{1}xi)
时间 shi^{2}jian^1	*n.* time
每 mei^3	*a.* every
天 tian^1	*n.* day; sky; heaven (opp. 地 di^4); time; season; weather
每天 mei^{3}tian^1	*adv.* every day
…点钟 dian^{3}zhong^1	…o'clock
几点钟 ji^{2}dian^{3}zhong^1	what time, when
起床 qi^{3}chuang^2	*v.* get up
刻 ke^4	*n.* a quarter of an hour
上班 shang^{4}ban^1	*v.* go to work (opp. 下班 xia^{4}ban^1)
时候 shi^{2}hou	*n.* time
睡觉 shui^{4}jiao^4	*v.* go to bed (opp. 起床 qi^{3}chuang^2); sleep
周 zhou^1	*n.* week
末 mo^4	*n.* end (opp. 始 shi^3)
周末 zhou^{1}mo^4	*n.* weekend (opp. 周日 zhou^{1}ri^4)
干 gan^4	*v.* do, work
gan^1	*a.* dry
	v. "bottoms up!"
干什么 gan^{4}shen^{2}me	what for, why
电视 dian^{4}shi^4	*n.* T.V.
呗 bei	*part.* expressing a clear fact or an agreement with reluctance
陪 pei^2	*v.* accompany
当然 dang^{1}ran^2	of course, certainly
当 dang^1	*v.* work as, be; ought, should (short for 应当 ying^{1}dang^1)
不过 bu^{2}guo^4	*conj.* but; *adv.* only; merely
	v. not exceed
马上 ma^{3}shang^4	*adv.* immediately

Supplementary Vocabulary and Expressions

arrive earlier	早到 (zao^{3}dao^4)
at a fixed time	定时 (ding^{4}shi^2)
clean the rooms	打扫房间 (da^{2}sao^3 fang^{2}jian^1)
do laundry	洗衣服 (xi^3 yi^{1}fu)
get up early and go to bed early	早起早睡 (zao^{2}qi^3 zao^{3}shui^4)
heavy work	重活 (zhong^{4}huo^2)
housework	家务 (jia^{1}wu^4)
light work	轻活 (qing^{1}huo^2)
live, get along	过日子 (guo^4 ri^{4}zi)
put on clothes	穿衣服 (chuan^1 yi^{1}fu)
relaxed	轻松 (qing^{1}song^1)
tired	累 (lei^4)
tooth brush	牙刷 (ya^{2}shua^1)
tooth paste	牙膏 (ya^{2}gao^1)
towel	毛巾 (mao^{2}jin^1)
soap	肥皂 (fei^{2}za^4)
wash face	洗脸 (xi^2 lian^3)
work overtime	加班 (jia^{1}ban^1)

What time is it now?
现在几点了? (Xian^{4}zai^4 ji^{2}dian^3 le?)

10. Exercises

I. Tone Practice: (Note: the two dots at the top of ü are omitted after j, q, x.)

qu^1 区 area   qu^2 渠 ditch   qu^3 取 take   qu^4 去 go

xu^1 须 must   xu^2 徐 slowly   xu^3 许 allow   xu^4 序 order

II. Put the following time into Chinese (Cf. Appendix 4.):

6:00	3:15	8:30	7:45
9:07	10:58	4:39	2:03

III. Make sentences with the words given below:

1. 每天   几点   睡觉   你
2. 上班   你太太   什么时候
3. 才   周末   我   十点   起床
4. 我   晚上   每天   所以   睡得晚   电视   看   太太

IV. Complete the following compound sentences and change 可是 into 不过 and vice versa:

1. 李小姐已经来了, 可是黄小姐_____.

2. 我喜欢中国小说, 不过我的中文_____.

3. 她喜欢看电视, 不过一看电视_____.

4. 我知道他家里的电话号码, 可是不知道他_____.

V. In which of the following questions 干什么 (gan^{4}shen^{2}me) should be changed into 为什么 (wei^{4}shen^{2}me)?

1. 你干什么要学广东话?
2. 已经十月了, 干什么还这么热?
3. 干什么喝茶有益健康?
4. 花儿干什么这样红?
5. 她干什么一来就走?
6. 干什么天热要多喝水?
7. 你干什么喝了这么多水?
8. 干什么多喝了咖啡, 想睡觉?
9. 他到书店去干什么?
10. 你知道不知道乌龙茶干什么能预防癌症?

十一. 请假

(电话铃响)

A: 喂!

B: 我要王经理听电话.

A: 我就[1]是.

B: 我是小张. 我今儿[2]不太舒服[3].
上午要去看大夫[4], 不能来上
班儿了, 要请假一天[5].

A: 行! 你哪儿不舒服?

B: 有点儿发烧. 可能是感冒了.

A: 喔, 你多喝些水, 好好儿地[6]休
息吧!

B: 谢谢. 明天见.

A: 明天见.

11. Qing³jia⁴

(Dian⁴hua⁴ ling² xiang³)

A: Wei²!

B: Wo³ yao⁴ Wang² jing¹li³ ting¹ dian⁴hua⁴.

A: Wo³ jiu⁴ shi⁴.

B: Wo³ shi Xiao³ Zhang¹. Wo³ jiər¹ bu²
tai⁴ shu¹fu. Shang⁴wu³ yao⁴ qu⁴ kan⁴
dai⁴fu, bu⁴ neng² lai² shang⁴bar¹ le.
Yao⁴ qing³jia⁴ yi⁴ tian¹.

A: Xing²! Ni² nar³ bu⁴ shu¹fu?

B: You² diar³ fa¹shao¹. Ke³neng² shi
gan³mao⁴ le.

A: O¹, ni³ duo¹ he¹ xie¹ shui³, hao²haor³
de xiu¹xi ba!

B: Xie⁴xie. Ming²tian¹ jian⁴.

A: Ming²tian¹ jian⁴.

11. Asking for Leave of Absence

(Phone ringing)

A: Hello!

B: May I speak to Mr. Wang, the manager?

A: This is he.

B: This is Xiao Zhang. I am not feeling

well today. I'm going to see my doctor;

I can't come to work. May I ask for a

day's leave?

A: Okay. What's wrong?

B: I have a slight fever. I may have caught

a cold.

A: Oh, drink a lot of water and get a lot of

rest.

B: Thank you. See you tomorrow.

A: See you tomorrow.

11. Notes

1. 就 (jiu⁴): exactly, precisely, used for emphasis Eg. **就** 在 这 儿 (jiu⁴ zai⁴ zher⁴) just here, **就** 在 那 儿 (jiu⁴ zai⁴ nar⁴) just there 她 **就** 要 这 个. (Ta¹ **jiu⁴** yao⁴ zhei⁴ ge.) This is just what she wants.

2. 今 儿 (jiər¹) today, colloq. for 今 天 (jin¹tian¹) Sometimes the character 个 (ge) is added to become 今 儿 个 (jiər¹ge). Note when *in* sound becomes retroflexed, its pronunciation is *iər*.

3. 不 太 舒 服 (bu² tai⁴ shu¹fu): not very well 不 舒 服 (bu⁴ shu¹fu) has two meanings: a. not comfortable b. sick

4. 大 夫 (dai⁴fu): medical doctor, same as 医 生 (yi¹sheng¹) Note the pronunciation of 大 here is dai⁴, not da⁴.

5. 请 假 一 天 (qing³ jia⁴ yi⁴ tian¹): = 请 一 天 假 (qing³ yi⁴ tian¹ jia⁴) The time word may be put before or after 假 (jia⁴).

6. 好 好 儿 地 (hao²haor³ de): to one's heart's content 你 累 了, 上 床 **好 好** 儿 **地** 睡 一 觉 吧! (Ni³ lei⁴le, shang⁴ chuang² **hao²haor³ de** shui⁴ yi² jiao⁴ ba!) You are tired. Get into bed and get a good rest. 请 把 这 房 间 **好 好** 儿 **地** 打 扫 一 下 儿. (Qing² ba³ zhe⁴ fang²jian¹ **hao²haor³ de** da²sao³ yi²xiar⁴.) Give the room a thorough cleaning, please. 地 (de) is a particle forming an adverbial with the word or words preceding it. Distinguish 地 (de) from 的 (de), which is used to form an attribute. Compare: 幸 福 **地** 生 活 (xing⁴fu² **de** sheng¹huo²) live happily and 幸 福 **的** 生 活 (xing⁴fu² **de** sheng¹huo²) a happy life

11. Vocabulary

请假 qing³jia⁴ — v. ask for leave of absence

假 jia⁴ — n. leave of absence; vacation

jia³ — a. false (opp. 真 zhen¹)

铃 ling² — n. bell

响 xiang³ — v. ring; a. loud

喂 wei⁴ — int. hello (As the 4th tone is too sharp, many people change it to the 2nd tone in answering phone calls.)

王 wang² — n. king; a family name

经理 jing¹li³ — n. manager

听 ting¹ — v. listen

听电话 ting¹ dian⁴hua⁴ — answer the phone

张 zhang¹ — n. a family name; meas. used with paper, sheet, etc.

今儿 jiər¹ — n., adv. today (colloq. of 今天 jin¹tian¹)

舒服 shu¹fu — a. well; comfortable

上午 shang⁴wu³ — n. morning, A.M. (opp. 下午 xia⁴wu³)

去 qu⁴ — v. (preceding a v.) be going to do sth; go, leave (opp. 来 lai²)

大夫 dai⁴fu — n. doctor (opp. 病人 bing⁴ren²)

行 xing² — int. O.K., all right

发烧 fa¹shao¹ — v. have a fever

烧 shao¹ — n. fever; v. burn; braise, cook

可能 ke³neng² — adv. possibly, maybe (opp. 一定 yi¹ding⁴)

感冒 gan³mao⁴ — v. catch a cold; n. cold

好好儿 hao²haor³ — all out, get the best out of, to one's heart's content; in perfectly good condition

地 de — part. forming an adverbial

di⁴ — n. earth (opp. 天 tian¹); place

休息 xiu¹xi — n. rest; v. take a rest (opp. 工作 gong¹zuo⁴)

明 ming² — a. bright (opp. 暗 an⁴); next (day, year, etc.)

明天 ming²tian¹ — adv., n. tomorrow (opp. 昨天 zuo²tian¹)

Supplementary Vocabulary and Expressions

have a (high, low) fever — 发 (高, 低) 烧 (fa¹ [gao¹, di¹] shao¹)

need two days' rest — 要休息两天 (yao⁴ xiu¹xi liang³ tian¹)

on vacation — 休假 (xiu¹jia⁴)

sick leave — 病假 (bing⁴jia⁴)

take medicines on time — 按时吃药 (an⁴shi¹ chi¹ yao⁴)

Need my help?
要我帮忙吗? (Yao⁴wo³ bang¹mang¹ ma?)
Please hold.
请稍等. (Qing³ shao¹ deng³.)
The fever is gone.
烧退了. (Shao¹ tui⁴ le.)
What happened? (asked by a doctor to his patient)
有什么不舒服? (You³ shen²me bu⁴ shu¹fu?)
Who is speaking? (on the phone)
您是谁? (Nin² shi shei²?)

11. Exercises

I. Give the phonetic spellings for the following words:

总是　　女　　结婚　　黄　　对不起

休息　　大夫　　舒服　　起床　　睡觉

II. Complete the following conversation on the phone:

1. A: 喂! _____ ?
   B: 他不在.
   A: _____ ?
   B: 他去看大夫了.
   A: 喔! _____ ?
   B: 他发烧了.

2. A: 喂! 小李在吗?
   B: 她在.
   A: 请她 _____ .
   B: 请稍等 (shao^1 deng^3: hold, wait a bit).
   C: 喂!
   A: 是小李吗?
   C: _____ .
   A: 你好吗? 小李!
   C: _____ , 谢谢!

III. Rewrite the sentences by replacing the underlined words with other expressions that have the same meaning:

Example: 您<u>哪儿</u>不舒服? → 您有什么不舒服?

1. 你爸爸每天<u>几点钟</u>睡觉?

2. 他家<u>不是个小家庭</u>.

3. 我太太一看电视<u>马上</u>睡觉.

4. 我看了《红楼梦》, <u>但是</u>还没有看《水浒》.

5. 今天她<u>不一定</u>会来.

44

十 二. 开 会

A: 王先生让我给你捎个信儿[1].

B: 什么事儿?

A: 今儿下午开会.

B: 几点钟?

A: 两点半.

B: 在哪儿?

A: 二楼会议室.

B: 开什么会?

A: 说是很重要的会, 大家不能迟
到.

B: 什么重要的会?

A: 别问了. 咱们[2] 一去
就知道了[3].

12. Kai[1] hui[4]

A: Wang[2] xian[1]sheng rang[4] wo[3] gei[2] ni[3]
shao[1] ge xiər[4].

B: Shen[2]me shər[4]?

A: Jiər[1] xia[4]wu[3] kai[1]hui[4].

B: Ji[2] dian[3]zhong[1]?

A: Liang[2] dian[3] ban[4].

B: Zai[4] nar[3]?

A: Er[4] lou[2] hui[4]yi[4]shi[4].

B: Kai[1] shen[2]me hui[4]?

A: Shuo[1] shi[4] hen[3] zhong[4]yao[4] de hui[4].
Da[4]jia[1] bu[4] neng[2] chi[2] da[4].

B: Shen[2]me zhong[4]yao[4] de hui[4]?

A: Bie[2] wen[4] le. Zan[2]men yi[2] qu[4] jiu[4]
zhi[1]dao le.

12. A Meeting

A: Mr. Wang told me to take a message

to you.

B: What message?

A: There will be a meeting this afternoon.

B: What time?

A: Two thirty.

B: Where?

A: In the second-floor meeting room.

B: Do you know what the meeting is about?

A: He said it's an important meeting.

Everyone must arrive on time.

B: What important meeting?

A: You don't have to ask. We'll know

what it's about when we get there.

12. Notes

1. 给 你 捎 个 信 儿 (gei^2 ni^3 shao^1 ge xiər^4) take a message to you 给 (gei^3) means (do sth.) *for* or *to* (sb.) 她 **给** 我 沏 了 茶. (Ta^1 **gei**^{2} wo^3 qi^1 le cha^2.) She made some tea for me. Sometimes "给 + sb.+ do sth." can be converted to "do sth.+ 给 + sb.". 给 你 捎 个 信 儿 (gei^2 ni^3 shao^1 ge xiər^4) = 捎 个 信 儿 给 你 (shao^1 ge xiər^4 gei^2 ni^3) 我 会 **给** 你 打 电 话. (Wo^3 hui^4 **gei**^{2} ni da^3 dian^{4}hua^4.) = 我 会 打 电 话 **给** 你. (Wo^3 hui^4 da^3 dian^{4}hua^4 **gei**^{2} ni.) I'll call you.

2. 咱 们 (zan^{2}men): we The pronoun 咱 们 (zan^{2}men) includes both the speaker and the person(s) spoken to, while 我 们 (wo^{3}men) may or may not include the person(s) spoken to. **咱 们** 商 量 一 下. (**Zan**^{2}**men** shang^{1}liang^2 yi^{2}xia^4.) Let's talk it over.

3. 一 去 就 知 道 了 (yi^2 qu^4 jiu^4 zhi^{1}dao le) = 去 了 就 知 道 了 (qu^4 le jiu^4 zhi^{1}dao le.) 一…就… (yi^1…jiu^4…): as soon as 你 一 看 **就** 懂. (Ni^3 yi^2 kan^4 **jiu**^{4} dong^3.) Once you read it, you understand it. 一… 就 … (yi^1...jiu^4...) means the same as 一… 马 上 (yi^1… ma^{3}shang^4) in Passage 10 (Note 5). 春 天 一 到, 我 **就** (or 马 上) 过 敏. (Chun^{1}tian^{1}yi^{2}dao^4, wo^3 **jiu**^{4} [*or* **ma**^{3}**shang**^{4}] guo^{4}min^3.) I always get allergies when spring comes. For more emphasis the word 马 上 (ma^{3}shang^4) and 就 (jiu^4) are used together. Cf. the use of 就 (jiu^4) in another pattern: 只 要 … 就 (zhi^{3}yao^4…jiu^4) in Note 5, Passage 4.

12. Vocabulary

开 kai^1	*v.* open; turn on (opp. 关 guan^1)
开会 kai^{1}hui^4	hold a meeting
先生 xian^{1}sheng	*n.* Mr.; teacher; husband (opp. 太太 tai^{4}tai) (Lit. earlier born)
先 xian^1	*adv.* earlier; before; at first, at the beginning (opp. 后 hou^4)
让 rang^4	*v.* let, allow
给 gei^3	*v.* give *prep.* for, to
捎 shao^1	*v.* bring
信 xin^4	*n.* message; letter *v.* believe
事 shi^4	*n.* thing, matter (or 事情 shi^{4}qing)
下午 xia^{4}wu^3	*n., adv.* afternoon, P.M. (opp. 上午 shang^{4}wu^3)
会议 hui^{4}yi^4	*n.* meeting
重 zhong^4	*a.* heavy (opp. 轻 qing^1)
chong^2	*adv.* again
重要 zhong^{4}yao^4	*a.* important
大家 da^{4}jia^1	*n.* everyone, all
迟 chi^2	*a., adv.* late
迟到 chi^{2}dao^4	*v.* be late
别 bie^2	don't (= 不要 bu^{2}yao^4)
咱们 zan^{2}men	*pron.* we, us
一…就 yi^1…jiu^4	*conj.* the instant, as soon as

Supplementary Vocabulary and Expressions

call a meeting	召集会议 (zhao^{4}ji^2 hui^{4}yi^4)
chairperson	主席 (zhu^{3}xi^2)
conclusion	结论 (jie^{3}lun^4)
debate	辩论 (bian^{4}lun^4)
discuss	讨论 (tao^{3}lun^4)
resolution	决议 (jue^{2}yi^4)
suggestion	建议 (jian^{4}yi^4)
vote against	投票反对 (tou^{2}piao^4 fan^{3}dui^4)
vote for	投票赞成 (tou^{2}piao^4 zan^{4}cheng^2)

Let's start the meeting.
现在开会. (Xian^{4}zai^4 kai^{1}hui^4.)
The meeting will start (end) at 4 PM.
会议下午四点开始 (结束).
(Hui^{4}yi^4 xia^{4}wu^3 si^4 dian^3 kai^{1}shi^3 [jie^{2}su^4].)
Three cobblers with their wits combined equal to Zhuge Liang, the mastermind. (A big group of people will always be more knowledgeable and smarter than just one expert.)
三个臭皮匠合一个诸葛亮. (San^1 ge chou^4 pi^{2}jiang he^2 yi^4 ge Zhu^{1}ge^2 liang^4.)

12. Exercises

I. Tone Practice:

fei¹ 飞 fly   fei² 肥 fat   fei³ 匪 bandit   fei⁴ 费 fee
lei¹ 勒 strap tight   lei² 雷 thunder   lei³ 蕾 bud   lei⁴ 累 tired

II. Fill in the following blanks with the words given below:

上班儿   理想   可是   马上   当然   好好儿   多半   …就

1. 快进去吧, _____ 就要开会了!

2. 都十点半了, 不要再看《红楼梦》了! _____ 地睡觉吧!

3. 学汉语 _____ 要下功夫.

4. 我很想去, _____ 我没有时间.

5. 他今天为什么不去 _____ ?

6. 当一个大夫是她的 _____ .

7. 你 _____ 说我的名字, 他 _____ 知道了.

8. 他这时候还不来, _____ 不会来了.

III. Complete the following dialogs:

1. A: 王大夫让我给你捎个信儿.
   B: _____ ?

2. A: 为什么还不开会? 我们是不是要等什么重要的人?
   B: _____ .

3. A: 今天下午我要陪我姐姐去看医生.
   B: _____ ?

4. A: 我的中文还不太好.
   B: _____ .

十三. 在书店

A: 我要买一本汉英词典.

B: 您瞧瞧这一本儿[1]. 新旧词汇

都收, 还有[2] 英文的用法说明.

很实用.

A: 让我看一下[3].

　……

这词典不错. 多少钱?

B: 十一块九毛九[4].

A: 我买一本. 这是十二块.

B: 这是找给您的零钱[5]. 您慢走[6]!

A: 再见!

13. Zai[4] Shu[1] Dian[4]

A: Wo[3] yao[4] mai[3] yi[4] ben[3] han[4]-ying[1]
ci[2]dian[3].

B: Nin[2] qiao[2]qiao zhei[4] yi[4] bər[3]. Xin[1] jiu[4]
ci[2]hui[4] dou[1] shou[1], hai[2]you[3] ying[1]wen[2]
de yong[4]fa[3] shuo[1]ming[1]. Hen[3] shi[2]yong[4].

A: Rang[4] wo[3] kan[4] yi[2]xia[4].
......
Zhe[4] ci[2]dian[3] bu[2]cuo[4]. Duo[1]shao qian[2]?

B: Shi[2] yi[2] kuai[4] jiu[3] mao[2] jiu[3].

A: Wo[2] mai[3] yi[4] ben[3]. Zhe[4] shi shi[2] er[4]
kuai[4].

B: Zhe[4] shi[4] zhao[3] gei[2] nin[2] de ling[2]qian[2].
Nin[2] man[4] zou[3].

A: Zai[4]jian[4]!

13. At a Book Store

A: I'd like to buy a Chinese-English dictionary.

B: Look at this one. It contains both current and older words and usage notes in English. It's very useful.

A: Let me take a look.

......

It's pretty good. How much is it?

B: Eleven *yuan* and ninety-nine.

A: I'll take it. Here are twelve *yuan*.

B: Here's your change. Have a good day!

A: You too.

13. Notes

1. 这 一 本 儿 (zhei⁴ yi⁴ bər³): this one (book) Here the word 一 (yi⁴) may be omitted. 这 本 书 (**zhei⁴** ben³ shu¹) this book, 这 杯 茶 (**zhei⁴** bei¹ cha²) this cup of tea 这 三 个 中 国 姑 娘 多 漂 亮! (**Zhei⁴** san¹ ge zhong¹guo² gu¹niang duo¹ piao⁴liang!) How beautiful these three Chinese girls are!

2. 还 有 (hai²you³): in addition, as well 他 买 了 咖 啡, 橙 汁 儿, **还 有** 乌 龙 茶. (Ta¹ mai³ le ka¹fei¹, cheng²zhər¹, **hai²you³** wu¹long² cha².) He bought coffee, orange juice, and some Oolong tea as well.

3. ... 一 下 (yi²xia⁴): following a *v.* to show a short action Eg. 让 我 想 一 下. (Rang⁴ wo² xiang³ **yi²xia⁴**.) Let me think a little bit. 请 你 尝 一 下 这 个 酒. (Qing² ni³ chang² **yi²xia⁴** zhei⁴ ge jiu³.) Won't you have a taste of this wine? Another way of expressing a short action is using two repeated verbs. 让 我 想 一 下. (Rang⁴ wo² **xiang³ yi²xia⁴**.) = 让 我 想 一 想. (Rang⁴ wo² **xiang³ yi⁴xiang³**.)

4. ...块 (kuai⁴)...毛 (mao²)...分 (fen¹): 块 is the colloquial for 元 (yuan²). 毛 is the colloquial for 角 (jiao³). 1 *yuan* = 10 *jiao*, 1 *jiao* = 10 *fen* Here 十 一 块 九 毛 九 (shi² yi² kuai⁴ jiu³ mao² jiu³) means eleven *yuan* nine *jiao* and nine *fen*.

5. 零 钱 (ling²qian²): change It usually means money in small units. Here it means 找 头 (zhao³tou), the money returned as the difference between the price and the sum tendered in payment.

6. 您 慢 走 (Nin² man⁴ zou³.): Good-bye! (Lit. you slowly walk away) Similar expressions: 您 走 好. (Nin² zou² hao³.) or 好 走. (Hao² zou³.) (Lit. You walk well.)

13. Vocabulary

店 dian[4]   *n.* store

买 mai[3]   *v.* buy (opp. 卖 mai:[4])

本 ben[3]   *meas.* used with books
n. root, the fundamental; capital, cost (not including profits)

汉 han[4]   *n.* the main nationality in China; short for 汉语 (han[4]yu[3]: Chinese language)

英 ying[1]   *n.* short for 英语 (ying[1]yu[3]: English) or 英国 (ying[1]guo[2]: Britain)

词 ci[2]   *n.* word

词 典 ci[2]dian[3]   *n.* dictionary

瞧 qiao[2]   *v.* look

新 xin[1]   *a.* new (opp. 旧 jiu[4] or 老 lao[3])

旧 jiu[4]   *a.* old (not referring to age)

词 汇 ci[2]hui[4]   *n.* vocabulary

收 shou[1]   *v.* collect, be collected; receive

还 有 hai[2]you[3]   *adv.* in addition

用 yong[4]   *v.* use
n. use

用 法 yong[4]fa[3]   *n.* usage

说 明 shuo[1]ming[1]   *n.* explanation

实 用 shi[2]yong[4]   *a.* practical, useful

一 下 yi[2] xia[4]   *adv.* (do sth.) for a short while

钱 qian[2]   *n.* money; a surname

块 kuai[4]   *meas.* piece; (colloq.) buck

毛 mao[2]   *n. jiao* (10 % of a *yuan*)

找 zhao[3]   *v.* give (change); look for, find; call on

零 钱 ling[2]qian[2]   *n.* change

慢 man[4]   *a.* slow
adv. slowly
(opp. 快 kuai[4])

Supplementary Vocabulary and Expressions

best seller	畅 销 书 (chang[4]xiao[1]shu[1])
book kiosk	书 亭 (shu[1]ting[2])
bookshelf	书 架 (shu[1]jia[4])
catalogue of books	书 目 (shu[1]mu[4])
editor	编 者 (bian[1]zhe[3])
foreign languages	外 文 (wai[4]wen[2])
magazine	杂 志 (za[2]zhi[4])
new edition	新 版 (xin[1]ban[3])
print	印 刷 (ying[4]shua[1])
publisher	出 版 社 (chu[1] ban[3] she[4])
reference books	参 考 书 (can[1]kao[3]shu[1])
revised edition	修 订 版 (xiu[1]ding[4]ban[3])
textbook	教 科 书 (jiao[4]ke[1]shu[1])

One will complain of having too few books only when one wants to use them.
书 到 用 时 方 嫌 少.
(Shu[1] dao[4] yong[4] shi[2] fang[1] xian[2] shao[3].)
When was the book published?
这 本 书 是 什 么 时 候 出 版 的?
(Zhei[4] ben[3] shu[1] shi[4] shen[2]me shi[2]hou chu[1]ban[3] de?)

13. Exercises

I. Tone Practice:

bo¹ 波 wave   bo² 薄 thin   bo³ 跛 lame   bo⁴ 柏 bark of cork tree
xi¹ 西 west   xi² 习 practice   xi³ 洗 wash   xi⁴ 细 thin

II. Substitution Drills:

他 让 我 你太太	瞧 听 用 坐 想 休息	一下.

III. Answer the following questions:

1. 你要买汉英词典还是英汉词典?

2. 你先生姓什么?

3. 他学了两年汉语, 可以用汉语说话了吧?

4. 你家里的那台 (tai² *meas*., used with machines) 新电视机是多少钱买的?

5. 在中国女人一结婚就用先生的姓吗?

IV. Compose sentences with the following words:

1. 再　我　让　好好儿　一下　地　想

2. 您　对不起　一下　请　等

3. 没来　了　张太太　张先生　来　不过

4. 味儿　知道　您　喝　就　一　不错

V. Fill in the blanks with 睡, 来, 会, or 回 (hui²: return):

他一学就 ＿＿＿.　他一请就 ＿＿＿.　他一去就 ＿＿＿.　他一回就 ＿＿＿.

52

十四. 三餐

A: 你每天早饭吃些什么?

B: 一个鸡蛋、两片烤面包、一杯[1]牛奶.

A: 午饭呢?

B: 午饭吃得很简单. 吃一、两块红烧肉[2],还吃些豆腐和绿色蔬菜.

A: 晚饭吃什么?

B: 吃点儿鱼、蔬菜、和水果.当然[3]还有米饭.

A: 中国的家常饭菜脂肪不多,有益[4]健康!

14. San[1] Can[1]

A: Ni[2] mei[3]tian[1] zao[3]fan[4] chi[1] xie[1] shen[2]me?

B: Yi[2] ge ji[1]dan[4], liang[3] pian[4] kao[3] mian[4]bao[1], yi[4] bei[1] niu[2]nai[3].

A: Wu[3]fan[4] ne?

B: Wu[3]fan[4] chi[1] de hen[2] jian[3]dan[1]. Chi[1] yi[4] liang[3] kuai[4] hong[2]shao[1]rou[4], hai[2] chi[1] xie[1] dou[4]fu he[2] lü[4]se[4] shu[1]cai[4].

A: Wan[3]fan[4] chi[1] shen[2]me?

B: Chi[1] diar[3] yu[2], shu[1]cai[4], he[2] shui[2]guo[3]. Dang[1]ran[2] hai[2]you[2] mi[3]fan[4].

A: Zhong[1]guo[2] de jia[1]chang[2] fan[4]cai[4] zhi[1]fang[2] bu[4] duo[1], you[3] yi[4] jian[4]kang[1]!

14. The Three Meals

A: What do you have for breakfast every morning?

B: An egg, two slices of toast, and a glass of milk.

A: And lunch?

B: I have a very simple lunch, just one or two pieces of braised pork, some bean curd, and greens.

A: And what do you have for dinner?

B: Some fish, vegetables, and fruit, with rice, of course.

A: The Chinese homely diet is less fattening and healthier for you!

14. Notes

1. 一 个..., 两 片..., 一 杯... (yi² ge⁴..., liang³ pian⁴..., yi⁴ bei¹...): 个 (ge⁴), 片 (pian⁴), and 杯 (bei¹) are all measure words. In Chinese, particular nouns require particular measure words. Cf. Appendix 2.

2. 肉 (rou⁴): meat Among Han people 肉 (rou⁴) refers to pork; when they talk about beef, the word 牛 (niu²: cow) is added before 肉 (rou⁴). 红 烧 肉 (hong²shao¹rou⁴) is a very popular homely dish in Chinese (Han) families.

3. 当然 (dang¹ran²): of course This phrase can be used independently as in Passage 10.
A: 你学习用功吗? (Ni³ xue²xi² yong⁴gong¹ ma?) Do you study hard?
B: **当然! (Dang¹ran²!)** Of course I do. It can also be used as an adverbial as in this text 他吃了这个药, **当然** 就会好的. (Ta¹ chi¹ le zhei⁴ ge yao⁴, **dang¹ran²** jiu⁴ hui⁴ hao³ de.) He will certainly recover if he takes this medicine.

4. 有益 (you³yi⁴): good for 开卷**有益**. (Kai¹ juan⁴ you³ yi⁴.) Reading is always profitable. It is often used with 对 (dui⁴: for, to) 运动 **对** 健康 **有益**. (Yun¹dong⁴ **dui⁴** jian⁴kang¹ **you³yi⁴**.) Exercise is good for the health. 牛奶 **对** 小孩儿的成长 **有益**. (Niu²nai³ **dui⁴** xiao³har² de cheng²zhang³ **you³yi⁴**.) Milk is good for children's growth. The opposite is 有害 (you³hai⁴). 抽烟对健康 **有害**. (Chou¹yan¹ dui⁴ jian⁴kang¹ **you³hai⁴**.) Smoking is harmful to the health.

14. Vocabulary

餐 can[1]   *n.* meal

早 zao[3]   *n.* morning
     a., adv. early (opp. 晚 wan[3] or 迟 chi[2]); long ago, for a long time
     int. good morning

早饭 zao[3]fan[4]   *n.* breakfast (opp. 晚饭 wan[3]fan[4])

鸡 ji[1]   *n.* chicken

蛋 dan[4]   *n.* egg

片 pian[4]   *meas.* used with slice-shaped things

烤 kao[3]   *v.* toast

面 mian[4]   *n.* flour; face
     pstp, showing side or direction

面包 mian[4]bao[1]   *n.* bread, loaf

牛 niu[2]   *n.* cow

奶 nai[3]   *n.* milk; breast

牛奶 niu[2]nai[3]   *n.* (cow's) milk

午饭 wu[3]fan[4]   *n.* lunch

简单 jian[3]dan[1]   *a.* simple (opp. 复杂 fu[4]za[2])

红烧肉 hong[2]shao[1]rou[4] *n.* pork braised in soy sauce

红烧 hong[2]shao[1]   *v.* braise in soy sauce (then the dish becomes red)

肉 rou[4]   *n.* meat

豆腐 dou[4]fu   *n. tofu,* bean curd

绿色蔬菜 lü[4]se[4] shu[1]cai[4]
     n. greens

绿 lü   *n., a. green*

色 se[4]   *n.* color

蔬菜 shu[1]cai[4]   *n.* vegetable

菜 cai[4]   *n.* vegetable; food; dish, course

晚饭 wan[3]fan[4]   *n.* dinner

鱼 yu[2]   *n.* fish

水果 shui[2]guo[3]   *n.* fruit

米饭 mi[3]fan[4]   *n.* (cooked) rice

米 mi[3]   *n.* (raw) rice

家常 jia[1]chang[2]   *a.* homely

饭菜 fan[4]cai[4]   *n.* meal, food, diet

脂肪 zhi[1]fang[2]   *n.* fat

有益 you[3]yi[4]   *a.* good for, beneficial to (opp. 有害 you[3]hai[4])

益 yi[4]   *n.* benefit
     a. beneficial (opp. 害 hai[4])

健康 jian[4]kang[1]   *n.* health (opp. 疾病 ji[2]bing[4])
     a. healthy (opp. 有病 you[3]bing[4])

Supplementary Vocabulary and Expressions

abstain from eating meat 吃素 (chi[1]su[4])

bean sprouts 豆芽 (dou[4]ya[2])

broccoli 甘蓝 (gan[1]lan[2])

cauliflower 菜花 (cai[4]hua[1])

cucumber 黄瓜 (huang[2]gua[1])

deep-fried twisted dough sticks 油条 (you[2]tiao[2])

dim sum 点心 (dian[3]xin[1])

green bean milk 豆汁儿 (dou[4]zhər)

greasy 油腻 (you[2]ni[4])

green pepper 青椒 (qing[1]jiao[1])

light, not greasy 清淡 (qing[1]dan[4])

meat and vegetables in proper proportions 荤素搭配 (hun[1] su[4] da[1]pei[4])

midnight snack 宵夜 (or 消夜) (xiao[1]ye[4])

mushroom 蘑菇 (mo[2]gu)

porridge 粥 (zhou[1]), 稀饭 (xi[1]fan[4])

soy bean milk 豆浆 (dou[4]jiang[1])

spinach 菠菜 (bo[1]cai[4])

steamed corn bun 窝窝头 (wo[1]wo tou[2])

tomato 番茄 (fan[1]qie[2]), 西红柿 (xi[1]hong[2]shi[4])

In the south the staple food is rice and in the north it is flour.
南方人主食是米, 北方人主食是面.
(Nan[2]fang[1]ren[2] zhu[3]shi[2] shi mi[3], bei[3]fang[1]ren[2] zhu[3]shi[2] shi mian[4].)

14 Exercises

I. Tone Practice:

hong[1] 烘 bake   hong[2] 红 red   hong[3] 哄 coax   hong[4] 讧 internal strife
tong[1] 通 through tong[2] 同 same   tong[3] 统 unite   tong[4] 痛 ache

II. Choose the right words to fill in the blanks:

咱们   陪   有益   得   就

1. 我 _____ 要买这个!
2. 小女孩要她妈妈 _____ 她睡觉.
3. 天儿不早了, _____ 走吧.
4. 他蔬菜吃 _____ 很多.
5. 多吃蔬菜和水果, _____ 健康.

III. Use "给 + somebody" to expand the following sentences:

Example: 他买了牛奶. → 他给我买了牛奶.

1. 妈妈买了水果.

2. 我要打电话.

3. 老黄捎了个信儿.

4. 李大夫瞧病 (qiao[2]bing[4]: see a patient).

5. 张先生说明了这本词典的用法.

IV. Translate the following sentences into English, paying attention to the meaning of 还有:

1. 这儿有一本词典, 那儿还有一本词典.

2. 你还有什么话儿, 明儿(colloq. = 明天) 再说吧!

3. 还有一个人没有来.

4. 那儿有两杯茶, 一杯是乌龙茶, 还有一杯也是乌龙茶.

5. 他请了老黄、老李、老张，还有小王.

十五. 避暑胜地

A: 今天天气很闷热!

B: 是啊. 天气预报说要到九十八度.

A: 好久[1] 没下雨了. 下一场雨就凉快了.

B: 也[2] 不一定[3]. 有时候[4] 会越下越[5] 热.

A: 这几天我天天[6] 游泳.

B: 游泳好啊! 游泳池是个避暑胜地. 泡在凉水里就不觉得热了.

15. Bi⁴shu³ Sheng⁴di⁴

A: Jin¹tian¹ tian¹qi⁴ hen³ men¹re⁴!

B: Shi⁴ a. Tian¹qi⁴ yu⁴bao⁴ shuo¹ yao⁴ dao⁴ jiu³ shi ba² du⁴.

A: Hao²jiu³ mei² xia⁴yu³ le. Xia⁴ yi⁴ chang² yu³ jiu⁴ liang²kuai⁴ le.

B: Ye³ bu⁴ yi²ding⁴. You³shi²hou hui⁴ yue⁴ xia⁴ yue⁴ re⁴.

A: Zhe⁴ ji³ tian¹ wo³ tian¹tian¹ you²yong³.

B: You²yong² hao³ a! You²yong³chi² shi⁴ ge bi⁴shu³ sheng⁴di⁴. Pao⁴ zai⁴ liang² shui³ li jiu⁴ bu⁴ jue²de re⁴ le.

15. A Summer Resort

A: It's awfully hot and humid today!

B: Yes. The weather forecast says the

high will be 98°F.

A: We haven't had rain for a long time.

It will be cooler after a rain.

B: Not necessarily. Sometimes when it

rains more, it gets hotter.

A: I go swimming every day these days.

B: It's good to go swimming. The

swimming pool is a good summer

resort. You won't feel hot in the cold

water.

15. Notes

1. 好久 (hao²jiu³): quite long 好 (hao³) is placed before words denoting length of time to indicate a long time. 好久没见你了! (**Hao²jiu³** mei² jian⁴ ni le!) Haven't seen you for a long time! 他学了好几年汉语了. (Ta¹ xue³ le **hao³** ji³ nian² han⁴yu³ le.) He's been studying Chinese for quite a few years. 我等了你好半天! (Wo² deng³ le ni³ **hao³** ban⁴tian¹!) I've been waiting for you quite a while! 好 (hao³) is also used before adjectives and adverbs to denote high degree or large amount. 今儿个好冷啊! (Jiər¹ ge **hao²** leng³ a!) How cold it is today! 这几天我好忙啊! (Zhe⁴ ji³ tian¹ wo² **hao³** mang² a!) I have been so busy these days! 你好傻! (Ni² **hao²** sha³!) How stupid you are!

2. 也 (ye³): It usually means *also, too*. It is also used in sentences expressing concession, meaning (*although…,) still…* 你不告诉我, 我也知道. (Ni³ bu² gao⁴su wo³, wo² **ye³** zhi¹dao.) You don't have to tell me. I know it already. 他请我, 我也不去. (Ta¹ qing³ wo³, wo² **ye²** bu² qu⁴.) I won't go even if he asks me to.

3. 不一定 (bu⁴ yi²ding⁴): not sure 他不一定会来. (Ta¹ **bu⁴ yi²ding⁴** hui⁴ lai⁴.) I am not sure if he will come. The phrase 不见得 (bu² jian⁴de) means roughly the same. 不见得 (bu² jian⁴de) is more emphatic than 不一定 (bu⁴ yi²ding⁴). 他不见得会来. (Ta **bu² jian⁴de** hui⁴ lai².) It is not likely that he will come.

4. 有时候 (you³shi²hou): sometimes 她有时候喜欢这个, 有时候又喜欢那个. (Ta¹ **you³shi²hou** xi³huan zhei⁴ ge, **you³shi²hou** you⁴ xi³huan nei⁴ ge.) She likes sometimes the one and sometimes the other.

5. 越…越 (yue⁴…yue⁴): the more… the more… 越快越好. (**Yue⁴** kuai⁴ **yue⁴** hao³.) The sooner, the better. 他越说越快. (Ta¹ **yue⁴** shuo¹ **yue⁴** kuai⁴.) He speaks faster and faster. Another useful expression is 越来越… (yue⁴lai²yue⁴…): more and more, by more stages, degrees, etc. 故事越来越好看了. (Gu⁴shi **yue⁴lai²yue⁴** hao³ kan⁴ le.) The story is getting more and more exciting.

6. 天天 (tian¹tian¹): = 每天 (mei³tian¹) every day 我天天见她. (Wo³ **tian¹tian¹** jian⁴ ta¹.) I see her every day. 我们天天见面. (Wo³men **tian¹tian¹** jian⁴mian⁴.) We see each other every day.

15. Vocabulary

避暑 bi⁴shu³ — v. be away for the hot summer days

胜地 sheng⁴di⁴ — n. resort

今天 jin¹tian¹ — n., adv. today

天气 tian¹qi⁴ — n. weather

闷热 men¹re⁴ — a. stifling, close (opp. 凉快 liang²kuai⁴)

预报 yu⁴bao⁴ — n., v. forecast

到 dao⁴ — v. reach; arrive; adv. (following a v.) showing a result is achieved

度 du⁴ — n. degree; limit, extent

久 jiu³ — adv. long

好久 hao²jiu³ — for a long time

雨 yu³ — n. rain

下雨 xia⁴yu³ — v. rain

场 chang² — meas. used with rain, snow, dream, etc. (of sth. which has happened)

chang³ — meas. used with film show, ball game, etc. (of sports and recreation)

凉 liang² — a. cool

凉快 liang²kuai⁴ — a. pleasantly cool

有时候 you³shi²hou — adv. sometimes

越...越 yue⁴... yue⁴ — conj. the more... the more

这几天 zhe⁴ji³ tian¹ — adv. these days

天天 tian¹tian¹ — adv. every day

游泳 you²yong³ — v., n. swim

游泳池 you²yong³chi² — n. swimming pool

泡 pao⁴ — v. soak, immerse

觉得 jue²de — v. feel

Supplementary Vocabulary and Expressions

climate — 气候 (qi⁴hou)

cold front — 寒潮 (han²chao²)

dry — 干燥 (gan¹zao⁴)

humid — 潮湿 (chao²shi¹)

moderate rain — 中雨 (zhong¹yu³)

overcast with occasional drizzle 阴有小雨 (yin¹ you² xiao²yu³)

sunny and occasionally cloudy 晴天间多云 (qing²tian¹ jian⁴ duo¹ yun²)

thunder storm — 雷阵雨 (lei²zhen⁴yu³)

In nature there are unexpected storms, and in life, unpredictable vicissitudes.
天有不测风云, 人有旦夕祸福.
(Tian¹ you³ bu²ce⁴ feng¹yun², ren² you³ dan⁴xi¹ huo⁴fu².)
It looks like rain.
看来要下雨了. (Kan⁴lai² yao⁴ xia⁴yu³ le.)
It's clearing up.
天气转晴了. (Tian¹qi⁴ zhuan³ qing² le.)
The thick clouds passed overhead, but the rain kept off.
密云不雨. (Mi⁴ yun² bu⁴ yu³.)
The weather is changing.
天气要变. (Tian¹qi⁴ yao⁴ bian⁴.)

15. Exercises

I. Tone practice:

jia^1 家 home   jia^2 夹 lined   jia^3 假 fake   jia^4 价 price
qia^1 掐 pinch   qia^2 --   qia^3 卡 get stuck   qia^4 恰 proper

II. Pattern Drill:

今天我起得		早.
游泳池里的水		凉.
他喝了		多水.
七月的天气	好	热.
我早饭吃得		简单.
今天的会		重要啊!

III. Translate the following sentences into English, paying attention to the word 天:

1. 今天是星期天.
2. 她天天吃鱼和蔬菜.
3. 天儿不早了, 我该走了. 我明天再来.
4. 你几天能看完那本书?
5. 我要请假一天.
6. 天知道他在那儿住了几天!
7. 这几天天天下雨.
8. 你每天都说来看我, 来看我, 可是哪天来了?
9. 天气预报说今天白天要下大雨, 您瞧这天, 会下雨吗?
10. A: 下雨天, 留客天, 留我不留? (留 liu^2: ask sb. to stay, put up sb. for the night; 客 ke^4: guest, visitor)
    B: 下雨, 天留客; 天留, 我不留.

IV. Fill in the blanks in the following sentences containing 越 … 越 or 越来越 with appropriate words:

1. 书总是越多越 _____ .
2. 雨越下越 _____ 了.
3. 他累 (lei^4: be tired) 了. 越走越 _____ 了.
4. 她天天游泳. 越游越 _____ 了.
5. 你越问, 她越不肯 _____ .
6. 十一月了, 天越来越 _____ 了.
7. 中国的人口越来越 _____ 了.
8. 她烧的菜越来越好 _____ 了.

十六. 订机票 [1]

A: 我下星期五 [2] 要上 [3] 纽约.

B: 哦! 机票订好了没 [4]?

A: 订好了.

B: 哪个航空公司?

A: 东西航空公司.

B: 单程还是来回票?

A: 来回票.

B: 多少钱?

A: 一百七十块.

B: 不贵.

A: 这是廉价票, 打了六折 [5], 不然 [6],
要三百多块.

16. Ding [4] Ji [1] piao [4]

A: Wo [3] xia [4] xing [1] qi [1] wu [3] yao [4] shang [4]
Niu [3] yue [1].

B: O [4]! Ji [1] piao [4] ding [4] hao [3] le mei [2]?

A: Ding [4] hao [3] le.

B: Nei [3] ge hang [2] kong [1] gong [1] si [1]?

A: Dong [1] xi [1] hang [2] kong [1] gong [1] si [1].

B: Dan [1] cheng [2] hai [2] shi lai [2] hui [2] piao [4]?

A: Lai [2] hui [2] piao [4].

B: Duo [1] shao qian [2]?

A: Yi [4] bai [3] qi [1] shi kuai [4].

B: Bu [2] gui [4].

A. Zhe [4] shi lian [2] jia [4] piao [4] da [3] le liu [4] zhe [2],
bu [4] ran [2], yao [4] san [1] bai [3] duo [1] kuai [4].

16. Booking Plane Tickets

A: I'm going to New York next Friday.

B: Oh! Have you booked the plane ticket yet?

A: Yes, I have.

B: Which airline are you with?

A: Eastwest Airlines.

B: One way or round trip?

A: Round trip.

B: How much did it cost?

A: 170 dollars.

B: That's not expensive.

A: This is a lower price ticket. I got 40 per cent off. Otherwise, it would be over 300.

16. Notes

1. 机票 (ji¹ piao⁴): plane ticket, short for 飞机票 (fei¹ji¹ piao⁴) 飞机 (fei¹ji¹): airplane (Lit. flying machine)

2. 下星期五 (xia⁴ xing¹qi¹ wu³): next Friday 下 (xia⁴) *adj.* is *next*. 下个月 (xia⁴ ge yue⁴) next month *Next week* is 下星期 (xia⁴ xin¹qi¹). But in oral Chinese *next year* is 明年 (ming²nian²), not 下年 (xia⁴ nian²).

3. 上 (shang⁴): go to 你上哪儿去? (Ni³ **shang⁴** nar³ qu⁴?) Where are you going? 我上街. (Wo³ **shang⁴**jie¹.) I am going shopping. 我上图书馆. (Wo³ **shang⁴** tu²shu¹guan³.) I'm going to the library. 他们上北京了. (Ta¹men **shang⁴** Bei³jing¹ le.) They went to Beijing. 我要上法院. (Wo³ yao⁴ **shang⁴** fa³yuan⁴.) I want to go to court. 我上厕所去. (Wo³ **shang⁴** ce⁴suo³ qu⁴.) I am going to the restroom. When 上 (shang⁴) means *go to*, it is used only with certain definite objects.

4. 订好了没? (Ding⁴ hao³ le mei²?) Have you booked it? ...好了 (hao³le) is used after verbs to denote some action has been done, corresponding to the present perfect tense. 你饭吃好了没? (Ni³ fan⁴ chi¹ **hao³le** mei²?) Have you finished your meal? 没 (mei²) is short for 没有 (mei²you³) have not. 他来了没? (Ta¹ lai² le **mei²**?) = 他来了没有? (Ta¹ lai² le **mei²you³**?) or = 他有没有来? (Ta¹ you³mei²you³ lai²?) Has he come yet?

5. 打...折 (da³...zhe²): at a discount of... 20% off is 打八折 (da³ ba¹zhe²); 15% off is 打八五折 (da³ ba¹wu⁵zhe²); 50% off is 打对折 (da³ dui⁴zhe²).

6. 不然 (bu⁴ran²): otherwise 快走, **不然**, 要迟到了. (Kuai⁴ zou³, **bu⁴ran²**, yao⁴ chi²dao⁴ le.) Hurry up, or else you will be late. 叫你干什么, 你就干什么, **不然**, 等着挨骂吧! (Jiao⁴ ni³ gan⁴ shen²me, ni³ jiu⁴ gan⁴ shen²me, **bu⁴ran²**, deng³ zhe ai¹ma⁴ ba!) Do what you've been told; otherwise you will get a scolding.

16. Vocabulary

订 ding[4]   *v.* book
机 票 ji[1]piao[4]   *n.* plane ticket
票 piao[4]   *n.* ticket
纽 约 niu[3]yue[1]   *n.* New York
哦 o[4]   *int.* Oh (expressing
             understanding)
航 空 hang[2]kong[1]   *n.* aviation
公 司 gong[1]si[1]   *n.* company
东 dong[1]   *n.* east
西 xi[1]   *n.* west
单 dan[1]   *a.* single (opp. 双
             shuang[1])
             n. list, form, bill
程 cheng[2]   *n.* journey, trip
单 程 dan[1]cheng[2]   *n.* one way
回 hui[2]   *v.* return; answer, reply,
             (of head) turn around
来 回 lai[2]hui[2]   *n.* round trip
百 bai[3]   *num.* hundred
贵 gui[4]   *a.* expensive
             (opp. 便 宜 pian[2]yi)
廉 价 票 lian[2]jia[4] piao[4]   *n.* ticket at a lower
               price
打…折 da[3]…zhe[2]   take a discount of…%
不 然 bu[4]ran[2]   *conj.* otherwise

Supplementary Vocabulary and Expressions

additional charge	加 钱 (jia[1]qian[2])
business class	商 务 舱 (shang[3]wu[4] cang[1])
coach class	普 通 舱 (pu[3]tong[1] cang[1])
economy class	经 济 舱 (jing[1]ji[4] cang[1])
first class	头 等 舱 (tou[2]deng[3] cang[1])
free ticket	免 费 票 (mian[3] fei[4] piao[4])
including airport tax	包 括 机 场 费 (bao[1]kuo[4] ji[1]chang[3]fei[4])
mileage point	里 程 点 (li[3]cheng[2] dian[3])
non-stop	直 达 (zhi[2]da[2])
transit	中 转 (zhong[1]zhuan[3])
travel agency	旅 行 社 (lü[3]xing[2] she[4])

The flight date cannot be changed.
不 得 改 期 (Bu[4]de[2] gai[3]qi[1].)
The ticket is non-refundable.
不 退 票. (Bu[2] tui[4]piao[4].)

16. Exercises

I. Tone Practice:

tun¹ 吞 swallow   tun² 囤 store up   tun³ 氽 deep-fry   tun⁴ 褪 slip out of
cun¹ 村 village   cun² 存 deposit   cun³ 忖 think over   cun⁴ 寸 inch

II. Rewrite the following questions by using …没 at the end:

   1. 你词典买了吗?
   2. 他零钱给你了吗?
   3. 她走了没有?
   4. 你有没有请假?
   5. 他有没有上纽约?

III. Make questions with 还是 to which the following sentences are the answers:

   1. A: _____?
      B: 我买的是单程票.

   2. A: _____?
      B: 我下星期五不上北京, 去纽约.

   3. A: _____?
      B: 会上我用了中文.

   4. A: _____?
      B: 我喜欢吃面包.

   5. A: _____?
      B: 天气预报说明天不下雨.

IV. Choose the best words for the blanks:

   1. 对不起! 让你 _____ 等了.   (a. 慢   b. 久   c. 多)

   2. 他 _____ 中国饭的味道不错.   (a. 觉得   b. 嫌   c. 当然)

   3. 中国饭他越吃越 _____ .   (a. 买   b. 感冒   c. 喜欢)

   4. 我要去 _____ 买《西游记》.   (a. 会议室   b. 饭店   c. 书店)

   5. 我爸爸八十多了, 可是很 _____ .   (a.健康   b. 简单   c. 没有癌症)

64

十七. 肺癌

A: 咱们有日子¹没见面了. 你好吗?

B: 我很好, 谢谢你. 你好吗?

A: 我也很好. 你听说²老黄³进医院了吗?

B: 没听说. 是什么病?

A: 得了肺癌.

B: 哎哟! 要动手术吗?

A: 还不知道.

B: 他烟抽得太多了⁴!

A: 八成儿是乌龙茶喝得太少了!

17. Fei⁴ai²

A: Zan²men you³ ri⁴zi mei² jian⁴mian⁴ le. Ni² hao³ ma?

B: Wo² hen² hao³. Xie⁴xie ni. Ni² hao³ ma?

A: Wo² ye² hen² hao³. Ni³ ting¹shuo¹ Lao³ Huang² jin⁴ yi¹yuan⁴ le ma?

B: Mei² ting¹shuo¹. Shi⁴ shen²me bing⁴?

A: De² le fei⁴ai².

B: Ai¹yo¹! Yao⁴ dong⁴ shou³shu⁴ ma?

A: Hai² bu⁴ zhi¹dao.

B: Ta¹ yan¹ chou¹ de tai⁴ duo¹ le!

A: Ba¹ chĕr² shi⁴ wu¹long²cha² he¹ de tai⁴ shao³ le!

17. Lung Cancer

A: Haven't seen you for a long time!

How are you doing?

B: I'm fine. Thank you. How are you

doing?

A: I'm fine too. Have you heard Lao

Huang is in hospital now?

B: No, I haven't. What happened?

A: He has lung cancer.

B: Oh no! Does he need a surgery?

A: Don't know yet.

B: He smoked too much!

A: Perhaps he didn't drink enough

Oolong!

17. Notes

1. 有日子 ($you^3 ri^4 zi$): for a long time = 好久 ($hao^2 jiu^3$) 我有日子没去纽约了. (Wo^2 **$you^3 ri^4 zi$** $mei^2 qu^4 Niu^3 yue^1 le$.) I haven't been to New York for a long while. 他走了有些日子了. ($Ta^1 zou^3 le$ **$you^3 xie^1 ri^4 zi$** le.) He's been away for some time.

2. 听说 ($ting^1 shuo^1$): be told, hear of (Lit.: hear say) 我从来没听说过那个地方. ($Wo^3 cong^2 lai^2 mei^2$ **$ting^1 shuo^1$** $guo nei^4 ge di^4 fang$.) I've never heard of the place. 听说中国的经济发展得很快. (**$Ting^1 shuo^1$** $zhong^1 guo^2 de jing^1 ji^4 fa^1 zhang^3 de hen^3 kuai^4$.) I heard that China's economy is developing very fast.

3. 老黄 ($lao^3 huang^2$): 老 (lao^3: *old*) is put before the name of a person not too young to express intimacy. Chinese people call Americans 老美 ($lao^2 mei^3$) and call foreigners 老外 ($lao^3 wai^4$). The word 老 (lao^3: *old*) does not necessarily carry any negative sense of old age. Some Chinese call themselves 老中 ($lao^3 zhong^1$), as 中 ($zhong^1$) means China or Chinese.

4. 他烟抽得太多了. ($Ta^1 yan^1 chou^1 de tai^4 duo^1 le$.): He smoked too much. In the pattern shown in Note 3, Passage 9 the verbs are intransitive. Here the verb 抽 ($chou^1$) is transitive and takes an object 烟 (yan^1). Then the pattern becomes "subject + object + *v.* + 得 (de) + complement". The object is put before the transitive verb. Eg. 他乌龙茶喝得太少. ($Ta^1 wu^1 long^2 cha^2 he^1$ **de** $tai^4 shao^3$.) He drinks too little *Oolong*. 毕先生棋下得很好. ($Bi^4 xian^1 sheng qi^2 xia^4$ **de** $hen^2 hao^3$.) Mr. Bi is a good chess player.

17. Vocabulary

肺 fei^4 — *n.* lung

有 日 子 you^3 ri^{4}zi — for quite a few days

日 子 ri^{4}zi — *n.* day, time; life

见 面 jian^{4}mian^4 — *v.* meet, see

听 说 ting^{1}shuo^1 — *v.* hear of, be told

老 lao^3 — *a.* old (opp. 小 xiao^3 or 少 shao^4: young; 新 xin^1: new)
pref. used with names of people
adv. for a long time; always

医 yi^1 — *n.* medicine; doctor
v. treat (disease)

医 院 yi^{1}yuan^4 — *n.* hospital

病 bing^4 — *n.* disease
v. be sick

哎 哟 ai^{1}yo^1 — *int.* O, expressing surprise

动 dong^4 — *v.* perform; move; act

术 shu^4 — *n.* technique, art

手 术 shou^{3}shu^4 — *n.* surgery

烟 yan^1 — *n.* cigarette; smoke, mist

抽 chou^1 — *v.* draw; smoke

八 成 ba^{1}cheng^2 — *adv.* most probably (Lit. 80%)

成 cheng^2 — *n.* 10 per cent
v. become; accomplish (opp. 败 bai^4)

Supplementary Vocabulary and Expressions

benign — 良 性 (liang^{2}xing^4)

BPH (Benign Prostatic Hyperplasia) — 前 列 腺 肥 大 (qian^{2}lie^{4}xian^4 fei^{2}da^4)

carcinogenic — 致 癌 的 (zhi^{4}ai^2 de)

colorectal cancer — 大 肠 /直 肠 癌 (da^{4}chang^2/zhi^{2}chang^{2}ai^2)

CT (Computed Tomography) — X 光 断 层 扫 描 (X guan^1 duan^{4}ceng^2 sao^{3}miao^2)

cyst — 囊 肿 (nang^{2}zhong^3)

ECG — 心 电 图 (xin^{1}dian^{4}tu^2)

esophagus — 食 道 (shi^{2}dao^4)

kidney — 肾 (shen^4)

M.R.I. (Magnetic Resonance Imaging) — 核 磁 共 振 (he^{2}ci^{2}gong^{4}zhen^4)

malignant — 恶 性 (e^{4}xing^4)

pancreas — 胰 (yi^2)

PET (Positron Emission Tomography) — 阳 电 子 放 射 性 断 层 扫 描 (yang^2 dian^{4}zi^3 fang^{4}she^{4}xing^4 duan^{4}ceng^2 sao^{3}miao^2)

polyp — 息 肉 (xi^{1}rou^4)

silent killer — 无 声 杀 手 (wu^{2}sheng^1 sha^{1}shou^3)

spleen — 脾 (pi^2)

stomach — 胃 (wei^4)

tumor — 肿 瘤 (zhong^{3}liu^2)

ultrasound — 超 声 波 (chao^{1}sheng^{1}bo^1)

windpipe — 气 管 (qi^{4}guan^3)

X ray — 爱 克 斯 光 (ai^{4}ke^{4}si^1 guan^1)

Health is valued only when one is sick.
有 病 方 知 健 时 仙.
(You^3 bing^4 fang^1 zhi^1 jian^4 shi^1 xian^1.)

17. Exercises

I. Tone Practice:

zhi[1] 汁 juice   zhi[2] 值 worth   zhi[3] 纸 paper   zhi[4] 痣 mole

chi[1] 吃 eat   chi[2] 迟 late   chi[3] 齿 tooth   chi[4] 翅 wing

shi[1] 狮 lion   shi[2] 十 ten   shi[3] 屎 dung   shi[4] 事 matter

II. Pattern Drill:

Subject	Object	Verb Transitive	Particle	Adverb or Adjective Complement
钱先生 王小姐	机票	订	得	早.
	中文	说		好.
	晚饭	吃		很简单.
	中文书	看		不少.

III. Fill in the blanks with appropriate words:

1. 我好, 你好, 他 _____ 很好.
2. 你好, 我好, 大家 (everyone It does not mean a "big family".) _____ 好!
3. 我 _____ 说抽烟的人容易得癌症.
4. 有时候我去她那儿, _____ 她来我这儿.
5. 你爱吃什么就吃 _____.
6. 你瞧! 大家都 _____ 喝茶.
7. 下雨了. 八 _____ 儿他不会来了.
8. 我有日子 _____ 见到你妈妈了, 她好吗?
9. A: 到纽约的单程票要三百八十块钱一张.
    B: 那太 _____ 了.
10. 少抽点儿烟吧! _____ 要得癌症了.

十八. 到中国去[1]旅游

A: 我下个月要到中国去.

B: 好啊. 是出差还是旅游?

A: 去旅游.

B: 你准备去哪些地方?

A: 去北京、西安、上海[2].

B: 好. 这几个地方都是值得一[3]
去的. 祝你一路平安[4]!

A: 谢谢! 回来后再见!

B: 再见!

18. Dao[4] Zhong[1]guo[2] Qu[4] Lü[3]you[2]

A: Wo[3] xia[4] ge yue[4] yao[4] dao[4] zhong[1]guo[2]
qu[4].

B: Hao[3] a. Shi[4] chu[1]chai[1] hai[2]shi lü[3]you[2]?

A: Qu[4] lü[3]you[2].

B: Ni[2] zhun[3]bei[4] qu[4] nei[3]xie[1] di[4]fang?

A: Qu[4] Bei[3]jing[1], Xi[1]an[1], Shang[4]hai[3].

B: Hao[3]. Zhe[4] ji[3] ge di[4]fang dou[1] shi[4]
zhi[2]de yi[2] qu[4] de. Zhu[4] ni[3] yi[2]lu[4]
ping[1]an[1]!

A: Xie[4]xie! Hui[2]lai[2] hou[4] zai[4]jian[4]!

B: Zai[4]jian[4]!

69

18. Going to China for Sight-seeing

A: I'm going to China next month.

B: Good. Are you going on business or

for pleasure?

A: For pleasure.

B: Which places are you planning to visit?

A: Beijing, Xi'an, and Shanghai.

B: Good. These are all places worth

visiting. Have a good trip!

A: Thank you! See you after I come

back.

B: See you then!

18. Notes

1. 到…去 (dao^4…qu^4) = 去 (qu^4)… go to (some place) 她 **到** 加拿大 **去** 了. (Ta^1 **dao^4** Jia^{1}na^{2}da^4 **qu^4** le.) = 她 **去** 加拿大了. (Ta^1 **qu^4** Jia^{4}na^{2}da^4 le.) She has gone to Canada.

2. 北京、西安、上海: (Bei^{3}jing^1, Xi^{1}an^1, Shang^{4}hai^3): Beijing is the capital of China. Its most famous historical sites are the Great Wall, the Forbidden City and the Temple of Heaven. Xi'an is an ancient capital of 12 dynasties. One of the world's wonders, the terracotta warriors and horses, is there. Shanghai, like New York, is the economic and commercial center of China.
It is interesting to note the ideogram 安 (an^1: safe) is composed of two parts: the upper part is the roof of a home (家 jia^1); the lower part is a woman (女 nü^3, whose shape expresses a woman's beautiful dancing posture). It means when there is a woman (wife) at home, there will be a safe family.

3. 值得一… (zhi^{2}de yi^1…): be worth 这本书 **值得一** 读. (Zhei^4 ben^3 shu^1 **zhi^{2}de yi^4** du^2.) The book is worth reading. 这是一场 **值得一** 做的 梦. (Zhe^4 shi yi^4 chang^2 **zhi^{2}de yi^2** zuo^4 de meng^4.) It is a dream worth dreaming.

4. 祝你一路平安! (Zhu^4 ni^3 yi^{2}lu^4 ping^{1}an^1!): Have a nice journey! *Bon voyage!* 一路 (yi^{2}lu^4) is *all the way*. 他们 **一路** 上有说有笑. (Ta^{1}men yi^2**lu^4** shang you^3 shuo^1 you^3 xiao^4.) They were chatting cheerfully all the way.

18. Vocabulary

到...去 dao⁴ ...qu⁴   *v.* go to

旅游 lü³you²   *n.* trip for pleasure
    v. have a trip for pleasure

月 yue⁴   *n.* month; moon

出差 chu¹chai¹   *n.* trip for business
    v. have a trip for business

准备 zhun³bei⁴   *v.* prepare, plan

哪些 nei³xie¹   *pron.* which (pl.)

地方 di⁴fang   *n.* place

北 bei³   *n.* north (opp. 南 nan²)

京 jing¹   *n.* capital

北京 bei³jing¹   *n.* Beijing

西安 xi¹an¹   *n.* Xi'an¹

安 an¹   *a.* safe; peaceful
    n. safety (opp. 危 wei¹)

上海 shang⁴hai³   *n.* Shanghai

海 hai³   *n.* sea

值得 zhi²de   *v.* worth
    a. worthwhile

祝 zhu⁴   *v.* wish

路 lu⁴   *n.* road; journey

平安 ping¹an¹   *a.* safe and sound
    n. safety (opp. 危险 wei¹xian³)

一路平安! Yi²lu⁴ ping¹an¹!   Have a good trip!

回来 hui²lai²   *v.* return, come back (opp. 出去 chu¹qu)

...后 hou⁴   *adv.* after, later (opp. ...前 qian²)

Supplementary Vocabulary and Expressions

busy season	旺季 (wang⁴ji⁴)
free for people over 68	68 岁以上的老人免费 (liu⁴shi ba¹ sui⁴ yi³shang⁴ de lao³ren² mian³fei⁴)
local products	土产 (tu²chan³)
slack season	淡季 (dan⁴ji⁴)
souvenir	纪念品 (ji⁴nian⁴pin³)
stand in the line	排队 (pai²dui⁴)

The more, the merrier. 人越多越热闹. (Ren² yue⁴ duo¹ yue⁴ re⁴nao.)

There are too many tourists at the attractions. 景点游客太多. (Jing²dian³ you²ke⁴ tai⁴ duo¹.)

Where is the ticket office? 哪儿买门票? (Nar² mai³ men²piao⁴?)

Which way should we go? 往哪边儿走? (Wang⁴ nei³ biar¹ zou³?)

18. Exercises

I. Give the phonetic spellings of the following words:

哪儿   哪些   多少   医院   先生

孩子   咱们   瞧   来回   哎哟

II. Fill in the blanks with words used in the text of this passage:

1. 一年有十二个 _____ .

2. 西安是 _____ 的好地方.

3. 我们 _____ 下星期去中国.

4. 《三国》这本小说 _____ 一看.

5. _____ 你健康!

III. Change the structure of the following sentences by replacing 去 … with 到 … 去 or vice versa:

1. 我们明年去中国.

2. 你到哪儿去吃饭?

3. 你去北京吗?

4. 你想到纽约去还是到上海去?

5. 老黄去医院了.

72

十九. 看电影

A: 星期六我想去看一场电影[1]儿.

B: 我昨天刚看了一部中国电影儿, 好看得很[2].

A: 电影儿叫什么名字?

B: 叫《男人, 女人和孩子》.

A: 在哪儿看的?

B: 在村民电影院. 这电影儿好极了[3], 我还得[4]再看一遍.

A: 得[5], 星期六咱们一块儿[6]去看.

19. Kan[4] Dian[4]ying[3]

A: Xing[1]qi[1]liu[4] wo[2] xiang[3] qu[4] kan[4] yi[4] chang[3] dian[4]yiěr[3].

B: Wo[3] zuo[2]tian[1] gang[1] kan[4] le yi[2] bu[4] zhong[1]guo[2] dian[4]yiěr. Hao[3] kan[4] de hen[3].

A: Dian[4]yiěr[3] jiao[4] shen[2]me ming[2]zi?

B: Jiao[4] "Nan[2]ren, Nü[3]ren he[2] Hai[2]zi".

A: Zai[4] nar[3] kan[4] de?

B: Zai[4] Cun[1]min[2] Dian[4]ying[3]yuan[4]. Zhe[4] dian[4]yiěr[3] hao[3] ji[2]le, wo[3] hai[2] dei[3] zai[4] kan[4] yi[2] bian[4].

A: De[2], xing[1]qi[1]liu[4] zan[2]men yi[2]kuar[4] qu[4] kan[4].

19. Going to the Movies

A: I am going to see a movie on Saturday.

B: I just watched a Chinese movie yesterday. It was very good.

A: What's its name ?

B: *Men, Women and Children.*

A: Where did you watch it?

B: At the Villagers' Cinema. The film was really excellent. I'd like to see it again.

A: Good. Let's go together on Saturday.

19. Notes

1. 一**场** 电 影 (yi⁴ **chang**³ dian⁴ying³): a film show, 一 **部** 电 影 (yi² **bu**⁴ dian⁴ying³) a film Note the two different measure words that are used with the same noun but mean different things.

2. 好 看 **得** 很 (hao³ kan⁴ de hen³): very nice …**得** 很 following adjectives or adverbs means *very*. 好 吃 **得** 很 (hao³ chi¹ **de hen**³) very delicious, 好 玩 **得** 很 (hao³ wan² **de hen**³) very amusing, 苦 **得** 很 (ku³ **de hen**³) very bitter 得 (de) in this construction is unstressed.

3. 好 极 了 (hao³ ji²le): excellent …极 了 (ji²le) expresses the highest degree. 差 **极** 了 (cha¹ **ji²le**) very, very bad, 高 兴 **极** 了 (gao¹xing⁴ **ji²le**) extremely happy 这 中 药 味 道 苦 **极** 了! (Zhe⁴ zhong¹yao⁴ wei⁴dao ku³ **ji²le!**) This Chinese medicine tastes very bitter!

4. 得 (dei³): need, have to 我 们 **得** 快 走, 不 然 要 淋 雨 了. (Wo³men **dei³** kuai⁴ zou³, bu⁴ran² yao⁴ lin²yu³ le.) We have to hurry, or we'll get wet in the rain.

5. 得 (de²): OK When used independently at the beginning of a sentence, it means *all right*. **得**, 就 这 么 办. (**De²**, jiu⁴ zhe⁴me ban⁴.) All right. Just go ahead.

6. 一 块 儿 (yi²kuar⁴): together 我 们 在 一 块 儿 工 作. (Wo³men zai⁴ **yi²kuar**⁴ gong¹zuo⁴.) We are working together. 她 们 一 **块** 儿 出 去 散 步 了. (Ta¹men **yi²kuar**⁴ chu¹qu san⁴bu⁴ le.) They went out for a walk together.

74

19. Vocabulary

电影 dian⁴ying³   *n.* movie

昨天 zuo²tian¹   *n., adv.* yesterday

刚 gang¹   *adv.* just, not long ago

部 bu⁴   *meas.* used with film, book, etc.
    n. part

…得 很 de hen³   *adv.* very…

男 人 nan²ren²   *n.* man

女 人 nü³ren²   *n.* woman

村 cun¹   *n.* village

民 min²   *n.* people

村 民 cun¹min²   *n.* villager

电 影 院 dian⁴ying³yuan⁴   *n.* cinema

极 ji²   *adv.* extremely

…极 了 ji²le   *adv.* extremely

遍 bian⁴   *meas.* showing the whole duration
    prep. all over

一 块 yi²kuai⁴   *adv.* together (opp. 各自 ge⁴zi⁴)

Supplementary Vocabulary and Expressions

best picture award   最 佳 影 片 奖 (zui⁴ jia¹ ying³pian⁴ jiang³)

caption   字 幕 (zi⁴mu⁴)

director   导 演 (dao²yan³)

feature film   故 事 片 (gu⁴shi pian⁴)

leading actor (actress)   主 演, 主 要 演 员 (zhu²yan³, zhu³yao⁴ yan³yuan²)

movie star   明 星 (ming²xing¹)

plot   情 节 (qing²jie²)

Odd numbers are on the left; even numbers are on the right.
单 号 在 左 边 儿, 双 号 在 右 边 儿.
(Dan¹hao⁴ zai⁴ zuo³ biar¹, shuan¹hao⁴ zai⁴ you⁴ biar¹.)

19. Exercises

I. Tone practice:

zi^1 资 capital	zi^2 -	zi^3 紫 purple	zi^4 自 self
ci^1 疵 defect	ci^2 词 word	ci^3 此 this	ci^4 次 time
si^1 丝 silk	si^2 -	si^3 死 die	si^4 四 four

II. Fill in the following blanks with appropriate words:

1. 我今天上午有点儿不 _____, 可能发烧了.

2. 感冒、发烧要多喝水, 多 _____ .

3. 我到上海去出差, 不买单程票, 总是买 _____ 票.

4. 他们在一 _____ 上班.

III. Complete the following sentences with 不太好, 还好, 好得很, or 好极了:

1. 大夫的手术 _____ ! 病人上午动手术, 下午病就好了.

2. 总的来说, 他们都 _____. 但年龄大了, 总有些病 .

3. 今天天气 _____ , 可能会下雨.

4. 那家中国饭店的菜 _____, 大家都爱吃.

IV. Reconstruct the sentences by using … 得很:

Example: 中国有很多值得旅游的地方. → 中国值得旅游的地方多得很.

1. 红烧鱼很好吃.

2. 今天天气很闷热.

3. 游泳池里的水好凉啊!

4. 她睡觉不早.

5. 中国的家常饭菜脂肪不多.

二十. 汽车故障

A: 昨天早晨我的车在路上抛锚[1]了.

B: 什么毛病[2]?

A: 引擎[3]坏了.

B: 那你怎么办[4]?

A: 我打电话给修车公司, 要他们来拖车, 等了一个多小时,[5] 他们才来人.

B: 那你没车用了?

A: 他们说明天可以修好.

20. Qi[4]che[1] Gu[4]zhang[4]

A: Zuo[2]tian[1] zao[3]chen[2] wo[3]de che[1] zai[4] lu[4]shang pao[1]mao[2] le.

B: Shen[2]me mao[2]bing[4]?

A: Yin[3]qing[2] huai[4] le.

B: Na[4] ni[3] zen[2]me ban[4]?

A: Wo[2] da[3] dian[4]hua[4] gei[3] xiu[1] che[1] gong[1]si[1], yao[4] ta[1]men lai[2] tuo[1] che[1], deng[3] le yi[2] ge duo[1] xiao[3]shi[2], ta[1]men cai[2] lai[2] ren[2].

B: Na[4] ni[3] mei[2] che[1] yong[4] le?

A: Ta[1]men shuo[1] ming[2]tian[1] ke[2]yi[3] xiu[1] hao[3].

20. Car Trouble

A: My car broke down on the road

yesterday morning.

B: What happened?

A: The engine blew out.

B: What did you do then?

A: I called the auto repair shop to tow it,

but no one came until after more than

an hour.

B: So you don't have a car right now?

A: They said the repairs would be done

by tomorrow.

20. Notes

1. 抛 锚 (pao¹mao²): (of a vehicle) break down, (of a ship) cast anchor

2. 毛病(mao²bing⁴): illness; trouble, breakdown 他 的 胃 有 毛病. (Ta¹de wei⁴ you³ **mao²bing⁴**.) He has a stomach disease. 引 擎 出 了 毛病. (Yin³qing² chu¹ le **mao²bing⁴**.) There's some trouble with the engine. 这 家 伙 神经 是 不 是 有 毛病? (Zhe⁴ jia¹huo shen²jing³ shi⁴bushi⁴ you³ **mao²bing⁴**?) Is that guy not quite right in the head?

3. 引 擎 (yin³qing²): a transliteration of *engine*. The more formal word is 发 动 机 (fa¹dong⁴ji¹).

4. 怎 么 办 (zen²me ban⁴): what to do
   A: 现 在 **怎 么 办**? (Xian⁴zai⁴ **zen³me ban⁴**?) What shall we do now?
   B: 你 爱 **怎 么 办** 就 **怎 么 办**. (Ni³ ai⁴ **zen³me ban⁴** jiu⁴ **zen³me ban⁴**.) Do as you like.

5. 一 个 多 小 时 (yi² ge duo¹ xiao³shi²): more than one hour When the word 多 (duo¹) is put after a numeral, it may mean *more, over*. 他 已 经 八 十 **多** 了. (Ta¹ yi³jing ba¹shi **duo¹** le) He is already over eighty. 这 本 会 话 书 有 二 百 **多** 页. (Zhei⁴ ben³ hui⁴hua⁴ shu¹ you³ er⁴bai³ **duo¹** ye⁴.) This conversation book has 200 odd pages. (Cf. "三 百 多 块" in Passage 16.)

20. Vocabulary

汽车 qi⁴che¹   *n.* car, automobile

车 che¹   *n.* vehicle

故障 gu⁴zhang⁴   *n.* trouble

早晨 zao³chen²   *n., adv.* morning (opp. 晚上 wan³shang)

抛锚 pao¹mao²   *v.* break down

毛病 mao²bing⁴   *n.* trouble; disease

引擎 yin³qing²   *n.* engine

坏 huai⁴   *v.* not work, be out of order
adj. bad, mean (opp. 好 hao³)

怎么 zen³me   *adv.* how
int. (expressing surprise) why

打 da³   *v.* make (phone call); beat, strike, hit; play (cards, ball, mahjong); practice (shadow-boxing)

打电话 da³ dian⁴hua⁴   make a phone call

修 xiu¹   *v.* repair, fix

拖 tuo¹   *v.* tow

小时 xiao³shi²   *n.* hour

来人 lai² ren²   some one comes

Supplementary Vocabulary and Expressions

discharged battery   蓄电池没电了 (xu¹dian⁴chi² mei² dian⁴ le)

flat tire   车胎瘪了 (che¹tai¹ bie³ le)

ignition system   点火系统 (dian²huo³ xi⁴tong³)

jump starting   跳接起动 (tiao⁴jie¹ qi³dong⁴)

jumper cable   跳接用的电线 (tiao⁴jie¹ yong⁴ de dian⁴xian⁴)

maintenance   维护 (wei²hu⁴)

tune up   调整 (tiao²zheng³)

A fuse is blown.
一根保险丝断了.
(Yi⁴ geng¹ bao²xian³si¹ duan⁴ le.)

20. Exercises

I. Tone Practice:

guan¹ 关 shut   guan² --   guan³ 馆 shop   guan⁴ 罐 jar

yuan¹ 冤 injustice   yuan² 圆 round   yuan³ 远 far   yuan⁴ 愿 wish

II. Translate the following phrases into Chinese, using 在, which denotes position or location:

1. in New York   2. at home   3. in the plane

4. upstairs   5. under the car   6. on the way back

III. Translate the following phrases into Chinese, using 多, which means *more, over* :

1. more than ten people
2. three months and more
3. over eighty years old
4. more than 30 days

IV. Complete the following sentences containing 那 (na⁴) with any expression that makes sense:

1. 你们能来, 那 _____.

2. 你说好, 那就 _____!

3. 你不去医院, 那_____ ?

4. 你要和我们一块儿走, 那_____.

5. 你不爱吃, 那我_____.

二十一. 味道好极了!

A: 小白! 昨天晚上我下中国馆子[1] 吃饭了.

B: 吃了些什么菜?

A: 我要了三个菜: 宫爆鸡丁儿、鱼香肉丝儿、麻婆儿豆腐.

B: 味道怎么样?

A: 宫爆鸡丁儿不怎么样[2].鱼香肉丝儿和麻婆儿豆腐的味道好极了! 我一口气儿把[3]这三个菜全吃完了.

B: 你一顿吃这三个菜, 不怕胆固醇高吗?

A: 难得吃吃也没关系[4]啦! 再说[5], 我们的身体也需要一些胆固醇.

21. Wei[4]dao Hao[3] Ji[2]le!

A: Xiao[3] Bai[2]! Zuo[2]tian[1] wan[3]shang wo[3] xia[4] zhong[1]guo[2] guan[3]zi chi[1]fan[4] le.

B: Chi[1] le xie[1] shen[2]me cai[4]?

A: Wo[3] yao[4] le san[1] ge cai[4]: gong[1]bao[4] ji[1]diər[1], yu[2]xiang[1] rou[4]sər[1], ma[2]por[2] dou[4]fu.

B: Wei[4]dao zen[3]meyang[4]?

A: Gong[1]bao[4] ji[1]diər[1] bu[4] zen[3]me yang[4], yu[2]xiang[1] rou[4]sər[1] he[2] ma[2]por[2] dou[4]fu de wei[4]dao hao[3] ji[2]le! Wo[3] yi[4]kou[3]qiər[4] ba[3] zhei[4] san[3] ge cai[4] quan[2] chi[1] wan[2] le.

B: Ni[3] yi[2] dun[4] chi[1] zhei[4] san[1] ge cai[4], bu[2] pa[4] dan[3]gu[4]chun[2] gao[1] ma?

A: Nan[2]de chi[1]chi ye[3] mei[2] guan[1]xi la! Zai[4]shuo[1], wo[3]men de shen[1]ti[3] ye[3] xu[1]yao[4] yi[4]xie[1] dan[3]gu[4]chun[2].

21. They Taste Fantastic!

A: Xiao Bai! Yesterday evening I went to a Chinese restaurant.

B: What did you eat?

A: I ordered three dishes: *kungbao* chicken, fish-flavored pork slices, and *mapo tofu*.

B: How did they taste?

A: The *kungpao* chicken was so so. The other two tasted fantastic! I finished them in one breath.

B: You finished all three of these dishes in one meal! Are you not afraid of high cholesterol?

A: I only eat them once in a while, so it's okay. Besides, our body needs some cholesterol.

21. Notes

1. 下馆子 (xia^4 guan^{3}zi): go to a restaurant 下 (xia^4) means *go to*. It is used with certain objects only. 她先生每天下橱房. (Ta^1 xian^{1}sheng mei^{3}tian^1 **xia^4** chu^{2}fang^2.) Every day her husband does the cooking. Its opposite word 上 (shang^4) may also mean *go to*, and it takes its own particular objects too. (Cf. Note 3, Passage 16.)

2. 不怎么样 (bu^4 zen^{2}me yang^4): not very good, only so-so 他球踢得**不怎么样**. (Ta^1 qiu^2 ti^1 de **bu^4 zen^{2}me yang^4**.) He is a very indifferent footballer. Another expression with similar meaning is 一般 (yi^{4}ban^1). 这台相机很便宜,可是质量**不怎么样** (or 一般). (Zhei^4 tai^2 xiang^{4}ji^1 hen^3 pian^{2}yi, ke^{3}shi^4 zhi^{4}liang^4 **bu^4 zen^{2}me yang^4** [or **yi^{4}ban^1**].) This camera is inexpensive, but the quality is mediocre.

3. 把 (ba^3): used to form an inverted structure with the object placed before the transitive verb 请**把**门关上. (Qing^2 **ba^3** men^2 guan^1 shang^4.) =请关上门. (Qing^3 guan^1 shang^4 men^2.) Please shut the door. 请洗洗衣服吧. (Qing^2 xi^{3}xi yi^{1}fu ba.) =请**把**衣服洗洗吧. (Qing^3 **ba^2** yi^{1}fu xi^{2}xi ba.) Please wash the clothes. This disposal construction with 把 describes how an action is carried out on the object, and thus focus is laid on the object, not on the action.

4. 没关系 (mei^2 guan^{1}xi): not matter, be of no importance 这药早上吃还是晚上吃都**没关系**. (Zhe^4 yao^4 zao^{3}shang chi^1 hai^{2}shi wan^{3}shang chi^1 dou^1 **mei^2 guan^{1}xi**.) It doesn't matter whether the medicine is taken in the morning or at bed time. 这**没**有多大**关系**. (Zhe^4 **mei^2**you^3 duo^1 da^4 **guan^{1}xi**.) It doesn't matter much.

5. 再说 (zai^{4}shuo^1): besides, in addition 现在给她打电话太晚了,**再说**,她也不一定在家. (Xian^{4}zai^4 gei^3 ta^1 da^3 dian^{4}hua^4 tai^4 wan^3 le, **zai^{4}shuo^1**, ta^1 ye^3 bu^4 yi^{2}ding^4 zai^{4}jia^1.) It's too late to call her; besides, she may not be at home.

21. Vocabulary

白 bai^2 — *n.* a surname; *n., a.* white (opp. 黑 hei^1);

馆 guan^3 — *n.* shop; hall

馆子 guan^{3}zi — *n.* restaurant

宫 gong^1 — *n.* palace, (recipe, etc.) from royal court

爆 bao^4 — *v.* quick-fry

鸡丁 ji^{1}ding^1 — *n.* chicken cubes

香 xiang^1 — *n.* aroma, fragrance, flavor *a.* fragrant; delicious

丝 si^1 — *n.* shredded meat or vegetables; silk

麻 ma^2 — *a.* pockmarked

婆 po^2 — old woman; grandma; a woman's mother-in-law (opp. 公 gong^1)

麻婆 ma^{2}po^2 — *n.* a legendary pockmarked woman who was good at making very delicious spicy bean curd

怎么样 zen^{3}meyang^4 — *adv.* how

不怎么样 bu^4 zen^{2}me yang^4 — *a., adv.* only fair, not up to much

一口气 yi^{4}kou^{3}qi^4 — *adv.* in one breath, at a stretch

把 ba^3 — *prep.* used to form an inverted structure *meas.* used with 劲 (jin^4: energy), 年纪 (nian^{2}ji^4: age), 钥匙 (yao^{4}shi: key), etc.

全 quan^2 — *a.* complete *adv.* wholly

顿 dun^4 — *meas.* used with meals

怕 pa^4 — *v.* be afraid of *adv.* perhaps

胆固醇 dan^{3}gu^{4}chun^2 — *n.* cholesterol

高 gao^1 — *a.* high, tall (opp. 低 di^1)

难得 nan^{2}de — *adv.* seldom (opp. 经常 jing^{1}chang^2)

关系 guan^{1}xi — *n.* relationship, bearing

没关系 mei^2 guan^{1}xi — it does not matter

啦 la — *part.* a combination of 了 (le) and 啊 (a)

再说 zai^{4}shuo^1 — *adv.* besides, moreover, plus

身体 shen^{1}ti^3 — *n.* body; health

需要 xu^{1}yao^4 — *v.* need, require

一些 yi^{4}xie^1 — *pron., a.* some

Supplementary Vocabulary and Expressions

beef with oyster sauce — 蚝油牛肉 (hao^{2}you^2 niu^{2}rou^4)

crisp fried duck — 香酥鸭 (xian^{3}su^{2}ya^1)

fotiaoqiang (steamed abalone, shark's fin, and fish, etc. mixed together) — 佛跳墙 (fo^{2}tiao^{4}qiang^2, Lit. Buddha will jump over the wall to eat it.)

lamb — 羊肉 (yang^{2}rou^4)

pan fried flounder — 干煎龙利 (gan^{1}jian^1 long^{2}li^4)

roast Beijing duck — 北京烤鸭 (Bei^{3}jing^1 kao^3 ya^1)

sea cucumber — 海参 (hai^{3}shen^1)

seafood — 海鲜 (hai^{3}xian^1)

steamed pullet — 清蒸子鸡 (qing^{1}zheng^1 zi^{3}ji^1)

sweet and sour pork — 糖醋里脊 (tang^{3}cu^4 li^{3}ji)

twice cooked pork — 回锅肉 (hui^{2}guo^{1}rou^4)

Green food, fresh air, regular exercise, and a cheerful frame of mind are good for your health. 绿色食品, 新鲜空气, 经常运动, 和愉快的心情对健康有益. (Lü^{4}se^4 shi^{2}pin^3, xin^{1}xian^1 kong^{1}qi^4, jing^{1}chang^2 yun^{4}dong^4, he^2 yu^{2}kuai^4 de xin^{1}qing^2 dui^4 jian^{4}kang^1 you^3 yi^4.)

21. Exercises

I. Tone Practice:

wei[1] 危 danger	wei[2] 围 surround	wei[3] 伟 great	wei[4] 味 taste
yong[1] 佣 servant	yong[2] 喁 (fish) sticking mouth out	yong[3] 永 forever	yong[4] 用 use

II. Give the antonyms of the following words:

1. 好　　2. 天　　3. 上　　4. 来　　5. 没
6. 少　　7. 大　　8. 早　　9. 晚上　　10. 难得

III. Fill in the blanks with any word or words that make sense:

1. 你在书店买了些什么好_____ ?
2. 你吃了些什么 _____ ?
3. 你喝了些什么 _____ ?
4. 你说了些什么 _____ ?
5. 你请了些什么 _____ ?

IV. Rewrite the following sentences by using 把 (ba[3]):

Example: 请先吃了水果. → 请先把水果吃了.

1. 他修好了我的汽车.
2. 我叫她 "大姐".
3. 他忘了开会的时间. (忘 wang[4]: forget)
4. 学完第一本, 再学第二本.

V. Answer the following questions according to the text:

1. 昨天晚上你上哪儿了?
2. 你吃了几个菜?
3. 你吃了鱼吗?
4. 你喜欢吃肉吗?
5. 你吃蔬菜了没?
6. 味儿不错吧?
7. 你胆固醇高吗?
8. 那你干什么一顿吃三个菜, 吃了鸡, 还要吃肉?

二十二. 看电视

A: 电视是每家不可缺少的东西[1]. 可是我的孩子一回家就看电视, 一看至少就是两、三个小时.

B: 那不太好, 会看坏眼睛[2]的. 再说, 有些节目也不适合小孩儿看.

A: 你的孩子不看电视吗?

B: 平时[3]我不让他们看. 只有星期六下午和星期天上午可以看一些儿童节目.

22. Kan⁴ Dian⁴shi⁴

A: Dian⁴shi⁴ shi⁴ mei³jia¹ bu⁴ ke³ que¹shao³ de dong¹xi, ke³shi⁴ wo³de hai²zi yi⁴ hui²jia¹ jiu⁴ kan⁴ dian⁴shi⁴, yi² kan⁴ zhi⁴shao³ jiu⁴shi⁴ liang³ san¹ ge xiao³shi².

B: Na⁴ bu² tai⁴ hao³, hui⁴ kan⁴ huai⁴ yan³jing de. Zai⁴shuo¹, you³xie¹ jie²mu⁴ ye³ bu² shi⁴he² xiao³har² kan⁴.

A: Ni³de hai²zi bu² kan⁴ dian⁴shi⁴ ma?

B: Ping²shi² wo³ bu² rang⁴ ta¹men kan⁴. Zhi² you³ xing¹qi¹ liu⁴ xia⁴wu³ he² xing¹qi¹tian¹ shang⁴wu³ ke²yi³ kan⁴ yi⁴xie¹ er²tong² jie³mu⁴.

22. Watching TV

A: TV is something no family can do

without, but my children watch TV

as soon as they come home and once

they turn it on, they keep watching

for at least two to three hours straight.

B: That's not good because it's bad for

their eyes. Besides, some programs are

not suited to children.

A: Your children do not watch TV, do

they?

B: I don't allow them to watch any TV

on weekdays. They may watch

children's programs on Saturday

afternoons and Sunday mornings

only.

22. Notes

1. 东西 (dong¹xi): thing It is mostly used
to denote concrete things. 这是谁的
东西? (Zhe⁴ shi shei² de **dong¹xi?**)
Whose things are they? 她出去买东
西了. (Ta¹ chu² qu⁴ mai³ **dong¹xi** le.)
She's out shopping. 他知道一些东
西, 就是不肯说. (Ta¹ zhi¹dao yi⁴xie¹
dong¹xi, jiu⁴shi⁴ bu⁴ ken³ shuo¹.) He
knows something, but he is not willing
to say anything about it. When used of
a person or animal, it expresses an
emotion of affection or hatred. 她是个
可爱的小东西. (Ta¹ shi⁴ ge ke³ai⁴
de xiao³ **dong¹xi**.)   She's a sweet little
thing.

2. 看坏眼睛 (kan⁴ huai⁴ yan³jing):
hurt the eyes by watching … Note the
sentence pattern: the objective
complement precedes the object. 小心
不要打破玻璃. (Xiao³xin¹ bu² yao⁴
da³ po⁴ bo¹li.) Be careful not to break
the glass. 医生治死了病人.
(Yi¹sheng¹ **zhi⁴ si³** le bing⁴ren².) The
doctor killed the patient with his
maltreatment. 他的话儿让人笑掉
大牙. (Ta¹de huar⁴ rang⁴ ren² **xiao⁴
diao⁴** da⁴ ya².) His words are ridiculous
enough to make people laugh their
heads off.

3. 平时 (ping²shi²): at ordinary times
她平时只吃蔬菜, 不吃肉. (Ta¹
ping²shi² zhi³ chi¹ shu¹cai⁴, bu⁴ chi¹
rou⁴.) She normally eats only vegetables,
no meat. "平时不烧香, 急来抱佛
脚." (**Ping²shi²** bu⁴ shao¹xiang¹, ji² lai²
bao⁴ fo² jiao³.) Never burn joss-sticks
when all is well, but clasp Buddha's leg
when in distress.

22. Vocabulary

缺 少 que^{1}shao^3	*v.* lack (opp. 多 余 duo^{1}yu^2)
东 西 dong^{1}xi	*n.* thing
回 家 hui^{2}jia^1	*v.* come home, return (opp. 出 门 chu^{1}men^2)
至 少 zhi^{4}shao^3	*adv.* at least (opp. 至 多 zhi^{4}duo^1)
眼 睛 yan^{3}jing	*n.* eye
节 目 jie^{2}mu^4	*n.* program
适 合 shi^{4}he^2	*v.* fit
小 孩 xiao^{3}hai^2	*n.* child (opp. 大 人 da^{4}ren^2)
平 时 ping^{2}shi^2	*adv.* at ordinary times
只 有 zhi^2 you^3	*adv. a.* only
星 期 天 xing^{1}qi^{1}tian^1	*n.* Sunday
儿 童 er^{2}tong^2	*n.* children

antenna	天 线 (tian^{1}xian^4)
broadcast	广 播 (guan^{3}bo^1)
digital TV	数 位 电 视 (shu^{4}wei^4 dian^{4}shi^4)
HD (high definition)	高 清 晰 度 (gao^1 qing^{1}xi^{1}du^4)
LCD TV	液 晶 电 视 (ye^{4}jing^1 dian^{4}shi^4)
live	实 况 广 播 (shi^{2}kuang^4 guan^{3}bo^1)
plasma TV	电 浆 电 视 (dian^{4}jiang^1 dian^{4}shi^4)
rebroadcast	重 播 (chong^{2}bo^1)
relay	转 播 (zhuan^{3}bo^1)
satellite TV	卫 星 电 视 (wei^{4}xing^1 dian^{4}shi^4)
wide screen	宽 屏 幕 (kuan^1 ping^{2}mu^4)

I can't believe she is still watching TV.
我 不 能 相 信 她 还 在 看 电 视.
(Wo^3 bu^4 neng^2 xiang^{1}xin^4 ta^1 hai^2 zai^4 kan^4 dian^{4}shi^4.)

22. Exercises

I. Give the phonetic spelling of each word before parentheses:

大 (　　) 鱼　大 (　　) 夫　　觉 (　　) 得　　　睡觉 (　　　　)

地 (　　) 方　好好地 (　　)　生 (　　) 小孩　张先生 (　　　)

II. Pattern Drills:

Verb Transitive	Objective Complement	Object
看	坏	眼睛
修	好	汽车
刷	白	牙齿

III. Fill in the following blanks with 至多 (*at most*) or 至少 (*at least*):

1. 为了学好汉语, 我每天 _____ 要学两个小时.
2. 孩子们每天 _____ 只能看一个小时的电视.
3. 我们爱吃中国饭, 每周 _____ 要下一次中国馆子.
4. 为了少吃脂肪, 我们每周 _____ 下一次馆子.
5. 她还小, _____ 不过十八岁.
6. 在中国的农村里, 每家 _____ 有一台电视机.

IV. Fill in the blanks with words used in the text:

1. 他每顿饭肉是 _____ 的.
2. 他每天至少要睡八个 _____.
3. _____ 我胆固醇不高, 可是不知道为什么昨天高得很.
4. 昨天晚会 (evening entertainment) 上的 _____ 好看吗?
5. 你不去, _____ 我也不去了.
6. _____ 她妈妈知道她为什么不结婚.
7. 这本书很有用, _____, 钱也不贵.
8. 他马上要下班儿了. 现在 (xian^{4}zai^4: now) 去办公室找他, 时间不 _____.

二十三. 探望亲人 [1]

A: 那位漂亮的姑娘是谁啊?

B: 是我的表妹. 她刚从台湾回来.

A: 她去台湾干吗 [2]?

B: 去探亲的. 去看她的奶奶, 他们
已经十几 [3] 年没见面了. 她奶奶
可想她 [4] 呢.

A: 我和爷爷、奶奶也好几年没见
面了. 我小时候他们可疼我呢.
我今年一定要去看看他们啦!

23. Tan[4]wang[4] Qin[1]ren[2]

A: Ne[4] wei[4] piao[4]liang de gu[1]niang shi[4]
shei[2] a?

B: Shi[4] wo[3]de biao[3]mei[4]. Ta[1] gang[1] cong[1]
Tai[2]wan[1] hui[2]lai.

A: Ta[1] qu[4] Tai[2]wan[1] gan[4]ma[2]?

B: Qu[4] tan[4]qin[1] de. Qu[4] kan[4] ta[1]de nai[3]nai.
Ta[1]men yi[3]jing shi[2] ji[3] nian[2] mei[2]
jian[4]mian[4] le. Ta[1] nai[3]nai ke[2] xiang[3] ta
ne.

A: Wo[3] he[2] ye[2]ye, nai[3]nai ye[2] hao[2] ji[3]
nian[2] mei[2] jian[4]mian[4] le. Wo[2] xiao[3]
shi[2]hou ta[1]men ke[3] teng[2] wo[3] ne. Wo[3]
jin[1]nian[2] yi[2]ding[4] yao[4] qu[4] kan[4]kan
ta[1]men la !

23. Visiting Family Members

A: Who is that pretty girl?

B: My cousin. She just came back from

   Taiwan.

A: Why did she go there?

B: She went to visit her grandma. She

   hadn't seen her for over ten years.

   Her grandma missed her very much.

A: I haven't seen my grandparents for

   years either. They loved me so much

   when I was a kid. I will go to visit them

   sometime this year!

23. Notes

1. 探望亲人 (tan^{4}wang^4 qin^{1}ren^2): (usually to go to one's native place) to visit one's family or relatives The objects of the verb 探望 (tan^{4}wang^4) are usually seniors, patients, or people you have not seen for a long time. The contracted form of **探望亲人** (tan^{4}wang^4 qin^{1}ren^2) is 探亲 (tan^{4}qin^1).

2. 干吗 (or 干嘛 gan^4 ma^2): why It is more colloquial than 干什么 (gan^{4}shen^{2}me). Cf. Note 3, Passage 10. 她去台湾干吗? (Ta^1 qu^4 Tai^{2}wan^1 **gan^{4}ma^2**?) = 她干吗去台湾? (Ta^1 **gan^{4}ma^2** qu^4 Tai^{2}wan^1?) For what purpose did she go to Taiwan? Note the two possible positions of 干吗 (gan^{4}ma^2) in the above sentences. 干吗 (gan^{4}ma^2) also means *what to do*. 今儿下午干吗? (Jiər^1 xia^{4}wu^3 **gan^{4}ma^2**?) What are we going to do this afternoon?

3. 十几 (shi^{2}ji^3): over ten, same as 十多 (shi^{2}duo^1) Cf. Note 5, Passage 20.

4. 可想她 (ke^2 xiang^3 ta): miss her very much 可 (ke^3) is used for emphasis. 可别忘了! (**Ke^3** bie^2 wang^4 le!) Mind you don't forget it! 他的汉语讲得可地道啦! (Ta^{1}de han^{4}yu^2 jiang^3 de **ke^2** di^{4}dao^4 la!) His Chinese is excellent.

23. Vocabulary

探望 tan^{4}wang^4 — *v.* visit

亲人 qin^{1}ren^2 — *n.* family members

那 na^4 — *pron.* that

When it is used independently (as in 那是谁？ Na^4[or Ne^4] shi shei^2? Who is that person ?) or is followed by nouns, it is pronounced as na^4 or ne^4; if it is followed by measure words or numerals + measure words, or when it is in the following set combinations: 那个 (that), 那会儿 (at that time), 那些 (those), and 那样 (like that), it is usually pronounced as nei^4 or ne^4. In 那么 (like that; then), 那么些 (so many, so few), 那么点儿 (so little, so few), and 那么着 (like that), it is usually pronounced as ne^4. As a *conj.*, it is always pronounced as na^4, as in Note 5, Passage 6.

位 wei^4 — *meas.* used with people, showing respect

漂亮 piao^{4}liang — *a.* beautiful (opp. 难看 nan^{2}kan^4)

姑娘 gu^{1}niang — *n.* girl

谁 shei^2 — *pron.* who

…是谁? shi^4 shei^2 — who is (are)…?

表妹 biao^{3}mei^4 — *n.* (younger, female) cousin

她 ta^1 — *pron.* she, her

从 cong^1 — *prep.* from (opp. 到 dao^4)

台湾 tai^{2}wan^1 — *n.* Taiwan

干吗 gan^{4}ma^2 — *adv.* why

奶奶 nai^{3}nai — *n.* grandma (father's mother)

已经 yi^{3}jing — *adv.* already (opp. 还没有 hai^{2}mei^{2}you^3)

十几 shi^2 ji^3 — *a.* more than ten

年 nian^2 — *n.* year

爷爷 ye^{2}ye — *n.* grandpa (father's father)

好几年 hao^2 ji^3 nian^2 — *n., adv.* quite a few years

小时候 xiao^3 shi^{2}hou — when one is a child

可 ke^3 — *adv.* very much (for emphasis) *conj.* but *v.* may, can

疼 teng^2 — *v.* love dearly; ache, be painful *a.* painful

Supplementary Vocabulary and Expressions

as closely linked as flesh and blood — 骨肉相连 (gu^{3}rou^4 xiang^{1}lian^2)

family happiness — 天伦之乐 (tian^{1}lun^{2}zhi^{1}le^4)

family reunion — 家人团聚 (jia^{1}ren^2 tuan^{2}ju^4), 合家欢 (he^{2}jia^{1}huan^1)

homesick — 想家 (xiang^{3}jia^1), 思乡 (si^{1}xiang^1)

loving mother — 慈母 (ci^{2}mu^3)

person residing far away from home — 游子 (you^{2}zi^3)

stern father — 严父 (yan^{2}fu^4)

The moon is brighter in the home town.
月是故乡明.
(Yue^4 shi^4 gu^{4}xiang^1 ming^2.)

23. Exercises

I. Tone Practice:

gua¹ 瓜 melon   gua² --   gua³ 寡 widow   gua⁴ 挂 hang
hua¹ 花 flower   hua² 划 row   hua³ --   hua⁴ 画 drawing

II. Fill in the following blanks:

1. 爸爸的妈妈就是我的 _____.
2. 我叫爸爸的爸爸 _____.
3. 你刚才说谁刚 _____ 台湾回来?
4. 我小 _____ 和奶奶一起住在中国的一个农村里.
5. 我来美国以后, 和奶奶难得 _____ 了.

III. Translate the underlined words in the following sentences into English:

1. 你好!
2. 三天以后汽车修好了.
3. 修这个车要好几百块.
4. 他来了好一会儿了.
5. 单程的机票好贵啊!
6. 我表妹是个好姑娘.
7. 你的表姐好漂亮啊!
8. 你请了好多人?
9. 她喝了好多咖啡, 想睡觉了.
10. 天气预报说今天是好天.
11. 她头疼. 休息了一会儿, 好一点儿了.
12. 他爷爷的病好了.
13. 鱼香肉丝儿不好吃.
14. 那些节目好看吗?
15. A: 咱们去吃中国菜吧!
　　 B: 好! 咱们走!

IV. Insert the word 可 into each of the following sentences to make the word following it more emphatic:

1. 我奶奶对我好!
2. 昨儿 (= 昨天) 夜里的雨下得大!
3. 你来了, 让我好等啊!
4. 你知道李小姐要结婚了?
5. 这不是我说的.
6. 我没这么说.

92

二十四. 看牙医

A: 我的牙又不行[1]了.

B: 怎么了[2]? 有虫牙?

A: 虫牙倒[3]没有, 就是[4]每次刷牙,
牙肉都出血.

B: 可能有结石, 你得去洗牙了.

A: 洗牙? 我两年前[5]刚洗过[6]!

B: 两年前? 六个月就该洗一次了,
至少得每年洗一次.

A: 是吗? 那我明天就去看牙医.

24. Kan[4] Ya[2]yi[1]

A: Wo[3]de ya[2] you[4] bu[4]xing[2] le.

B: Zen[3]me le? You[3] chong[2]ya[2]?

A: Chong[2]ya[2] dao[4] mei[2]you[3], jiu[4]shi[4]
mei[3]ci[4] shua[1]ya[2], ya[2]rou[4] dou[1] chu[1]xie[3].

B: Ke[3]neng[2] you[3] jie[2]shi[2], ni[2] dei[3] qu[4] xi[3]
ya[2] le.

A: Xi[3] ya[2]? Wo[2] liang[3] nian[2] qian[2] gang[1]
xi[3] guo!

B: Liang[3] nian[2] qian[2]? Liu[4] ge yue[4] jiu[4]
gai[1] xi[3] yi[2]ci[4] le. Zhi[4]shao[3] ye[2] dei[3]
mei[3] nian[2] xi[3] yi[2]ci[4].

A: Shi[4] ma? Na[4] wo[3] ming[2]tian[1] jiu[4] qu[4]
kan[4] ya[2] yi[1].

24. Seeing a Dentist

A: There's something wrong again with my teeth.

B: What's wrong? Do you have any cavities?

A: No cavities, but my gum bleeds each time I brush my teeth.

B: Maybe you have some plaque build-up. You may need a cleaning.

A: Cleaning? I *just* had my teeth cleaned two years ago!

B: Two years ago? You should have them cleaned every six months, or at least once every year.

A: Really? Then I'll go see my dentist tomorrow.

24. Notes

1. 不行 (bu⁴xing²): no good 他的汉语**不行**. (Ta¹de han⁴yu³ **bu⁴xing²**.) His Chinese is not good. 我的听力**不行**. (Wo³de ting¹li⁴ **bu⁴xing²**.) My hearing is poor. Another meaning: won't do 这绝对**不行**. (Zhe⁴ jue²dui⁴ **bu⁴xing²**.) This will never do.

2. 怎么了 (zen³me le): What's wrong? 你今儿气色这么难看.**怎么了**? (Ni³ jiər¹ qi⁴se⁴ zhe⁴me nan²kan⁴. **Zen³me** le?): You are looking so sick today. What happened?

3. 倒 (dao⁴): used to indicate an opposite effect or something contrary to what is known or expected 请的客人还没有到, 不速之客**倒**有两个. (Qing³ de ke⁴ren² hai² mei²you³ dao⁴, bu² su⁴ zhi¹ ke⁴ **dao⁴** you³ liang³ ge.) The invited guests have not come; two uninvited guests are here.
   A: 我太太在橱房做饭, 没打麻将. (Wo³ tai⁴tai zai⁴ chu²fang² zuo⁴fan⁴, mei² da³ ma²jiang⁴.) My wife is fixing dinner in the kitchen, not playing mahjong.)
   B: 这**倒**新鲜! (Zhe¹ **dao⁴** xin¹xian¹!) What a surprise!

4. 就是 (jiu⁴shi⁴): only that 她本来会考好的, **就是**太紧张了. (Ta¹ ben³lai² hui⁴ kao² hao³ de, **jiu⁴shi⁴** tai⁴ jin³zhang¹ le.) She would probably have done well in the exam, only that she got too nervous. Cf. the 就是 (jiu⁴shi⁴) in Passage 11 for different use.

5. 前 (qian²): before, ago 三天**前** (san¹ tian¹ **qian²**) three days ago, 天黑**前** (tian¹ hei¹ **qian²**) before dark, 饭**前**服 (fan⁴ **qian²** fu²) take (medicine) before meals In the first two examples before 前 (qian²) the word 以 (yi³) can be added. 三天**前** (san¹ tian¹ **qian²**) = 三天**以前** (san¹ tian¹ **yi³qian²**) But in the third example 以 cannot be added. We cannot say 饭以前 (fan⁴ yi³qian²); but we may say 吃饭以前 (chi¹ fan⁴ yi³qian²).

6. 洗过 (xi³ guo): have cleaned 过 is a *part.* put after a *v.* to form a perfect tense. 我去**过**了. (Wo³ qu⁴ **guo** le.) I have been there. 我吃**过**午饭就去 (Wo³ chi¹ **guo** wu³fan⁴ jiu⁴ qu⁴.) I'll go right after lunch.

24. Vocabulary

牙医 ya²yi¹   *n.* dentist

牙 ya²   *n.* tooth

又 you⁴   *adv.* again

不行 bu⁴xing²   *a.* (be) no good, (sth. is) wrong

int. no, won't do, be out of the question

怎么了 zen³me le   what's wrong

虫牙 chong²ya²   *n.* (also 蛀牙 zhu⁴ya²) decayed tooth

倒 dao⁴   *adv.* used to indicate an opposite effect

每次 mei³ci⁴   *adv., conj.* each time

次 ci⁴   *n.* time, occasion

刷牙 shua¹ya²   *v.* brush teeth

牙肉 ya²rou⁴   *n.* gum

出血 chu¹xie³   *v.* bleed

血 xie³, xue⁴   *n.* blood

结石 jie²shi²   *n.* plaque

洗 xi³   *v.* clean, wash

...前 qian²   *adv.* ... ago (opp. ... 后 hou⁴)

过 guo   *suff.* after a *v.*, showing an action has been done

guo⁴   *v.* go across; spend; live (a life)

adv. too much, over

医生 yi¹sheng¹   *n.* doctor, (also called 大夫 dai⁴fu)

Supplementary Vocabulary and Expressions

English	Chinese
canine tooth	犬牙 (quan³ya²)
denture	假牙 (jia³ya²)
extraction	拔牙 (ba²ya²)
filling	补牙 (bu³ya²)
front tooth	门牙 (men²ya²)
gingivitis	牙龈炎 (ya²yin² yan²)
implant	植牙 (zhi²ya²)
molar	槽牙 (cao²ya²)
orthodontics	齿列矫形 (chi³lie⁴ jiao³xing²)
periodontitis	牙周炎 (ya²zhou¹yan²)
pus	脓 (nong²)
root canal	根管治疗 (gen¹guan³ zhi⁴liao²)

Brush and floss only those teeth that you want to keep.

对要保住的牙齿, 每天得刷牙,用牙线.

(Dui⁴ yao⁴ bao³zhu⁴ de ya²chi³, mei³tian¹ dei³ shua¹ya², yong⁴ ya²xian⁴.)

24. Exercises

I. Tone Practice:

you[1] 忧 worry   you[2] 游 swim   you[3] 有 have   you[4] 右 right

wen[1] 温 warm   wen[2] 文 language   wen[3] 吻 kiss   wen[4] 问 ask

II. Form sentences with the words given:

1. 白   刷   牙齿   越   越
2. 每年   探亲   中国   都   要   到   去   他
3. 就   了   出血   牙肉   不会   经常   洗牙
4. 了   前   过   小时   半   吃   午饭   我
5. 来   你   让   等   我   才   好   啊

III. Use the words in parentheses to give the response:

1. A: 一天该刷几次牙?
   B: (至少)
2. A: 我头很疼.
   B: (可能)
3. A: 我经常头疼. 怎么办?
   B: (得)
4. A: 我发烧了三天了.
   B: (干吗不 …)
5. A: 他老爸快不行了.
   B: (岁数)

IV. Rewrite the following sentences by using 倒:

1. 她来了. 我没有想到她会来.

2. 他花了不少钱, 病没有治好.

3. 钱花得不多. 饭菜很好吃.

4. 我奶奶没有什么大毛病, 但小毛小病很多.

5. 他奶奶快九十了, 身体还健康.

二十五. 问路

A: 大爷¹, 麻烦您², 请问³, 到健康
素菜馆怎么走?

B: 一直走. 看到红绿灯, 往右拐,
再过⁴两个街口, 往左拐, 你会
看到 一家银行和一个小旅馆.
中间有一 栋绿色的房子, 那就
是⁵健康素菜馆.

A: 要多久⁶可以走到?

B: 大约五分钟.

A: 谢谢!

B: 不谢!

25. Wen⁴lu⁴

A: Da⁴ye², ma²fan nin², qing³wen⁴, dao⁴
Jian⁴kang¹ Su⁴cai⁴ Guan³ zen³me zou³?

B: Yi⁴zhi² zou³, kan⁴dao⁴ hong²lü⁴ deng¹,
wang³ you⁴ guai³, zai⁴ guo⁴ liang³ ge
jie¹kou³, wang³ zuo² guai³, ni³ hui⁴
kan⁴dao⁴ yi⁴ jia¹ yin²hang² he² yi² ge
xiao³ lü²quan³. Zhong¹jian¹ you³ yi²
dong⁴ lü⁴ se⁴ de fang²zi, na⁴ jiu⁴ shi⁴
Jian⁴kang¹ Su⁴cai⁴ Guan³.

A: Yao⁴ duo¹jiu³ ke²yi³ zou³ dao⁴?

B: Da⁴yue¹ wu³ fen¹zhong¹.

A: Xie⁴xie!

B: Bu²xie⁴!

25. Asking for Directions

A: Excuse me, sir! How do I get to the
Jiankang Vegetable Restaurant?

B: Keep straight and make a right at the
light. After two blocks make a left and
you will see a green house between a
bank and a small hotel. That is the
restaurant.

A: How long will it take to get there?

B: About five minutes.

A: Thank you!

B: You're welcome!

25. Notes

1. 大爷 (da⁴ye²): Original meaning is father's elder brother. Here it is a respectful term of direct address to elderly men.

2. 麻烦您! (Ma²fan nin²!): Sorry to bother you! an expression often used before or after asking sb. to do sth.

3. 请问 (qing³wen⁴): excuse me, please This is a polite form used before asking a question.

4. 过 (guo⁴): *v.* pass, cross, go across 过马路要小心! (**Guo⁴**ma³lu⁴ yao⁴ xiao³xin¹!) Be careful to go across the road. 过 (guo⁴) is a word with multiple meanings. In Note 2, Passage 48 there is a summary of its use.

5. 就是 (jiu⁴shi⁴): indicating the exact thing that someone wants or asks about or the exact person that is mentioned, not other things or persons 瞧! **就是** 那个人! (Qiao²! **Jiu⁴shi⁴** ne⁴ ge ren².) Look, that's the man! The 就是 (jiu⁴shi⁴) here is different from that in Passage 24 (Note 4), where 就是 (jiu⁴shi⁴) means *only that*. The 就 (jiu⁴) here stresses 是 (shi⁴). It is the same as the 就 (jiu⁴) in Passage 11 (Note 1), but it is different from that in Passage 22, where it is a part of the idiom 一 … 就… (explained in Note 3, Passage12).

6. 多久 (duo¹jiu³): how long Here 多 (duo¹) is *how...?* 多快 (duo¹ kuai⁴) how soon, 多大 (duo¹ da⁴) how big; how old (See Note 3, Passage 8.)

25. Vocabulary

问 wen^4	*v.* ask (opp. 答 da^2)
问 路 wen^{4}lu^4	*v.* ask the way
大 爷 da^{4}ye^2	*n.* polite form used in addressing an elderly man
麻 烦 ma^{2}fan	*v., n.* trouble, bother
麻 烦 您 ma^{2}fan nin^2	sorry to put you to trouble; excuse me
素 菜 su^{4}cai^4	*n.* vegetable dish (opp. 荤 菜 hun^{1}cai^4)
一 直 yi^{4}zhi^2	*adv.* straight (opp. 拐 弯 guai^{3}wan^1); continuously
看 到 kan^{4}dao^4	*v.* see, catch sight of
红 绿 灯 hong^{2}lü^4 deng^1	*n.* traffic light
灯 deng^1	*n.* light, lamp
往 wang^3	*prep.* toward *v.* go toward
右 you^4	*n., a., adv.* right (opp. 左 zuo^3)
拐 guai^3	*v.* turn
往 右 拐 wang^3 you^4 guai^3	turn to the right
街 jie^1	*n.* street
街 口 jie^{1}kou^3	*n.* crossing, intersection
左 zuo^3	*n., a., adv.* left
银 行 yin^{2}hang^2	*n.* bank
旅 馆 lü^{2}quan^3	*n.* hotel
栋 dong^4	*meas.* used with houses
房 fang^2	*n.* house; room
房 子 fang^{2}zi	*n.* house
多 久 duo^{1}jiu^3	*adv.* how long
大 约 da^{4}yue^1	*adv.* about, probably
分 钟 fen^1 zhong^1	*n.* minute
不 谢 bu^{2}xie^4	you are welcome, (a response to "thank you")

Supplementary Vocabulary and Expressions

GPS	全 球 定 位 系 统 (quan^{2}qiu^2 ding^{4}wei^4 xi^{4}tong^3)
no outlet	此 路 不 通 (ci^3 lu^4 bu^{4}tong^1)
slow down	慢 下 来 (man^4 xiao^{4}lai^2)

Here we are. Let's get off.
到 了. 下 车 吧! (Dao^4 le. Xia^{4}che^1 ba.)
Please drive slowly.
请 开 慢 一 点 儿. (Qing^3 kai^1 man^4 yi^{4}diar^3.)
Stop here.
在 这 儿 停 车. (Zai^4 zher^4 ting^2 che^1.)
We have lost our way.
咱 们 迷 路 了. (Zan^{2}men mi^{2}lu^4 le.)
We'll be there in a moment.
马 上 就 到 了. (Ma^{3}shang^4 jiu^4 dao^4 le.)
You can't miss it.
你 不 会 错 过 的. (Ni^3 bu^{2}hui^4 cuo^4 guo de.)

25. Exercises

I. Tone Drills:

ke^1 科 department   ke^2 --   ke^3 壳 shell   ke^4 课 lesson

huang^1 慌 flurried   huang^2 黄 yellow   huang^3 谎 lie   huang^4 晃 sway

II. Choose the best answer:

1. A: 对不起, 麻烦您了!
   B: _____. (a.没关系   b. 谢谢你   c. 越麻烦越好)
2. A: 请问, 到西京饭店怎么走?
   B: _____. (a. 马上就到   b. 要走快一点儿   c. 一直走, 再往左拐)
3. A: 到东京饭店要过几个街口?
   B: _____. (a. 两个   b. 大约八分钟   c.要看到红绿灯)
4. A: 要多久可以走到?
   B: _____. (a. 一点四十三分   b. 十个半小时   c. 大约六分钟)

III. Fill the blanks with 东, 南, 西, or 北:
(面 mian^4 and 边 bian^1 mean the same, showing position, side or direction, used together with 东, 南, 西, 北, 左, 右, 前, 后, 上, 下, 里, 外 etc.

If you face the sun at 12 o'clock at noon in New York, then:
   1. 你的前面是 _____ .
   2. 你的后面是 _____ .
   3. 你的左边是 _____ .
   4. 你的右边是 _____ .
(部 bu^4 means *part*, also used with 东, 南, 西, 北, 中, etc.)
   5. 上海在中国的 _____ 部.
   6. 北京在中国的 _____ 部.
   7. 旧金山 (Jiu^{4}jin^{1}shan^1: San Francisco) 在美国的 _____ 部.

A: 您在中国呆了多久?

B: 呆了两年.

A: 您住在哪个城市?

B: 苏州住了一年, 杭州[1]住了一年.

A: 苏州、杭州都是好地方啊!是鱼米之乡[2].

B: 是啊! 是江南[3]水乡.在那儿人人都过着安定幸福的生活.

A: 您喜欢中国吗?

B: 挺喜欢. 中国的地方很美丽,人民很友好.

A: 您说得对[4]. 在中国您最不喜欢的是什么?

B: 中国[5]抽烟的人太多了,到处[6]都是烟雾腾腾[7]!

26. Zhong¹guo² de Yin⁴xiang⁴

A: Nin² zai⁴ zhong¹guo² dai¹ le duo¹jiu³?

B: Dai¹ le liang³ nian².

A: Nin² zhu⁴ zai⁴ nei³ ge cheng²shi⁴?

B: Su¹zhou¹ zhu⁴ le yi⁴ nian², Hang²zhou¹ zhu⁴ le yi⁴ nian².

A: Su¹zhou¹, Hang²zhou¹ dou¹ shi⁴ hao³ di⁴fang a! Shi⁴ yu²mi³ zhi¹ xiang¹.

B: Shi⁴ a! Shi⁴ jiang¹nan² shui³xiang¹. Zai⁴ nar⁴ ren²ren² dou¹ guo⁴ zhe an¹ding⁴ xing⁴fu² de sheng¹huo².

A: Nin² xi³huan zhong¹guo² ma?

B: Ting² xi³huan. Zhong¹guo² de di⁴fang hen² mei³li⁴, ren²min² hen² you²hao³.

A: Nin² shuo¹ de dui⁴. Zai⁴ zhong¹guo² nin² zui⁴ bu⁴ xi³huan de shi⁴ shen²me?

B: Zhong¹guo² chou¹yan¹ de ren² tai⁴ duo¹ le, dao⁴chu⁴ dou¹ shi⁴ yan¹wu⁴ teng²teng²!

26. Impressions of China

A: How long did you live in China?

B: Two years.

A: Which city did you live in?

B: One year in Suzhou and one year in

Hangzhou.

A: Oh, they are nice places, the land of

fish and rice.

B: Yes, a region of rivers and lakes in

the south of the Yangtze. People arc

leading a stable and happy life there.

A: Do you like China?

B: Yes, very much. China has a beautiful

landscape and the people there are

friendly.

A: You're right. What do you dislike

most about China?

B: There are too many smokers in China.

The smoke makes it hazy everywhere!

26. Notes

1. 苏州、杭州 （Su¹zhou¹, Hang²zhou¹): two beautiful historical cities in the Yangtze Delta, the richest region in China "Heaven is above, Suzhou and Hangzhou below." "上有天堂,下有苏杭." (Shang⁴ you³ tian¹tang², xia⁴ you³ su¹ hang².), as the saying goes.

2. 鱼米之乡 (yu²mi³ zhi¹ xiang¹): a land of fish and rice, meaning a land of plenty The basic meaning of 乡 (xiang¹) is country, opposite to 城市 (cheng²shi⁴: city); it also means region, area. 苏杭是鱼米之乡,也是丝绸之乡. (Su¹ Hang² shi⁴ yu²mi³ zhi¹ **xiang¹**, ye³ shi si¹chou² zhi¹ **xiang¹**.) Suzhou and Hangzhou are a land of fish and rice; they are also the home of silk. 乡 (xiang¹) also means the native place. Eg: 回乡探亲 (hui² **xiang¹** tan⁴qin¹) return to one's native place to visit family members 乡音未改. (**Xiang**¹yin¹ wei⁴ gai³.) The native accent is still there.

3. 江南 (jiang¹nan²): south of the (lower reaches of the Yangtzc) river 江 (jiang¹) means river. It usually refers to 长江 (Chang²**jiang**¹, the Yangtze River). The literal meaning of 长江 (Chang²**jiang**¹) is *long river*. The character 江 (jiang¹) is usually used to show rivcrs that are bigger than 河 (he²), but the Yellow River which is as big as the Yangtze is named 黄河 (huang²**he**²) . The Chinese translation for big rivers in the world is 河 (he²), not 江 (jiang¹). Eg. The Amazon is 亚马孙河 (Ya⁴ma³sun¹he²). The Mississippi is 密西西比河 (Mi⁴xi¹xi¹bi³he²). The Nile is 尼罗河 (Ni²luo²he²).

4. 您说得对. (Nin² shuo¹ de dui⁴.): Yes. You are right. What you said is correct. Cf. Note 3, Passage 9. This expression is the same as 您说对了. (Nin² shuo¹ dui⁴ le.)

5. 中国 (zhong¹guo²): = 在中国 (zai⁴ zhong¹guo²) in China In Chinese nouns can sometimes be used as adverbials of place, that is, the *prep.* 在 (zai⁴) is omitted.

6. 到处 (dao⁴chu⁴): everywhere 我**到处**都找过了. (Wo³ **dao**⁴**chu**⁴ dou¹ zhao³ guo le.) I have looked everywhere for it. 在纽约**到处**都能碰上中国人. (Zai⁴ Niu³yue¹ **dao**⁴**chu**⁴ dou¹ neng² pen⁴shang⁴ zhong¹guo² ren².) You will see Chinese people everywhere in New York.

7. 烟雾腾腾 (yan¹wu⁴ teng²teng²): smoke laden or 烟雾缭绕 (yan¹wu⁴ liao²rao⁴), 烟雾弥漫 (yan¹wu⁴ mi²man⁴), 烟雾蒙蒙 (yan¹wu⁴ meng²meng²). They all mean dense smoke (or fog) suspended in the atmosphere and difficult to see through.

26. Vocabulary

印象 yin⁴xiang⁴   *n.* impression
呆 dai¹   *v.* stay
   a. slow-witted
城市 cheng²shi⁴   *n.* city
苏州 su¹zhou¹   *n.* Suzhou
杭州 hang²zhou¹   *n.* Hangzhou
鱼米之乡 yu²mi³ zhi¹ xiang¹   *n.* a land of fish and rice
之 zhi¹   *part.* used between an attributive and the noun it modifies, same as 的, a literary word
乡 xiang¹   *n.* village, countryside
江 jiang¹   *n.* river
水乡 shui³xiang¹   *n.* region of rivers and lakes
人人 ren²ren²   *n.* everyone
安定 an¹ding⁴   *a.* stable
幸福 xing⁴fu²   *a.* happy
生活 sheng¹huo²   *n.* life
   v. live
挺 ting²   *adv.* very
美丽 mei³li⁴   *a.* beautiful
人民 ren²min²   *n.* people
友好 you²hao³   *a.* friendly
到处 dao⁴chu⁴   *adv.* everywhere
烟雾 yan¹wu⁴   *n.* smoke, mist
腾腾 teng²teng²   *a.* hazy with smoke

Supplementary Vocabulary and Expressions

capitalism	资本主义 (zi¹ben³zhu³yi⁴)
common people	老百姓 (lao²bai³xing⁴)
communist party	共产党 (gong⁴chan² dang³)
comparatively well-off	小康 (xiao³kang¹)
developed country	发达国家 (fa¹da² guo²jia¹)
developing country	发展中国家 (fa¹zhan³ zhong¹ guo²jia¹)
economic recession	经济衰退 (jing¹ji⁴ shuai¹tui⁴)
economic reform	经济改革 (jing¹ji⁴ gai³ge²)
freedom and democracy	自由民主 (zi⁴you² min²zhu³)
government official	官 (guan¹)
ideology	意识形态 (yi⁴shi² xing²tai⁴)
illiterate	文盲 (wen²mang²)
intellectual	知识分子 (zhi¹shi fen⁴zi³)
objective	客观 (ke⁴guan¹)
political reform	政治改革 (zheng⁴zhi⁴ gai³ge²)
prosperous economy	经济繁荣 (jing¹ji⁴ fan²rong²)
socialism	社会主义 (she⁴hui⁴zhu³yi⁴)
stagnant economy	经济停滞 (jing¹ji⁴ ting²zhi⁴)
subjective	主观 (zhu³guan¹)

First impression is often misleading.
第一个印象往往是错误的.
(Di⁴yi² ge yin⁴xiang⁴ wang²wang³ shi⁴ cuo⁴wu⁴ de.)

26. Exercises

I. Tone Practice:

lin¹ -- lin² 邻 neighbor lin³ 凛 cold lin⁴ 吝 stingy
ling¹ 拎 carry in hand ling² 铃 bell ling³ 领 lead ling⁴ 另 other

II. Fill the blanks in the following sentences containing 得 with the proper words from the list below: 大, 晚, 贵, 好, 久, 早, 多, 舒服

1. 您说得 _____!
2. 他睡得 _____.
3. 她起得 _____.
4. 那本词典新词收得_____.
5. 她在北京呆得_____.
6. 这场雨下得 _____.
7. 车太小, 坐得不 _____.
8. 那本书你买(得) _____了.

III. Expand each of the following characters into a phrase and give the phonetic spelling of the phrase:

Examples: 美 → 美丽 (mei³li⁴); 烟 → 烟雾腾腾 (yan¹wu⁴ teng²teng²)

1. 到 → (   )
2. 喜 → (   )
3. 友 → (   )
4. 值 → (   )
5. 麻 → (   )
6. 印 → (   )
7. 打 → (   )
8. 素 → (   )
9. 简 → (   )
10. 探 → (   )

IV. Choose the right words from the list below to fill in the blanks:
节目   天气   大鱼大肉   姑娘   水果   会议

1. 美丽的小_____
2. 我最爱吃的_____
3. 一个重要的_____
4. 多么闷热的_____
5. 挺好看的_____
6. 胆固醇高的_____

104

二十七. 定房间

A: 先生, 早!

B: 早! 我要一个单人房间.

A: 请您填一下这张旅客登记表:
姓名、地址、电话号码儿.可以
看一看带相片儿的身份证明
吗?

B: 可以.

A: 请给[1]我您的信用卡.

......

三一四 (314) 号房间. 这是您的
钥匙.您的行李马上给您送到
您的房间.

B: 谢谢.

A: 不客气[2].

27. Ding[4] Fang[2]jian[1]

A: Xian[1]sheng, zao[3]!

B: Zao[3]! Wo[3] yao[4] yi[2] ge dan[1]ren[2]
fang[2]jian[1].

A: Qing[3] nin[2] tian[2] yi[2]xia[4] zhei[4] zhang[1]
lü[3]ke[4] deng[1]ji[4] biao[3]: xing[4]ming[2],
di[4]zhi[3], dian[4]hua[4] hao[4]mar[3]. Ke[2]yi[3]
kan[4]yikan[4] dai[4] xiang[4]piar[1] de shen[1]fen
zheng[4]ming[2] ma?

B: Ke[2]yi[3].

A: Qing[2] gei[2] wo[3] nin[2]de xin[4]yong[4]ka[3].
......
San[1] yao[1] si[4] (314) hao[4] fang[2]jian[1].
Zhe[4] shi nin[2]de yao[4]shi. Nin[2] de xing[2]li
ma[3]shang[4] gei[2] nin[2] song[4] dao[4] nin[2] de
fang[2]jian[1].

B: Xie[4]xie.

A: Bu[2] ke[4]qi.

27. Booking a Room

A: Good morning, sir!

B: Good morning! I need a single room.

A: Fill out this guest registration form, please: name, address, and phone number.

May I see your photo ID?

B: Sure.

A: May I have your credit card please?
......
Room 314. Here's your key. Your luggage will be carried to your room just now.

B: Thanks.

A: You're welcome.

27. Notes

1. 给 (gei³): give The verb 给 (gei³) can take two objects. The pattern is: 给 + sb. + sth. Eg. 她**给**了**我**那本**书**. (Ta¹ **gei³** le **wo³** ne⁴ ben³ **shu¹**.) She gave me that book. If the direct object (sth.) is placed before the indirect object (sb.), then the word 把 (ba³) must be used. The pattern becomes: 把 + sth. + 给 + sb. The above sentence becomes: 她**把**那本**书给**了**我**. (Ta¹ **ba³** ne⁴ ben³ **shu¹ gei³** le **wo³**.) She gave that book to me. Cf. another use of 给 (gei³) in Note 1, Passage 12. Also cf. Note 3, Passage 21 for the 把 structure.

2. 不客气. (Bu² ke⁴qi.) or 不用客气. (Bu²yong⁴ ke⁴qi.), 甭客气 (Beng² ke⁴qi.): You're welcome. In response to *thank you*, another alternative is 不谢. (Bu² xie⁴.) Some people use 没事儿. (Mei² shər⁴.: It's nothing.) or 没关系. (Mei² guan³xi.: It doesn't matter.) to respond to 谢谢. (Xie⁴xie.: Thank you.), but these responses seem not to be appropriate. They should be used to respond to apologies, not gratitude.

定 ding⁴ — *v.* book (seat, ticket, etc.), order (same as 订); decide, short for 决定 (jue²ding⁴)

房间 fang²jian¹ — *n.* room

单人 dan¹ren² — *n.* single person (opp. shuang¹ren²)

填 tian² — *v.* fill out

旅客 lü³ke⁴ — *n.* hotel guest, traveler

登记 deng¹ji⁴ — *n.* registration; *v.* register

表 biao³ — *n.* form; wrist watch

带 dai⁴ — *prep.* with, having (sth.) attached; *v.* bring, take, carry; *n.* belt

相片 xiang⁴pian¹ — *n.* photo

身份 shen¹fen — *n.* identification

证明 zheng⁴ming² — *n.* evidence, proof; certificate

信用 xin⁴yong⁴ — *n.* credit

卡 ka³ — *n.* card

钥匙 yao⁴shi — *n.* key

行李 xing²li — *n.* luggage

送 song⁴ — *v.* deliver, carry; give as a gift; see (sb.) off

客气 ke⁴qi — *a.* modest, courteous, polite

不客气 bu²ke⁴qi — You are welcome. (a response to "thank you"); Do not stand on ceremony. Make yourself at home.

call a taxi — 叫计程车 (jiao⁴ ji⁴cheng²che¹)

check in — 办入住手续 (ban⁴ ru⁴zhu⁴ shou³xu⁴)

check out — 办离店手续 (ban⁴ li² dian⁴ shou³xu⁴)

double bed — 双人床 (shuang¹ren² chuang²)

escalator — 电动扶梯 (dian⁴dong⁴ fu¹ti¹)

extra bed — 加铺 (jia¹pu⁴)

five-star — 五星级 (wu³xing¹ ji²)

hotel, inn — 旅馆 (lü²guan³), 酒店 (jiu³dian⁴)

operator — 接线员 (jie¹xian⁴yuan²),

operator's room — 总机室 (zong³ji¹ shi⁴)

suite — 套间 (tao⁴jian¹)

How many days are you going to stay here?
您准备住几天? (Nin² zhun³bei⁴ zhu⁴ ji³ tian¹?)
The elevator is on the right.
电梯在右边. (Dian⁴ti¹ zai⁴ you⁴bian¹.)
What is the rate per night?
多少钱一个晚上? (Duo¹shao qian² yi² ge wan³shang?)

27. Exercises

I. Tone Practice:

wai¹ 歪 crooked   wai² --   wai³ 崴 sprain   wai⁴ 外 outside
pai¹ 拍 pat   pai² 牌 plate   pai³ 迫 near   pai⁴ 派 dispatch

II. Fill in the blanks of the following sentences with proper verbs:

1. 他机票 _____ 得早.
2. 他游泳 _____ 得快.
3. 他烟 _____ 得太多.
4. 你蔬菜 _____ 得太少.
5. 他汉语_____ 得好.
6. 老黄手术 ____ 得不理想.

III. Change the structure of the following sentences by replacing "给 sb. sth." with "把 sth. 给 sb." or vice versa:

Example: 我把我的信用卡给了他. ←→ 我给了他我的信用卡.

1. 他给了我房间的钥匙.

2. 她奶奶把她爷爷的相片儿给了她.

3. 爷爷给了我一本最好看的书.

4. 奶奶把最好的菜给她吃.

IV. Change the following sentences into polite questions with 可以:

1. 让我看一下你的相片儿.

2. 把你的词典给我用一下.

3. 我要定一个单人房间.

4. 我想在这儿抽烟.

5. 告诉我你今年多大了.

二十八. 我 得 了 肝 炎!

A: 最近老是浑身不得劲儿. 头昏

脑涨, 腰酸背痛, 胃口也不好, 见

了鱼和肉就恶心.

B: 大小便怎么样?

A: 大小便倒还正常.

B: 睡觉好不好?

A: 要么乱做恶梦, 要么[1]就失眠.

我看, 我准是得了肝炎.

B: 我看, 你不是得了什么[2]肝炎,

而是活动得太少了. 整天坐

着[3]打麻将, 没病也要坐出病来[4]

了.

28. Wo^3 De^2 le Gan^{1}yan^2!

A. Zui^{4}jin^4 lao^{3}shi^4 hun^{2}shen^1 bu^4 de^{2}jiər^4.

Tou^{2}hun^1 nao^{3}zhang^4, yao^{1}suan^2

bei^{4}tong^4, wei^{4}kou^3 ye^3 bu^4 hao^3. Jian^4

le yu^2 he^2 rou^4 jiu^4 e^{3}xin.

B: Da^{4}xiao^{3}bian^4 zen^{3}meyang^4?

A: Da^{4}xiao^{3}bian^4 dao^4 hai^2 zheng^{4}chang^2.

B: Shui^{4}jiao^4 hao^{3}buhao^3?

A: Yao^{4}me luan^4 zuo^4 e^{4}meng^4, yao^{4}me

jiu^4 shi^{1}mian^2. Wo^3 kan^4, wo^2 zhun^3 shi^4

de^2 le gan^{1}yan^2.

B: Wo^3 kan^4, ni^3 bu^2 shi^4 de^2 le shen^{2}me

gan^{1}yan^2, er^2 shi^4 huo^{2}dong^4 de tai^4

shao^3 le. Zheng^{3}tian^1 zuo^{4}zhe da^3

ma^{2}jiang^4, mei^2 bing^4 ye^3 yao^4 zuo^4 chu^1

bing^4 lai^2 le.

28. I've Got Hepatitis!

A: I feel tired all the time these days. I feel dizzy in the head and painful in the lower back. I have no appetite, and feel like vomiting at the sight of fish and meat.

B: How are your bowel movement and urination?

A: They are normal.

B: How's your sleep?

A: I either have a lot of bad dreams, or get insomnia. I'm sure I've got hepatitis!

B: I don't think you have any hepatitis, but I think you're not getting enough exercise. You get sick because you just sit around all day playing mahjong!

28. Notes

1. 要么…要么 (yao^{4}me…yao^{4}mc): either … or 要么他来, 要么我去, 我们总得见个面. (**Yao^{4}me** ta^1 lai^2, **yao^{4}me** wo^3 qu^4, wo^{3}men zong^2 dei^3 jian^4 ge mian^4.) Either he comes here or I go there; in any case we need to see each other. 他要么是发疯了, 要么是喝醉了. (Ta^1 **yao^{4}me** shi^4 fa^{1}feng^1 le, **yao^{4}me** shi^4 he^{1}zui^4 le.) He is either mad or drunk. Another pair of correlative conjunctions with the same meaning is 不是…就是 (bu^{2}shi^4…jiu^{4}shi^4). 不是你的狗就是你的猫把蛋糕吃了. (**Bu^{2}shi^4** ni^{3}de gou^3 **jiu^{4}shi^4** ni^{3}de mao^1 ba^3 dan^{4}gao^1 chi^1 le.) Either your dog or your cat has eaten the cake.

2. 什么 (shen^{2}me): what IIcrc 什么 (shen^{2}me) is not really a question word; it shows disagreement to what the other party just said. 什么不知道! 你这是装糊涂罢了! (**Shen^{2}me** bu^4 zhi^{1}dao! Ni^3 zhe^4 shi^4 zhuang^1 hu^{2}tu ba^4 le!) What do you mean by you don't know? You're pretending.

3. 坐着 (zuo^4 zhe): sitting 着 (zhe) *part.*, always unstressed, shows an action or a condition is continuing. 别站着, 请坐下吧! (Bie^2 zhang^4 **zhe**, qing^3 zuo^4 xia ba!) Don't stand there. Please sit down! 请让门开着. (Qing^3 rang^4 men^2 kai^1 **zhe**!) Please leave the door open! 她开着窗睡觉. (Ta^1 kai^1 **zhe** chuang^1 shui^{4}jiao^4.) She sleeps with open windows.

4. 坐出病来 (zuo^4 chu^1 bing^4 lai^2): sit (too long) and get sick 出…来 (chu^1…lai^2) after verbs indicates that certain results are produced by certain action. 这个汤里你喝出什么怪味儿来了吗? (Zhei^4 ge tang^1 li ni^3 he^1 **chu^1** shen^{2}me guai^4 wər^4 **lai^2** le ma?) Can you taste anything strange in the soup? Sometimes the character 来 (lai^2) is omitted.

28. Vocabulary

肝 gan^1 — *n.* liver

炎 yan^2 — *n.* inflammation

肝炎 gan^{1}yan^2 — *n.* hepatitis

最近 zui^{4}jin^4 — *adv.* recently

老是 lao^{3}shi^4 — *adv.* always

浑身 hun^{2}shen^1 — *adv.* from head to foot, all over

劲 jin^4 — *n.* energy, strength

得劲 de^{2}jin^4 — *a.* full of energy, comfortable

不得劲 bu^4 de^{2}jin^4 — *v.* feel slack

头 tou^2 — *n.* head (opp. 脚 jiao^3); the front

昏 hun^1 — *a.* dizzy

脑 nao^3 — *n.* brain

涨 zhang^4 — *v.* become swollen, bloated; (of one's face) become (red)

头昏脑涨 tou^{2}hun^1 nao^{3}zhang^4 — feel one's head swimming

腰 yao^1 — *n.* the small of the back

酸 suan^1 — *a.* sour; ache

背 bei^4 — *n.* back

痛 tong^4 — *v.* ache; *a.* painful

腰酸背痛 yao^{1}suan^1 bei^{4}tong^4 — have a pain in the back

胃口 wei^{4}kou^3 — *n.* appetite

恶心 e^{3}xin — *n.* nausea; *v.* feel like vomiting

大小便 da^{4}xiao^3 bian^4 — *n.* bowel movement (大便 da^{4}bian^4) and urination (小便 xiao^{3}bian^4)

便 bian^4 — *n.* convenience

正常 zheng^{4}chang^2 — *a.* normal

要么…要么 yao^{4}me … yao^{4}me — *conj.* either…or

乱 luan^4 — *a., adv.* in disorder

恶梦 e^{4}meng^4 — *n.* nightmare

恶 e^4 — *a.* bad, evil

做梦 zuo^{4}meng^4 — *v.* have a dream

失眠 shi^{1}mian^2 — *n.* insomnia

我看 wo^3 kan^4 — I think (used parenthetically)

准 zhun^3 — *adv.* definitely, accurately

不是…而是 bu^{2}shi^4 …er^{2}shi^4 — *conj.* not…but

活动 huo^{2}dong^4 — *n.* activity

活 huo^2 — *v.* live; *a.* living; *n.* work

整天 zheng^{3}tian^1 — *adv.* all day long

着 zhe — *part.* showing an action is going on

麻将 ma^{2}jiang^4 — *n.* mahjong, a tile game (Some people say where there are four Chinese, there is mahjong.)

出 chu^1 — *v.* go out; produce, occur, bring about (opp. 进 jin^4 or 入 ru^4)

Supplementary Vocabulary and Expressions

abdomen ache — 肚子疼 (du^{4}zi teng^2)

antibiotics — 抗生素 (kang^{4}sheng^{1}su^4)

blood test — 验血 (yan^4 xie^3)

call an ambulance — 叫救护车 (jiao^4 jiu^{4}hu^{4}che^1)

faint away — 晕过去 (yun^4 guoqu)

first aid, emergency — 急救 (ji^{2}jiu^4)

infection — 感染 (gan^{2}ran^3)

palpitate — 心慌 (xin^{1}huang^1)

short of breath — 气急 (qi^{4}ji^2)

top-heavy — 头重脚轻 (tou^{2}zhong^4 jiao^{3}qing^1)

Which medical insurance can give you the best benefits?
哪个医疗保险最好? (Nai^3 ge yi^{1}liao^2 bao^2 xian^3 zui^{4}hao^3?)

111

28. Exercises

I. Tone Drills:

qiang^1 枪 gun   qiang^2 强 strong   qiang^3 抢 rob   qiang^4 呛 irritate (nose)

yao^1 腰 waist   yao^2 摇 shake   yao^3 咬 bite   yao^4 药 medicine

II. Connect the following words to make compound sentences, by using 要么… 要么:

1. 这事儿他还不知道, 请人   给他   给他   捎个信儿   打个电话

2. 不知道   装糊涂   他

3. 进来   出去   站在门口   老   不要

4. 去   你自己定   你   跟我一起   呆在家里   你

III. Fill in the blanks with 站着, 听着, 瞧着, 开着 or 走着:

    1. 不要老是_____, 坐下吧!
    2. 你讲, 我 _____ 呢!
    3. 张经理他们正 _____ 会呢!
    4. 咱们 _____ 瞧! (We'll see who's right. Time will tell who's stronger. I'll teach you a lesson.)
    5. 你 _____ 办吧! (Do as you see fit!)

IV. 出…来 is usually used with verbs of human senses. Fill in the following blanks with the words given below:

看出 (kan^{4}chu^1: spot, make out)
喝出
闻出 (wen^2 chu^1: smell)
听出
摸出 (mo^{1}chu^1: learn after some studies)

    1. 我 _____ 他的破绽 (po^{4}zhan: flaw, vulnerable point) 来了.
    2. 我 _____ 她的真意(zhen^{1}yi^1: real idea) 来了.
    3. 我 _____ 乌龙的香味来了.
    4. 这茶现在已经 _____ 点味儿 来了.
    5. 你 _____ 窍门 (qiao^{4}men^2: knack) 来了吗?

二十九. 职业

A: 您在哪里[1]工作?

B: 在一家医院工作.

A: 您是大夫吗?

B: 是, 我是心脏科的大夫.您在哪儿工作?

A: 我在一个小学工作, 我是个老师. 您工作很忙吧?

B: 很忙. 我病人很多.

A: 您一定很辛苦?

B: 是. 但说实话, 钱也挣得不少.

A: 是, 难怪[2]这么多的人想当医生.

B: 但是, 老师的工作和医生一样重要. 医生是治病救人, 老师是塑造人的灵魂.

29. Zhi^{2}ye^4

A: Nin^2 zai^4 na^{3}li gong^{1}zuo^4?

B: Zai^1 yi^4 jia^1 yi^{1}yuan^4 gong^{1}zuo^4.

A: Nin^2 shi dai^{4}fu ma?

B: Shi^4. Wo^3 shi xin^{1}zang^4 ke^1 de dai^{4}fu. Nin^2 zai^4 nar^3 gong^{1}zuo^4?

A: Wo^3 zai^4 yi^2 ge xiao^{3}xue^2 gong^{1}zuo^4, wo^3 shi ge lao^{3}shi^1. Nin^2 gong^{1}zuo^4 hen^3 mang^2 ba?

B: Hen^3 mang^2. Wo^3 bing^{4}ren^2 hen^3 duo^1.

A: Nin^2 yi^{2}ding^4 hen^3 xin^{1}ku^3?

B: Shi^4. Dan^4 shuo^1 shi^{2}hua^4, qian^2 ye^3 zheng^4 de bu^{4}shao^3.

A: Shi^4, nan^{2}guai^4 zhe^{4}me duo^1 de ren^2 xiang^3 dang^1 yi^{1}sheng^1.

B: Dan^{4}shi^4, lao^{3}shi^1 de gong^{1}zuo^4 he^2 yi^{1}sheng^1 yi^{2}yang^4 zhong^{4}yao^4. Yi^{1}sheng^1 shi^4 zhi^{4}bing^4 jiu^{4}ren^2, lao^{3}shi^1 shi^4 su^{4}zao^4 ren^2 de ling^{2}hun^2.

A: Where you are working?

B: At a hospital.

A: Are you a doctor?

B: Yes. I am a cardiologist. Where do you work?

A: At an elementary school. I'm a teacher. You are always very busy, aren't you?

B: Yes, indeed. I have a lot of patients.

A: Then you have to work very hard.

B: Yes. But frankly I earn a lot of money.

A: Yes. That's why so many people want to be doctors.

B: But teachers' work is by no means less important than doctors'. Doctors cure the diseases to save people, while teachers mold people's soul.

1. 哪 里 (na³li): where Same as 哪 儿 (nar³), 哪 里 (na³li) is an interrogative adverb of place. Note its other uses:

a. In China you may frequently hear the question "你 到 哪 里 去 啊?" (Ni³ dao⁴ **na³li** qu⁴ a? Where are you going?), when you run into an acquaintance in the street. This question, like "你 吃 过 饭 了 吗?" (Ni³ chi¹ guo fan⁴ le ma? See Note 2, Passage 3.), is only an introductory statement to begin a sociable talk. You do not need to treat it as a real question; so your answer "I have sth. to do." or any other evasive answer will be OK.

b. 哪 里 (na³li) is used to form a rhetorical question. 我 **哪 里** 知 道 他 住 在 哪 里? (Wo² **na³li** zhi¹dao ta¹ zhu⁴ zai⁴ na³li?) How could I know where he lives?

c. It is also used as a self-depreciatory expression in response to praise.
A: 你 的 汉 语 讲 得 很 漂 亮! (Ni³de han⁴yu³ jiang³ de hen³ piao⁴liang!) You speak excellent Chinese!
B: **哪 里**, **哪 里**, 还 差 得 远 呢! (**Na³li**, **na³li**, hai² cha⁴ de yuan³ ne!) You flatter me. It leaves much to be desired!

2. 难 怪 (nan² guai⁴): no wonder, that's why (Lit. hard to blame), same as 怪 不 得 (guai⁴bude) 天 气 预 报 说 今 天 有 雷 阵 雨, **难 怪** (or **怪 不 得**) 空 气 这 么 闷 人. (Tian¹qi⁴ yu⁴bao⁴ shuo¹ jin¹tian¹ you³ lei²zhen⁴yu³, **nan²guai⁴** (or **guai⁴bude**) kong¹qi⁴ zhe⁴me men¹ ren².) The weather forecast says there will be thunderstorms today; that's why the air is so stifling. 你 这 么 爱 吃 肥 肉, **难 怪** 胆 固 醇 要 高 了. (Ni³ zhe⁴me ai⁴ chi¹ fei²rou⁴, **nan²guai⁴** dan³gu⁴chun² yao⁴ gao¹ le.) You like the fat on meat so much. No wonder you have high cholestrol.

29. Vocabulary

职业 zhi^{2}ye^4 — *n.* job, occupation

哪里 na^{3}li — *adv.* where

工作 gong^{1}zuo^4 — *v., n.* work (opp. 休息 xiu^{1}xi)

心 xin^1 — *n.* the heart; mind

心脏 xin^{1}zang^4 — *n.* heart (the organ)

科 ke^1 — *n.* department

小学 xiao^{3}xue^2 — *n.* elementary school

老师 lao^{3}shi^1 — *n.* teacher (opp. 学生 xue^{2}sheng)

忙 mang^2 — *a.* busy (opp. 闲 xian^2)

病人 bing^{4}ren^2 — *n.* patient (opp. 医生 yi^{1}sheng^1)

辛苦 xin^{1}ku^3 — *adv.* (work) hard *a.* tiring, toilsome (opp. 轻松 qing^{1}song^1)

说实话 shuo^1 shi^{2}hua^4 — to tell the truth (opp. 说假话 shuo^1 jia^{3}hua^4)

实 shi^2 — *a.* true (opp. 假 jia^3 or 虚 xu^1); solid (opp. 空 kong^1)

挣 zheng^4 — *v.* make (money), earn (opp. 赔 pei^2)

难怪 nan^{2}guai^4 — no wonder

怪 guai^4 — *v.* blame *a.* strange

一样 yi^{2}yang^4 — *a.* same *adv.* equally

治 zhi^4 — *v.* treat, cure

救 jiu^4 — *v.* rescue, save

塑造 su^{4}zao^4 — *v.* mold

灵魂 ling^{2}hun^2 — *n.* soul

Supplementary Vocabulary and Expressions

accountant — 会计师 (kuai^{4}ji^{4}shi^1)

air hostess — 空姐 (kong^{1}jie^3)

cashier — 收银员 (shou^{1}yin^{2}yuan^2)

CEO — 首席执行长 (shou^{3}xi^1 zhi^{2}xing^2 zhang^3)

clerk (doing office work) 文员 (wen^{2}yuan^2)

contractor — 承包商 (cheng^{2}bao^{1}shang^1)

designer — 设计师 (she^{4}ji^{4}shi^1)

garbage man — 垃圾工 (la^{1}ji^1 gong^1)

hairdresser — 理发师 (li^{3}fa^{4}shi^1)

lawyer — 律师 (lü^{4}shi^1)

nurse — 护士 (hu^{4}shi)

pilot — (飞机, 轮船) 驾驶员 ([fei^{1}ji^1, lun^{2}chuan^2] jia^{4}shi^{3}yuan^2)

police officer — 警察 (jing^{1}cha^2)

porter — 行李搬运员 (xing^{2}li ban^{1}yun^{4}yuan^2)

programer — 程序编制员 (cheng^{2}xu^4 bian^{1}zhi^4 yuan^2)

public relations — 公关 (gong^{1}guan^1)

realtor — 房地产经纪人 (fang^{3}di^{4}chan^3 jing^{1}ji^{4}ren^2)

receptionist — 接待员 (jie^{1}dei^{4}yuan^2)

reporter — 记者 (ji^{4}zhe^3)

secretary — 秘书 (mi^{4}shu^1)

sales clerk — 售货员 (shou^{4}huo^{4}yuan^2)

social worker — 社会工作者 (she^{4}hui^4 gong^{1}zuo^{4}zhe^3)

taxi driver — 出租车司机 (chu^{1}zu^{1}che^1 si^{1}ji^1)

tour guide — 导游 (dao^{3}you^2)

waiter, waitress — (餐馆) 服务员 (can^{1}guan^3) fu^{2}wu^4 yuan^2

Every profession produces its own leading authority.

行行出状元. (Hang^{2}hang^2 chu^1 zhuang^{4}yuan.)

29. Exercises

I. Tone Practice:

chan[1] 搀 help by arm   chan[2] 馋 greedy   chan[3] 产 produce   chan[4] 颤 quiver

chang[1] 鲳 butterfish   chang[2] 长 long   chang[3] 厂 factory   chang[4] 唱 sing

II. Which tone is the word 得 in the following sentences?

    1. 他中文学得 (　) 很好.

    2. 他对北京的印象好得 (　) 很.

    3. 这事儿我还得 (　) 想一想.

    4. 得 (　)! 就这么办.

    5. 不经常洗手容易得 (　) 病.

    6. 今天家里有事儿, 得 (　) 早点儿回去.

III. Complete the following sentences containing 不是 … 而是: (The word 而 may be omitted.)
   Example: 爷爷不是坐飞机来的, 而是<u>坐火车来的</u>.

    1. 他不是心脏科的大夫, 而是 _____.

    2. 你不是睡得不够, 而是 _____.

    3. 不是我不爱她, 而是 _____.

    4. 不是我不想买, 而是 _____.

    5. 我不是不想当医生, 而是 _____.

IV. Translate the following sentences into Chinese, using 难怪:

    1. You went to bed at two after midnight? No wonder you were so late today.
    2. No wonder he is so glad these days, he was just admitted (考上) to a medical college.
    3. He got sick, and no wonder, considering that he had been overworking for months.
    4. No wonder you can't find anybody here, they're all away at a meeting.

V. Read the following dialog between an American gentleman and a Chinese lady, learning the two different meanings of 哪里 (na[3]li):

A: 花小姐, 你真漂亮! (Hua[1]xiao[2]ie[3], ni[3] zhen[1] piao[4]liang!) Miss Hua, you are so beautiful!

C: 哪里, 哪里! (Na[3]li, na[3]li!) Thank you!

A: (Thinking that 哪里, 哪里 means *Where? Where?*, he wonders why Chinese women are so particular about the exact spot that is beautiful. To further flatter her, he answers:) Everywhere, everywhere! (每个地方都很漂亮! Mei[3] ge di[4]fang dou[1] hen[3] piao[4]liang!)

116

三十. 生日

A: 明天是我先生¹的生日, 家里
会来好多客人, 很热闹.

B: 祝他生日快乐!

A: 谢谢!

B: 你们庆祝生日是不是也吃生
日蛋糕?

A: 我们吃面条儿.

B: 吃面条儿有什么讲究儿?

A: 因为面条儿很长, 吃面条象征
长寿的意思.

B: 喔, 我明白了. 那么²面条儿应
该做得越长越好.

A: 您说对了.

A: Ming²tian¹ shi⁴ wo³ xian¹sheng de
sheng¹ri. Jia¹ li hui⁴ lai² hao³duo¹
ke⁴ren², hen³ re⁴nao.

B: Zhu⁴ ta¹ sheng¹ri kuai⁴le⁴!

A: Xie⁴xie!

B: Ni³men qing⁴zhu⁴ sheng¹ri shi⁴bushi⁴
ye³ chi¹ sheng¹ri dan⁴gao¹?

A: Wo³men chi¹ mian⁴tiaor².

B: Chi¹ mian⁴tiaor² you³ shen²me
jiang³jiur⁴?

A: Yin¹wei⁴ mian⁴tiaor² hen³ chang², chi¹
mian⁴tiaor² xiang⁴zheng¹ chang²shou⁴
de yi⁴si.

B: O¹, wo³ ming²bai le. Na⁴me mian⁴tiaor²
ying¹gai¹ zuo⁴ de yue⁴ chang² yue⁴
hao³.

A. Nin² shuo¹ dui⁴ le.

A: Tomorrow will be my husband's birthday. A lot of guests will come to our house and we will have a good time.

B: Happy birthday to him!

A: Thank you!

B: Do you also celebrate birthdays by eating birthday cake?

A: We eat noodles.

B: Why do you eat noodles?

A: Because the long noodles symbolize longevity.

B: Oh, I see. Then the longer the noodles are made the better.

A: Absolutely.

1. 先 生 (xian^{1}sheng): husband In addition to *husband*, 先 生 has three other meanings:
   a. Mr... (following a person's last name (See Note 1, Passage 8.)
   b. Sir (used independently), a polite form used in addressing a man to show respect (See Passage 27.)
   c. teacher (male or female), same as 老 师 (lao^{3}shi^1)

2. 那 么 (na^{4}me): in that case, then
   你 说 你 不 要 请 大 夫, **那 么** 怎 么 办? (Ni^3 shuo^1 ni^3 bu^2 yao^4 qing^3 dai^{1}fu, **na^{4}me** zen^{3}me ban^4?) You say you don't want to call a doctor. Then what do you want to do?
   A: 那 本 书 不 在 这 儿.
   (Ne^4 ben^3 shu^1 bu^2 zai^4 zher^4.)
   The book isn't here.
   B: **那 么** 一 定 在 隔 壁 房 间 里.
   (**Na^{4}me** yi^{2}ding^4 zai^4 ge^{2}bi^4 fang^{2}jian^1 li.) It must be in the next room, then. 那 么 (na^{4}me) can be contracted to 那 (na^4). (See Note 5, Passage 6.)

30. Vocabulary

生日 sheng^{1}ri   *n.* birthday
(opp. 死忌 si^{3}ji^4)

日 ri^4 *n.* day (opp. 夜 ye^4)
n. sun (opp. 月 yue^4)

好多 hao^{3}duo^1 *a.* many, much

客人 ke^{4}ren^2 *n.* guest (opp. 主人 zhu^{3}ren^2)

快乐 kuai^{4}le^4 *a.* happy (opp. 悲伤 bei^{1}shang^1)

庆祝 qing^{4}zhu^4 *v.* celebrate (opp. 哀悼 ai^{1}dao^4)

蛋糕 dan^{4}gao^1 *n.* cake

面条 mian^{4}tiao^2 *n.* noodle

讲究 jiang^{3}jiu^4 *n.* explanation, reason, sth. that should be carefully studied

因为 yin^{1}wei^4 *conj.* because

长 chang^2 *a.* long (opp. 短 duan^3)
zhang^3 *v.* grow; look (usu. with 得 de)
n. chief

象征 xiang^{4}zheng^1 *v.* symbolize, signify

长寿 chang^{2}shou^4 *n.* longevity (opp. 短命 duan^{3}ming^4)

意思 yi^{4}si   *n.* meaning, sense; idea

明白 ming^{2}bai   *v.* understand

那么 na^{4}me   *adv.* then

应该 ying^{1}gai^1 *v.* should

做 zuo^4 *v.* make, do

您说对了. Nin^2 shuo^1 dui^4 le.   Correct. What you said is correct.

Supplementary Vocabulary and Expressions

birthday gift   生日礼物 (sheng^{1}ri li^{3}wu^4)

birthday party   生日宴会 (sheng^{1}ri yan^{4}hui^4)

celebrate one's birthday   祝寿 (zhu^{4}shou^4)

elderly person whose birthday is being celebrated   寿星 (shou^{4}xing^1)

Wish you good health, longevity, and happiness!
祝你健康, 长寿, 快乐!
(Zhu^4 ni^3 jian^{4}kang^1, chang^{2}shou^4, kuai^{4}le^4!)

30. Exercises

I. Tone Practice:

fen[1] 分 divide　　fen[2] 坟 tomb　　fen[3] 粉 powder　　fen[4] 粪 feces
feng[1] 风 wind　　feng[2] 缝 sew　　feng[3] 讽 satirize　　feng[4] 凤 phoenix

II. Fill in the blanks with appropriate words:

　　1. 祝你生日 _____!
　　2. 祝你一路 _____!
　　3. 祝你健康 _____!
　　4. 祝你 _____!

III. Answer the following questions by using 因为:

　　1. 小张为什么今天不来上班?
　　2. 今天你为什么要买蛋糕?
　　3. 你怎么知道今天要下雨?
　　4. 为什么这么多的人想当医生?
　　5. 老黄为什么会想他得了肝炎?
　　6. 你家为什么总是很热闹?

IV. Rewrite the following sentences by replacing the underlined words with their antonyms:

　　Example: 你说对了. ➔ 你说错了.

　　1. 请出去.
　　2. 路难走.
　　3. 他家人很多.
　　4. 昨晚我做了个恶梦.
　　5. 你往左拐, 就看到那餐馆了.
　　6. 你感冒了. 要多喝水, 多活动.
　　7. 那个难看的姑娘是谁啊?
　　8. 今天天气很凉快.
　　9. 她每天九点种起床.
　　10. 她经常吃大鱼大肉.

三十一. 老家的房子

A: 你老家在哪儿?

B: 在中国西部山区的一个农村里.
我爷爷和奶奶还住在那儿.

A: 那儿的生活怎么样?

B: 以前¹苦得很, 几年前住的还是
茅草房².

A: 现在呢?

B: 改革后变化极大, 他们现在住
上³了两层楼的大房子, 有四个
卧房、两个半卫生间. 生活大
好⁴了.

A: 和以前真是大不一样⁵了!

31. Lao³jia¹ de Fang²zi

A: Ni² lao³jia¹ zai⁴ nar³?

B: Zai⁴ zhong¹guo² xi¹bu⁴ shan¹qu¹ de yi²
ge nong²cun¹ li. Wo³ ye²ye he² nai³nai
hai² zhu⁴ zai⁴ nar⁴.

A: Nar⁴ de sheng¹huo² zen³meyang⁴?

B: Yi³qian² ku³ de hen³, ji³ nian² qian²
zhu⁴ de hai² shi⁴ mao²cao³ fang².

A: Xian⁴zai⁴ ne?

B: Gai³ge² hou⁴ bian⁴hua⁴ ji² da⁴. Ta¹men
xian⁴zai⁴ zhu⁴shang⁴ le liang³ ceng²
lou² de da⁴ fang²zi, you³ si⁴ ge
wo⁴fang², liang³ ge ban⁴
wei⁴sheng¹jian¹. Sheng¹huo² da⁴ hao³
le.

A: He² yi³qian² zhen¹ shi⁴ da⁴ bu⁴
yi²yang⁴ le!

31. Our House in the Native Village

A: Where is your native town?

B: I lived in a village in the hills of west China. My grandparents still live there.

A: How's life there?

B: They used to have a hard life. Even a few years ago they were still living in a thatched-roof cottage.

A: And now?

B: Big changes have taken place since economic reform. Now they have a big two-story house with four bedrooms and two and a half bathrooms. Their life today is much, much better.

A: That's a world of difference!

31. Notes

1. 以前 (yi³qian²): in the past 以前她是个老师. (**Yi³qian²** ta¹ shi⁴ ge lao³shi¹.) She was a teacher before. A time word or a verb phrase can be placed before 以前 (yi³qian²). See Note 5, Passage 24.

2. 茅草房 (mao²cao³ fang²): thatched cottage Note the word 草 (cao³) cannot be omitted here, though 茅 (mao²) alone also means straw, as 茅房 (mao² fang²) usually means latrine.

3. 住上 (zhu⁴ shang⁴): (be able to) live in The word 上 (shang⁴) after a verb indicates achievement of one's goal or result of some occurrence. 他当上了医生. (Ta¹ dang¹ **shang**⁴ le yi¹sheng¹.) He succeeded in becoming a doctor. 上 (shang⁴) may also indicate an action that just starts and will continue. 他看上了一个北京姑娘. (Ta¹ kan⁴ **shang**⁴ le yi² ge Bei³jing¹ gu¹niang.) He took a fancy to a Beijing girl.

4. 大好 (da⁴hao³): much better 她的病大好了. (Ta¹ de bing⁴ **da**⁴**hao**³ le.) She is much better now. 大 is *much, greatly, fully*. 我爱祖国的大好河山. (Wo³ ai⁴ zu³guo² de da⁴hao³ he²shan¹.) I love the beautiful rivers and mountains of my country.

5. 大不一样 (da⁴ bu⁴ yi²yang⁴ or 大不相同 da⁴ bu⁴ xiang¹tong²): much different 今天的生活和五十年前大不一样. (Jin¹tian¹ de sheng¹huo² he² wu³shi² nian² qian² **da**⁴ **bu**⁴ **yi**²**yang**⁴. Life today is much different from life fifty years ago. 大不 (da⁴bu⁴) must not be confused with 不大 (bu²da⁴), which means *not very*. 她身体不大好. (Ta¹ shen¹ti³ **bu**²**da**⁴hao³.) She is not very well. 我不大清楚. (Wo³ **bu**²**da**⁴ qing¹chu.) I'm not quite clear about it.

31. Vocabulary

老家 lao^{3}jia^1 — *n.* native place

西部 xi^1 bu^4 — *n.* the western part

山 shan^1 — *n.* mountain, hill (opp. 水 shui^3)

区 qu^1 — *n.* district

农村 nong^{2}cun^1 — *n.* village (or 乡村 xiang^{1}cun^1, opp. 城市 cheng^{2}shi^4)

那儿 nar^4 — *adv.* there (opp. 这儿 zher^4)

以前 yi^{3}qian^2 — *adv.* in the past (opp. 以后 yi^{3}hou^4)

苦 ku^3 — *a.* bitter; (of life) difficult, painful (opp. 甜 tian^2 or 甘 gan^1)
n. bitterness

茅草 mao^{2}cao^3 — *n.* dried straw

茅草房 mao^{2}cao^{3}fang^2 — *n.* thatched cottage

现在 xian^{4}zai^4 — *adv.* now

改革 gai^{3}ge^2 — *n., v.* reform

变 bian^4 — *n., v.* change

变化 bian^{4}hua^4 — *n., v.* change

层 ceng^2 — *n.* story, floor

卧房 wo^{4}fang^2 — *n.* bedroom

卫生 wei^{4}sheng^1 — *n.* hygiene

卫生间 wei^{4}sheng^{1}jian^1 — *n.* bathroom

大好 da^4 hao^3 — *a.* much better, greatly improved, very good

真 zhen^1 — *adv.* really
a. true (opp. 假 jia^3)

大不一样 da^4 bu^4 yi^{2}yang^4 — differ widely

---

apartment	公寓 (gong^{1}yu^4)	
big mansion	豪宅 (hao^{2}zhai^2)	
condo	康斗 (kang^{1}dou^4), 自有公寓 (zi^{4}you^3 gong^{1}yu^4)	
finished basement	完成地库 (wan^{2}cheng^2 di^{4}ku^4)	
garage	车库 (che^{1}ku^4)	
kitchen	厨房 (chu^{2}fang^2)	
mortgage	贷款 (dai^{4}kuan^3)	
single-storied house	平房 (ping^{2}fang^2)	
situated in a quiet area among noisy surroundings	闹中取静 (nao^4 zhong^1 qu^3 jing^4)	
town house	非独立的住宅 (fei^1 du^{2}li^4 de zhu^{4}zhai^2)	
villa	别墅 (bie^{2}shu^3)	

There is a world of difference beween the present and the past.

现在和过去真有天壤之别. (Xian^{4}zai^4 he^2 guo^{4}qu^4 zhen^2 you^3 tian^1 rang^3 zhi^1 bie^2.)

31. Exercises

I. Tone Practice:

ban¹ 搬 move	ban² --	ban³ 板 board	ban⁴ 半 half
bang¹ 帮 help	bang² --	bang³ 绑 fasten	bang⁴ 磅 pound

II. Note the two different uses of 以前 with time words (…*ago*, …*before*) and 以前 without time words (*in the past*) in the following examples. Make two sentences with 以前 after the examples:

以前他们是住在这里. 三个月 (以) 前他们搬 (ban¹: move) 走了.
以前他是个学生. 半年 (以) 前他当了老师.
我以前没坐过飞机. 三天 (以) 前我第一次坐上了飞机.

III. Translate the following sentences into Chinese, using 吃上, 爱上, 考上 (be admitted to), 碰上 (peng⁴shang⁴: run into), 见上, and 交上 (jiao¹shang⁴: make friends with) respectively:

1. His grandson was accepted by Princeton.
2. Yesterday he ran into her in the street.
3. He fell in love with her at first sight.
4. I was too late for the meal.
5. She went to the country and met her old grandma, whom she had not seen for twenty years.
6. He learned Mandarin and made a lot of Chinese friends.

IV. Fill in the following blanks with 大不 (*greatly not*) or 不大 (*not very, not much, not too, not often*):

1. 他有病, _____ 出门 (go out).
2. 红茶和咖啡的味道 _____ 一样.
3. 他 _____ 爱说话.
4. 住茅草房和住楼房 _____ 相同 (xiang¹tong² = 一样).
5. 他经常出差, _____ 在家.
6. 你看出来了吗? 他今天的脸色 (lian³se⁴: look; facial expression Lit. face color) 好像 (hao³xiang⁴: seem) 有点儿 _____ 正常.
7. 你的脸色 _____ 对头 (dui⁴tou²: normal = 正常), 一定是病了.
8. 她的孩子才一岁, 还 _____ 会走路.

124

三十二. 换钱

A: 请问, 哪儿可以换钱?

B: 四号窗口.

C: 您好! 要办什么事儿?

A: 我要取五百美元, 再换成[1]人民币. 这是我的信用卡.

C: 请在这单儿上[2]签个名儿[3].

A: 好.

C: 今天的汇率是六点一一三二. 五百美元换人民币是三千零五十六元六角. 扣掉手续费四十元, 这儿是三千零一十六元六角.

A: 谢谢.

C: 请慢走!

32. Huan⁴ Qian²

A: Qing³wen⁴, nar³ ke²yi³ huan⁴ qian²?

B: Si⁴ hao⁴ chuang¹kou³.

C: Nin² hao³! Yao⁴ ban⁴ shen²me shər⁴?

A: Wo³ yao⁴ qu³ wu² bai³ mei³yuan², zai⁴ huan⁴cheng² ren²min²bi⁴. Zhe⁴ shi wo³de xin⁴yong⁴ka³.

C: Qing³ zai⁴ zhe⁴ dar¹ shang qian¹ ge miər².

A: Hao³.

C: Jin¹tian¹ de hui⁴lü⁴ shi⁴ liu⁴ dian³ yi¹ yi¹ san¹ er⁴. Wu² bai³ mei³yuan² huan⁴ ren²min²bi⁴ shi⁴ san¹ qian¹ ling² wu³ shi² liu⁴ yuan² liu⁴ jiao³. Kou⁴ diao⁴ shou³xu⁴ fei⁴ si⁴ shi yuan², zher⁴ shi⁴ san¹ qian¹ ling² yi⁴ shi² liu⁴ yuan² liu⁴ jiao³.

A: Xie⁴xie.

C: Qing³ man⁴ zou³!

32. Currency Exchange

A: Excuse me! Can you tell me where I

   can make a currency exchange?

B: Window No. 4.

C: Hi, sir! What can I do for you?

A: I want to exchange five hundred

   dollars for RMB. This is my credit

   card.

C: Please sign your name on this form.

A: OK.

C: Today's rate is 6.1132. Five hundred

   dollars are converted to three thousand

   and fifty six *yuan* and six *jiao*. With a

   fee of forty *yuan* deducted, here is three

   thousand and sixteen *yuan* and six *jiao*.

A: Thank you!

C: Bye!

32. Notes

1. 换成 (huan[4]cheng[2]): change into 成 (cheng[2]) means *becoming*, *turning into*. 雪化成水. (Xue[3] hua[4] **cheng**[2] shui[3].) Snow melts into water. 两鬓已成霜. (Liang[3] bin[4] yi[3] **cheng**[2] shuang[1].) The hair at the temples has turned grey. 成 (cheng[2]) is usually combined with another verb to form a two-character verb. 蔗糖是用甘蔗制成的. (Zhe[4]tang[2] shi[4] yong[4] gan[1]zhe **zhi**[4]**cheng**[2] de.) Cane sugar is made from sugar-cane. 丑小鸭长成了漂亮的白天鹅了. (Chou[2] xiao[3] ya[1] **zhang**[3]**cheng**[2] le piao[4]liang de bai[2] tian[1]e[2] le.) The ugly ducking has grown into a beautiful white swan.

2. …上 (shang, unstressed; used after nouns to indicate location): *pstp.* on, in, at… 墙上 (qiang[2] **shang**) on the wall, 地板上 (di[4]ban[4] **shang**) on the floor, 火车上 (huo[3]che[1] **shang**) on the train 请你把钱放在桌上. (Qing[2] ni[2] ba[3] qian[2] fang[4] zai[4] zhuo[1] **shang**.) Please put the money on the table. "世上无难事,只怕有心人." (Shi[4] **shang** wu[2] nan[2] shi[4], zhi[3] pa[4] you[3]xin[1]ren[2].) Nothing in the world is difficult for one who is set on doing it.

3. 签个名儿 (qian[1] ge miər[2]): short for 签一个名儿 (qian[1] yi[2] ge miər[2]) sign a name Cf. Note 6, Passage 1.

126

32. Vocabulary

换 huan^4 — v. change, exchange
窗口 chuang^{1}kou^3 — n. window, wicket
取 qu^3 — v. take, withdraw (opp. 存 cun^2)
美元 mei^{3}yuan^2 — n. U.S. dollar
换成 huan^{4}cheng^2 — v. convert into
人民币 ren^{2}min^{2}bi^4 — n. Renminbi (RMB)
签名 qian^{1}ming^2 — v. sign, n. signature
汇率 hui^{4}lü^4 — n. rate of exchange
千 qian^1 — num. thousand
扣掉 kou^{4}diao^4 — v. deduct (opp. 加上 jia^{1}shang^4)
手续 shou^{3}xu^4 — n. process, handling
费 fei^4 — n. fee

Supplementary Vocabulary and Expressions

appreciation — 升值 (sheng^{1}zhi^2)
British pound — 英镑 (ying^{1}bang^4)
depreciation — 贬值 (bian^{3}zhi^2)
Euro — 欧元 (ou^{1}yuan^2)
foreign currency trade — 外汇交易 (wai^{4}hui^4 jiao^{1}yi^4)
HKD — 港币 (gang^{3}bi^4)
Japanese yen — 日元 (ri^{4}yuan^2)
middle rate — 中间价 (zhong^{1}jian^{1}jia^4)
NTD — 台币 (tai^{2}bi^4)

The exchange rates fluctuate all the time.
汇率是不断地变动的.
(Hui^{4}lü^4 shi^4 bu^2 duan^4 de bian^{4}dong^4 de.)

32. Exercises

I. Tone Practice:

jin⁴ 进 enter   jin³ 紧 tight   jin² --   jin¹ 今 today

jing⁴ 静 silent   jing³ 景 scene   jing² --   jing¹ 京 capital

II. Answer the following questions:

1. 每个窗口都可以换钱吗?

2. 可以用信用卡换钱吗?

3. 美元可以换成人民币, 人民币也可以换成美元吗?

4. 换钱有什么手续?

5. 什么是汇率?

6. 银行要扣掉一些钱吗?

7. 他们为什么要扣钱?

8. 你知道在中国可以在取款机 (ATM; 款 kuan³: sum of money) 上取美元吗?

III. Fill the blanks with 换成, 变成, 结成, 说成, 办成, 病成, 煮 (zhu³: cook) 成, and 磨 (mo²: grind) 成:

1. 两年不见, 小女孩儿_____ 大姑娘了.
2. 事情 _____ 了没有?
3. 别把茅草房 _____ 了茅房.
4. 你 _____ 这样, 还不去看大夫!
5. 他们 _____ 朋友了.
6. 在上海机场 (机场 ji¹chang²: airport) 我把人民币又_____ 了美元.
7. 生米_____ 了熟 (shu²: cooked) 饭 (The uncooked rice has been made into cooked rice. -- a Chinese proverb What's done can't be undone.), 你还能说些什么啊?
8. 只要功夫深, 铁杵_____ 针. (Zhi³yao⁴ gong¹fu shen¹, tie²chu³ mo²cheng² zhen¹. Constant grinding can turn an iron rod into a needle. -- a Chinese proverb)

128

三十三. 航班延误[1]

A: 我们去看一看布告牌, 一三五
航班是不是准点儿.

B: 哎哟! 晚点啦. 九点半起飞, 晚
点一个多小时.

A: 我去问问是什么原因.

……

说[2]是目的地[3]的天气不好.

B: 那就到登机口去耐心等待吧!

A: 我正巧带了一份儿报纸和一
本儿杂志, 可以消磨时间.

B: 我没有东西看, 只能闭目养
神[4]了.

33. Hang²ban¹ Yan²wu⁴

A: Wo³men qu⁴ kan⁴yikan⁴ bu⁴gao⁴ pai²,
135 (yao¹ san¹ wu³) hang²ban¹
shi⁴bushi⁴ zhun²diar³.

B: Ai¹yo¹! Wan²dian³ la. Jiu² dian³ ban⁴
qi³fei¹, wan²dian³ yi² ge duo¹ xiao³shi².

A: Wo³ qu⁴ wen⁴wen shi⁴ shen²me
yuan²yin¹.
......
Shuo¹ shi⁴ mu⁴di⁴di⁴ de tian¹qi⁴ bu⁴
hao³.

B: Na⁴ jiu⁴ dao⁴ deng¹ji¹kou³ qu⁴ nai⁴xin¹
deng³dai⁴ ba!

A: Wo³ zheng⁴qiao³ dai⁴ le yi² fər⁴
bao⁴zhi³ he yi⁴ bər³ za²zhi⁴, ke²yi³
xiao¹mo² shi²jian¹.

B: Wo³ mei²you³ dong¹xi kan⁴, zhi³ neng²
bi⁴mu⁴ yang³shen² le.

33. Flight Delayed

A: Let's go look at the notice board to see

if Flight 135 is on time.

B: Ah! It's late. It'll depart at nine thirty,

more than one hour late.

A: Let me ask why it's delayed.

......

They say the weather at the destination

is not good.

B: Then let's go to the boarding gate and

wait patiently.

A: I happen to have a newspaper and a

magazine with me, so I can pass the

time reading.

B: I have nothing to read. I can only sit

and rest my eyes.

33. Notes

1. 延 误 (yan^{2}wu^4): late, also called 晚 点 (wan^{2}dian^3) or 误 点 (wu^{4}dian^3)

2. 说 (shuo^1): say This 说 (shuo^1) without any subject implies 他 们 说 (ta^{1}men shuo^1) they say or 据 说 (ju^4 shuo^1) it is said that.

3. 目 的 地 (mu^{4}di^{4}di^4): destination
The 的 here is not a particle. It is a noun meaning *target*. And its pronunciation is also different. 目 (mu^4) means *eye*; hence 目 plus 的 means *aim*, *goal*, or *objective*. And hence 目 的 地 means *destination*. It is interesting to note that the pictographic character 目 (mu^4) resembles an eye, but inverted. We are sure that the eye shape of the Chinese people has been normal, and when this character 目 (mu^4) was first constructed, it was not inverted, which can be proved from the primitive inscription of this character on tortoise shells of the Shang Dynasty (c.16th – 11th century B.C.). Later its shape gradually evolved perhaps from horizontal to slanted, and then to inverted. Were it not for the change, perhaps it would be difficult to distinguish it from the character 四 (si^4: four).

4. 闭 目 养 神 (bi^{4}mu^4 yang^{3}shen^2):
close one's eyes to rest one's mind
This is a set phrase. Chinese people do this to conserve energy and to have a good rest to attain mental tranquility.

33. Vocabulary

航班 hang²ban¹   *n.* flight

延误 yan²wu⁴   *a.* delayed (opp. 准点 zhun²dian³)

布告 bu⁴gao⁴   *n.* bulletin

牌 pai²   *n.* board; playing card, card game

准点 zhun²dian³   *a.* on time

晚点 wan²dian³   *a.* late

起飞 qi³fei¹   *v.* take off, depart (opp. 降落 jiang⁴luo⁴)

原因 yuan²yin¹   *n.* reason, cause (opp. 结果 jie²guo³)

目的地 mu⁴di⁴di⁴   *n.* destination (opp. 出发港 chu¹fa¹ gang³)

目 mu⁴   *n.* eye

的 di⁴   *n.* target

登机口 deng¹ji¹ kou³   *n.* boarding gate

耐心 nai⁴xin¹   *adv.* patiently

等待 deng³dai⁴   *v.* wait

正 zheng⁴   *adv.* just, precisely

正巧 zheng⁴qiao³   *v.* happen to

份 fen⁴   *meas.* used with newspaper, set meal, gift, etc.

报纸 bao⁴zhi³   *n.* newspaper

杂志 za²zhi⁴   *n.* magazine

消磨 xiao¹mo²   *v.* spend, kill (time)

闭 bi⁴   *v.* close (opp. 开 kai¹)

养 yang³   *v.* nourish, enrich; support (parents); keep (pet)

神 shen²   *n.* spirit, mind, energy

Supplementary Vocabulary and Expressions

aisle seat   靠走道的坐位 (kao⁴ zou³dao⁴ de zuo⁴wei¹)

arrival   到港 (dao⁴ gang³)

boarding pass   登机卡 (deng¹ji¹ ka³)

cancel   取消 (qu³xiao¹)

carry on luggage   手提行李 (shou³ti² xing²li)

check in luggage   托运行李 (tuo¹yun⁴ xing²li)

claim luggage   提取行李 (ti²qu³ xing²li)

concourse, terminal   航站区 (hang²zhan⁴ qu¹)

departure   离港 (li²gang³)

go through security check   过安检 (guo⁴ an¹jian³)

information window   问讯窗口 (wen⁴xun⁴ chuang¹kou³)

green (red) passage   绿(红)色通道 lü⁴ (hong²) se⁴ tong¹dao⁴

passport   护照 (hu⁴zhao⁴)

visa   签证 (qian¹zheng⁴)

window seat   靠窗口的坐位 (kao⁴ chuang¹kou³ de zuo⁴wei⁴)

Is it domestic or international?
国内航班还是国际航班?
(Guo²nei⁴ hang¹ban¹ hai³shi guo²ji⁴ hang¹ban¹?)
The Customs formalities are simple.
过海关的手续很简单.
(Guo⁴ hai³guan¹ de shou³xu⁴ hen² jian³dan¹.)
The lavatory is occupied / vacant.
盥洗室有/没人. (Guan⁴xi³shi⁴ you³ / mei² ren².)
What time is your flight?
你搭几点钟的飞机?
(Ni³ da¹ ji² dian³ zhong¹ de fei¹ji¹?)

33. Exercises

I. Tone Practice:

pu⁴ 铺 shop   pu³ 朴 simple   pu² 仆 servant   pu¹ 扑 pounce on
leng⁴ 愣 distracted   leng³ 冷 cold   leng² 棱 edge   leng¹ –

II. Fill each of the following blanks with 看一看, 听一听, 闻一闻, 尝一尝, 摸一摸, 想一 想, 猜一猜 (cai¹: guess), or 问一问: (The word 一 can be omitted.)

1. 你去 _____ 他们, 五三一航班是不是准点儿.
2. 不用问, 你去 _____ 布告牌, 就知道了.
3. 你 _____, 他在说什么!
4. 我有点儿不舒服, 你 _____ 我的头, 看是不是发烧了.
5. 你 _____, 我给你带来了什么好消息 (xiao¹xi: news).
6. 你去好好 _____, 这事怎么办?
7. 这个菜是我太太做的. 你 _____ 味儿怎么样?
8. 你 _____ 这花儿多香啊!

III. Answer the following questions according to the text:

1. 一三五航班是不是误点了?

2. 你怎么知道是误点了?

3. 你问过他们了吗? 为什么误点?

4. 要误点多久?

5. 那我们怎么办?

6. 怎么消磨时间呢?

7. 你倒好, 有东西看. 我什么都没带, 我怎么办呢?

三十四. 交通

A: 四十年前我来美国, 第一个印象就是交通很发达. 高速公路四通八达.

B: 是的. 听说中国的交通发展得也很快. 连世界屋脊--西藏高原也¹通了火车.

A: 是的. 在中国, 火车还是²主要的交通工具.

B: 我还听说中国到处都是自行车. 中国是个自行车王国.

A: 不错, 男女老少³都骑自行车. 百分之八十的人骑自行车上班儿.

B: 骑自行车好哇. 既省钱, 又锻炼身体, 还⁴不污染空气! 这叫"一箭三雕⁵".

34. Jiao¹tong¹

A: Si⁴ shi² nian² qian² wo³ lai² mei³guo², di⁴yi¹ ge yin⁴xiang⁴ jiu⁴ shi⁴ jiao¹tong¹ hen³ fa¹da². Gao¹su⁴ gong¹lu⁴ si⁴tong¹ ba¹da².

B: Shi⁴ de. Ting¹shuo¹ zhong¹guo² de jiao¹tong¹ fa¹zhan³ de ye² hen³ kuai⁴. Lian² shi⁴jie⁴ wu¹ji³ -- Xi¹zang⁴ gao¹yuan² ye³ tong¹ le huo³che¹.

A: Shi⁴ de. Zai⁴ zhong¹guo² huo³che¹ hai²shi⁴ zhu³ya⁴ de jiao¹tong¹ gong¹ju⁴.

B: Wo³ hai² ting¹shuo¹ zhong¹guo² dao⁴chu⁴ dou¹ shi⁴ zi⁴xing²che¹. Zhong¹guo² shi ge zi⁴xing²che¹ wang²guo².

A: Bu²cuo⁴, nan²nü³ lao³shao⁴ dou¹ qi² zi⁴xing²che¹. Bai³ fen¹ zhi¹ ba¹ shi² de ren² qi² zi⁴xing²che¹ shang⁴bar¹.

B: Qi² zi⁴xing²che¹ hao³ wa. Ji⁴ sheng³ qian², you⁴ duan⁴lian⁴ shen¹ti³, hai² bu⁴ wu¹ran³ kong¹qi⁴! Zhe⁴ jiao⁴ "yi² jian⁴ san¹ diao¹".

34. Transportation

A: The first impression I got after I came to the US forty years ago was that the transportation system was highly developed. The expressways extend to every corner of the nation.

B: Yes. I heard transportation in China is also developing very fast. Trains even go to the roof of the world, Tibet plateau.

A: Yes. In China trains are still the main means of transportation.

B: I also heard that you see bikes everywhere in China. China is the "Kingdom of Bicycles".

A: Yes. In China everyone, young and old, man or woman, rides a bike. 80% of people go to work by bike.

B: Bike riding is very good! It saves money, provides good physical exercise, and doesn't pollute the air! "It kills three birds with one stone".

34. Notes

1. 连… 也 (lian² …ye³): even 连 你 也 不 懂? (**Lian²** ni² **ye³** bu⁴ dong³?) Even you don't understand it? 就 连 小 孩 儿 也 可 以 看 懂 这 本 书. (Jiu⁴ **lian²** xiao³har² **ye²** ke²yi³ kan⁴ dong³ zhei⁴ ben³ shu¹.) Even a child can understand the book. 她 连 我 的 电 话 也 不 接! (Ta¹ **lian²** wo³de dian⁴hua⁴ **ye³** bu⁴ jie¹!) She didn't answer even my call! In this usage 也 (ye³) can be replaced by 都 dou¹ (dou¹).

2. 还 是 (hai²shi): still 尽 管 下 雨, 他 还 是 来 了. (Jin²guan³ xia⁴yu³, ta¹ **hai²shi** lai² le.) He managed to come despite the rain. This expression here consists of the *adv.* 还 (hai²: still) and the linking *v.* 是 (shi: be). It is different from the 还 是 (hai²shi) in Passage 1, where the two characters are closely combined to form a conjunction, meaning *or.*

3. 男 女 老 少 (nan² nü³ lao³ shao⁴): the old and young, men and women, everyone 在 北 京 男 女 老 少 都 爱 吃 豆 腐 脑 儿. (Zai⁴ Bei³jing¹ **nan² nü³ lao³ shao⁴** dou¹ ai⁴ chi¹ dou⁴funaor³.) Everyone in Beijing likes jellied bean curd.

4. 既…又… 还… (ji⁴… you⁴ … hai²): …, … and … as well 他 们 的 儿 子 既 聪 明, 又 用 功, 还 长 得 帅. (Ta¹mende er²zi **ji⁴** cong¹ming, **you⁴** yong⁴gong¹, **hai²** zhang³ de shuai⁴.) Their son is clever, hardworking, and handsome as well. 小 美, 嫁 给 我 吧! 我 既 年 轻, 又 好 看, 还 健 壮 如 牛. (Xiao² Mei³, jia⁴ gei² wo³ ba! Wo³ **ji⁴** nian⁴qing¹, **you⁴** hao³kan⁴, **hai²** jian⁴zhuang⁴ ru² niu².) Marry me, Xiao Mei. I'm young, good-looking, and well set up.

5. 一 箭 三 雕 (yi² jian⁴ san¹ diao¹): It kills three birds with one stone. This is a fabricated phrase from 一 箭 双 雕 (yi² jian⁴ shuang¹ diao¹). Kill two birds with one stone. 双 (shuang¹): a pair It is usually used as a *meas.* 一 双 鞋 (yi⁴ shuang¹ xie²) a pair of shoes, 三 双 筷 子 (san¹ shuang¹ kuai⁴zi) three pairs of chopsticks But a pair of glasses is 一 副 眼 镜 (yi² fu⁴ yan³jing⁴), not 一 双 眼 镜 (yi⁴ shuang¹ yan³jing⁴).

34. Vocabulary

交通 jiao¹tong¹ — *n.* transportation

美国 mei³guo² — *n.* the United States (Lit. beautiful country)

第一 di⁴yi¹ — *num.* first

发达 fa¹da² — *a.* developed (opp. 落后 luo⁴hou⁴)

速 su⁴ — *n.* speed

公路 gong¹lu⁴ — *n.* highway (Lit. public road)

四通八达 si⁴tong¹ ba¹da² — extend in all directions

发展 fa¹zhan³ — *v.* develop (opp. 衰退 shuai¹tui⁴)

连… 也 lian²… ye³ — *adv.* even

世 shi⁴ — *n.* world

世界 shi⁴jie⁴ — *n.* world

屋脊 wu¹ji³ — *n.* ridge of a roof

西藏 xi¹zang⁴ — *n.* Xi¹zang⁴ (Tibet)

高原 gao¹yuan² — *n.* plateau (opp. 平川 ping²chuan¹)

火车 huo³che¹ — *n.* train

主要 zhu³ya⁴ — *a.* main (opp. 次要 ci⁴yao⁴)

工具 gong¹ju⁴ — *n.* tool

交通工具 jiao¹tong¹ gong¹ju⁴ — *n.* means of transportation

自行车 zi⁴xing²che¹ — *n.* bicycle

王国 wang²guo² — *n.* kingdom

男女老少 nan²nü³ lao³shao⁴ — *n.* the old and young, men and women; everybody

骑 qi² — *v.* ride

百分之…bai³fen¹ zhi¹ — … per cent

哇 wa — *int.* same as 啊 (a¹), used after words ending in *u* or *ao* sound

既…又 ji⁴… you⁴ — *conj.* both…and

省 sheng³ — *v.* save

省钱 sheng³qian² — save money

锻炼 duan⁴lian⁴ — *v.* take exercise

锻炼身体 duan⁴lian⁴ shen¹ti³ — build up physical strength

污染 wu¹ran³ — *v.* pollute *n.* pollution

空气 kong¹qi⁴ — *n.* air

箭 jian⁴ — *n.* arrow

雕 diao¹ — *n.* vulture

Supplementary Vocabulary and Expressions

bus — 公共汽车 (gong¹gong⁴ qi⁴che¹)

commute — 通勤 (tong¹qin²), 上下班 (shang⁴xia⁴ ban¹)

lane — 车道 (che¹dao⁴)

motorcycle — 摩托车 (mo²tuo¹che¹)

parking lot — 停车场 (ting²che¹chang³)

parking space for the handicapped — 残疾人停车位 (can²ji²ren² ting²che¹wei⁴)

subway — 地铁 (di⁴tie³)

traffic jam — 堵车 (du³che¹)

walk — 步行 (bu⁴xing²)

There is always heavy traffic during rush hours.
上下班时间车总是特多.
(Shang⁴xia⁴ban¹ shi²jian¹ che¹ zong³ shi⁴ te⁴ duo¹.)

34. Exercises

I. Tone Practice:

xian⁴ 现 now   xian³ 险 risk   xian² 嫌 dislike   xian¹ 鲜 fresh
xiang⁴ 像 look like   xiang³ 想 think   xiang² 详 detailed   xiang¹ 香 fragrant

II. Add a character to the character given below to form a two-character word:

Examples: 交 → 交通   上 → 上班

到 →   王 →   高 →   听 →   庆 →
原 →   身 →   辛 →   航 →   现 →

III. Fill in the blanks with words from the text:

1. 飞机、汽车、火车、自行车都是交通 _____.
2. 中国和 _____ 是两个友好的国家.
3. 你刚去过中国, 对中国的 _____ 怎么样?
4. 中国是一个 _____ 中的国家.
5. 有人说中国是一个 _____ 的发展中的国家.
6. 在美国汽车是 _____ 的交通工具.
7. 在中国骑自行车是为了上、下班, 在美国骑自行车是为了 _____ 身体.
8. 在汉语里,"_____双雕" 也叫 "一举两得". (yi¹ju³liang³de²: achieve two aims at once 举 ju³: act, move)

IV. Use 既…又 to connect each of the following two parts to form a sentence, adding necessary contextual words:

1. 高   大
2, 漂亮   聪明
3. 快   好
4. 花钱   有害 (害 hai⁴: harmful) 健康

V. Translate the following sentences containing 连…也 (都) into English:

1. 连他爸爸都笑 (xiao⁴: smile)了.
2. 她连我的信也不回.
3. 他连头也不回, 走了.
4. 连老爷爷都出来瞧热闹了. (瞧热闹 = 看热闹 watch the fun, watch the excitement)
5. 她不好意思 (feel embarrassed), 连脸都涨红了.
6. 他打麻将打得连饭也不吃, 觉也不睡.

136

三十五. 过敏[1]

A: 这两天咳嗽、流鼻涕、打喷嚏,
还有头痛, 难受得很[2].

B: 你准是感冒了.

A: 不, 是过敏. 一到春天, 我就过
敏.

B: 你知道是什么过敏?

A: 花粉过敏.

B: 我也有过敏.

A: 也是花粉过敏吗?

B: 不, 我管它叫[3] "宠物过敏".
我姐姐家养了只猫, 妹妹家养
了条狗儿, 我一去她们家, 马上
就过敏. 严重的时候还会发烧.

A: 是吗?

35. Guo[4]min[3]

A: Zhe[4] liang[3] tian[1] ke[2]sou, liu[2] bi[2]ti[4], da[3]
pen[1]ti[4], hai[2]you[3] tou[2]tong[4], nan[2]shou[4]
de hen[3].

B: Ni[2] zhun[3] shi[4] gan[3]mao[4] le.

A: Bu[4], shi[4] guo[4]min[3]. Yi[2]dao[4] chun[1]tian[1],
wo[3] jiu[4] guo[4]min[3].

B: Ni[3] zhi[1]dao shi[4] shen[2]me guo[4]min[3]?

A: Hua[1]fen[3] guo[4]min[3].

B: Wo[2] ye[2] you[3] guo[4]min[3].

A: Ye[3] shi[4] hua[1]fen[3] guo[4]min[3] ma?

B: Bu[4], wo[2] guan[3] ta jiao[4] "chong[3]wu[4]
guo[4]min[3]". Wo[2] jie[3]jie jia[1] yang[3] le zhi[1]
mao[1], mei[4]mei jia[1] yang[3] le tiao[2] gour[3],
wo[3] yi[2] qu[4] ta[1]men jia[1], ma[3]shang[4] jiu[4]
guo[4]min[3]. Yan[2]zhong[4] de shi[2]hou hai[2]
hui[4] fa[1]shao[1].

A: Shi[4] ma?

137

35. Allergy

A: I have been suffering from coughing,

a runny nose, constant sneezes, plus

a headache these past two days.

B: You must have caught a cold.

A: No. It's allergies. I always get

allergies when spring comes.

B: What kind of allergy?

A: Pollen.

B: I am also allergic.

A: To pollen too?

B: No. I call it a "Pet Allergy".

One of my sisters has a cat and the other

has a dog. Each time I go to their homes,

I get allergic all at once. When the case

is serious, I get a fever.

A: Really?

35. Notes

1. 过 敏 (guo^{4}min^3): allergy, oversensitive 敏 (min^3) is *sensitive*; 过 (guo^4) is *over, too much, excessive(ly)*. 今 年 雨 水 **过** 多. (Jin^1 nian^2 yu^{2}shui^3 **guo^4** duo^1.) There's excessive rainfall this year. **过** 犹 不 及. (**Guo^4** you^2 bu^{4}ji^2.) Going too far is as bad as not going far enough. Other examples with 过 (guo^4):
过 奖 (guo^{4}jiang^3) over-praise
过 高 (guo^{4}gao^1) too tall, too high, too much
过 肥 (guo^{4}fei^2) overweight
过 谦 (guo^{4}qian^1) over-modest
过 快 (guo^{4}kuai^4) too fast
过 早 (guo^{4}zao^3) too early
过 量 (guo^{4}liang^4) too great an amount
过 虑 (guo^{4}lü^4) over-anxious
过 热 (guo^{4}re^4) over-heat
But oversleep is not 过 睡 (guo^{4}shui^4), but 睡 过 头 (shui^4 guo^{4}tou^2).

2. 难 受 得 很 (nan^{2}shou^4 de hen^3): = 很 难 受 (hen^3 nan^{2}shou^4) or 怪 难 受 的 (guai^4 nan^{2}shou^4 de). 难 受 (nan^{2}shou^4) is *feel sick*. 他 咳 得 厉 害, 很 **难 受**. (Ta^1 ke^2 de li^{4}hai, hen^3 **nan^{2}shou^4**.) The bad cough made him feel very sick. The opposite of 难 受 (nan^{2}shou^4) is 好 受 (hao^{3}shou^4). 我 吃 了 药 以 后, **好 受** 多 了. (Wo^3 chi^1 le yao^4 yi^{3}hou^4, **hao^{3}shou^4** duo^1 le.) I feel much better after taking the medicine. (Cf. Note 3, Passage 6.)

3. 管 … 叫… (guan^3… jiao^4…): call sb. or sth. … (a name) 大 伙 儿 **管** 他 **叫** "快 马". (Da^{4}huor^3 **guan^3** ta^1 **jiao^4** "Kuai^4 Ma^3".) = 大 伙 儿 **叫** 他 "快 马". (Da^{4}huor^3 **jiao^4** ta "Kuai^4 Ma^3".) Everybody calls him "Fast Horse". When 管 (guan^3) is used, the object precedes the verb 叫 (jiao^4), and when it is not used, the object follows the verb. Here 管 (guan^3) can be replaced by 把 (ba^3). (Cf. Note 3, Passage 21.)

35. Vocabulary

过 敏 guo⁴min³   *n.* allergy
敏 min³   *n.* sensitivity
    a. sensitive
咳 ke²   *v., n.* cough
咳 嗽 ke²sou   *v., n.* cough
流 鼻 涕 liu² bi²ti⁴   *v.* have a runny nose
打 喷 嚏 da³ pen¹ti⁴   *v.* sneeze
头 痛 tou²tong⁴   *n., v.* headache
受 shou⁴   *v.* get, receive; stand, endure
难 受 nan²shou⁴   *v.* feel sick, feel uncomfortable
春 天 chun¹tian¹   *n.* spring
花 hua¹   *n.* flower; a family name
    v. spend (time, money, energy)
    a. multicolored
粉 fen³   *n.* powder
花 粉 hua¹fen³   *v.* pollen
管…叫… guan³…jiao⁴…   call (sb., sth.)… (a name)
它 ta¹   *pron.* it
宠 物 chong³wu⁴   *n.* pet
猫 mao¹   *n.* cat
条 tiao²   *meas.* used with dog, news item, thin and long things
狗 gou³   *n.* dog
她 们 ta¹men   *pron.* they (females)
严 重 yan²zhong⁴   *a.* severe, serious

Supplementary Vocabulary and Expressions

antihistamine   抗 过 敏 药 (kang⁴ guo⁴min³yao⁴)
bacteria   细 菌 (xi⁴jun⁴)
cause   病 因 (bing⁴yin¹)
diarrhea   拉 稀 (la¹xi¹)
drug-induced allergy   药 物 过 敏 (yao⁴wu⁴ guo⁴min³)
dust /mold allergy   灰 尘 / 霉 菌 过 敏 (hui¹chen² /mei²jun⁴ guo⁴min³)
food allergy   食 物 过 敏 (shi²wu⁴ guo⁴min³)
itchiness in the nose   鼻 子 痒 (bie²zi yang³)
sore throat   嗓 子 疼 (sang³zi teng²)
stuffy nose   鼻 塞 (bi²se⁴)
symptoms   病 状 (bing⁴zhuang⁴)
virus   病 毒 (bing⁴ du²)
watery eyes   流 眼 泪 (liu² yan³lei⁴)

To avoid allergy, you must first of all find out the allergen.
要 避 免 过 敏, 先 要 找 出 过 敏 源.
(Yao⁴ bi⁴mian³ guo⁴min³, xian¹ yao⁴ zhao³chu¹ guo⁴min³ yuan².)

35. Exercises

I. Tone Practice:

guo⁴ 过 too   guo³ 果 fruit   guo² 国 country   guo¹ 锅 pot

huo⁴ 或 or   huo³ 火 fire   huo² 活 living   huo¹ 豁 slit

II. Change 很… into …得很 and vice versa:

1. 她唱得很好.
2. 美国的交通发达得很.
3. 你的意思我很明白.
4. 老师挣的钱少得很, 可是他们的工作很重要.
5. 以前他们的生活苦得很.

III. Pick up the suitable words from below to fill them in the blanks:

过奖   过高   过肥   过谦   过快   过早   过量

1. 你已经 _____ 了. 少吃些肉吧!
2. 这件事儿你办最好, 不必_____ 了.
3. A: 你才学了一年中文, 汉语说得这么好!
   B: 您 _____ 了.
4. 中国的经济发展得是不是有点 _____?
5. 喝酒 (jiu²: liquor) 不能 _____.
6. 对小孩儿不要要求 (yao¹qiu²: demand) _____.
7. 现在说谁对谁错, 还 _____ 了一些.

IV. Fill in the following blanks with words used in this text:

1. A: 天气变冷了, _____ 的人特别多.
   B: 是啊, 我也感冒了.
2. A: 这几天老是流鼻涕、打喷嚏, 不知道是感冒还是 _____.
   B: 你得去看医生.
3. A: 你有没有花粉过敏?
   B: 没有, 可是我有 _____ 过敏.
4. A: 什么叫宠物过敏?
   B: 就是一闻到宠物的味道 _____ 要过敏.
5. A: 有你说的这么 _____ 吗?
   B: 就是. 有时候还要发烧呢!

140

三十六. 可怜的奔驰[1]!

A: 昨天我出[2]车祸了.

B: 哎哟. 什么情况?

A: 在六十五号公路上, 我紧跟着前面的一辆面包车, 它突然刹车, 我的车就撞上[3]了.

B: 你受伤了吗?

A: 我倒没受伤, 可是我的可怜的、心爱的、全新的奔驰啊! 车头儿撞扁了, 车头灯罩儿撞破了, 水箱儿漏水了, 车门儿关不上了. ...还吃[4]了一张罚单儿, 罚款二百元, 还记了六个点儿, 还说我什么超速和尾随过紧.

B: 那你自认倒霉吧!

A: 不. 我一定要上法院, 要法官还[5]我一个公道.

36. Ke³lian² de Ben¹chi²!

A: Zuo²tian¹ wo³ chu¹ che¹huo⁴ le.

B: Ai¹yo¹. Shen²me qing²kuang⁴?

A: Zai⁴ liu⁴ shi² wu³ hao⁴ gong¹lu⁴ shang, wo² jin³ geng¹ zhe qian²mian de yi² liang⁴mian⁴bao¹ che¹, ta¹ tu¹ran² sha¹che¹, wo³de che¹ jiu⁴ zhuang⁴ shang⁴ le.

B: Ni³ shou⁴shang¹ le ma?

A: Wo³ dao⁴ mei² shou⁴shang¹, ke³shi⁴ wo³de ke³lian² de, xin¹ai⁴ de, quan²xin¹ de Ben¹chi² a! Che¹ tour² zhuang⁴ bian³ le, che¹ tou¹ deng¹zhaor⁴ zhuang⁴ po⁴ le, shui³xiār¹ lou⁴shui³ le, che¹ mər² guan¹ bu² shang⁴ le.... Hai² chi¹ le yi⁴ zhang¹ fa²dar¹, fa²kuan³ er² bai³ yuan², hai² ji⁴ le liu⁴ ge diar³, hai² shuo¹ wo³ shen²me chao¹su⁴ he² wei³sui² guo⁴ jin³.

B: Na⁴ ni³ zi⁴ ren⁴ dao³mei² ba!

A: Bu⁴. Wo³ yi²ding⁴ yao⁴ shang⁴ fa³yuan⁴, yao⁴ fa³guan¹ huan² wo³ yi² ge gong¹dao⁴.

36. My Poor Benz!

A: I had a car accident yesterday.

B: Oh. What happened?

A: I was driving behind a van on Highway 65. The driver suddenly hit the brake and my car ran into his.

B: Oh, no. Were you injured?

A: Fortunately I was not injured, but my poor, beloved, brand-new Mercedes! The front was crushed flat, the headlight covers were broken, the coolant reservoir was leaking, the front door wouldn't shut. … In addition, I got a ticket for two hundred dollars and six points. The alleged fault was speeding and tailgating.

B: Then you'd better accept your bad luck!

A: No, no. I'll go to court and ask the judge to bring justice to me.

36. Notes

1. 奔驰 (ben¹chi²): a transliteration of *Benz* The literal meaning of 奔驰 (ben¹chi²) is *run quickly*. Another popular translation is 宾士 (bin¹shi⁴), which is perhaps not a good translation, because 宾士 (bin¹shi⁴) sounds like 病逝 (bing⁴ shi⁴), meaning *die of a disease.*

2. 出车祸 (chu¹ che¹huo⁴): have a car accident 出 (chu¹) means *occur, take place,* usually of sth. unpleasant. 出事故 (**chu¹ shi¹gu⁴**) have an accident, 出毛病 (**chu¹ mao²bing⁴**) go out of order 出错 (**chu¹cuo⁴**) make mistakes, 出纰漏 (**chu¹ pi¹lou⁴**) make a slip 他的肺出问题了. (Ta¹de fei⁴ **chu¹** wen⁴ti² le.) There's something wrong with his lungs. 我的车出故障了. (Wo³de che¹ **chu¹** gu⁴zhang⁴ le.) My car is out of order. 出了什么事儿? (**Chu¹** le shen²me shər⁴?) What's up? Cf. Note 4, Passage 28.

3. 撞上 (zhuang⁴ shang⁴): run into, collide with 上 (shang⁴) indicates the occurrence of some result. 这门儿关不上. (Zhe⁴ mər² guan¹ bu² **shang⁴**.) The door won't shut. Cf. Note 3, Passage 31.

4. 吃 (chi¹): get (sth. bad) 他吃了批评. (Ta¹ **chi¹** le pi¹ping².) He was criticized. 他腿上吃了一枪. (Ta¹ tui³ shang **chi¹** le yi⁴ qiang¹.) He got a shot on the leg. 吃一堑, 长一智. (**Chi¹** yi² qian⁴, zhang³ yi² zhi⁴.) A fall into the pit, a gain in your wit.

5. 还 (huan²): *vt.* return This is a homograph with 还 (hai²: *adv.* still). 我还有一本儿书要还. (Wo³ **hai²** you³ yi⁴ bər³ shu¹ yao⁴ **huan²**.) I still have a book to return.

36. Vocabulary

可怜 ke³lian²	*a.* poor, pitiful
奔驰 ben¹chi²	*n.* (Mercedes) Benz
车祸 che¹huo⁴	*n.* traffic accident
情况 qing²kuang⁴	*n.* situation, condition
情 qing²	*n.* situation; feeling, affection, love
紧 jin³	*a.* close; tight *adv.* closely (opp. 松 song¹)
跟 geng¹	*v.* follow *conj.* and *prep.* with
前面 qian²mian	*a., adv.* in the front (opp. 后头 hou⁴tou)
辆 liang⁴	*meas.* used with vehicles
面包车 mian⁴bao¹che¹	*n.* mini-bus, van (or 厢型车 xiang¹xing²che¹)
突然 tu¹ran²	*adv.* suddenly
刹车 sha¹che¹	*v.* slam on the brakes *n.* brake
撞 zhuang⁴	*v.* hit, run into
受伤 shou⁴shang¹	*v.* be injured
心爱的 xin¹ai⁴de	*a.* beloved
全新 quan² xin¹	*a.* brand new
扁 bian³	*a.* flat
罩 zhao⁴	*n.* cover
破 po⁴	*v.* break *a.* broken
水箱 shui³xiang¹	*n.* coolant reservoir, water tank
漏 lou⁴	*v.* leak
门 men²	*n.* door
关 guan¹	*v.* shut, close
罚 fa²	*v.* punish, penalty
罚款 fa²kuan³	*n., v.* fine
罚单 fa²dan¹	*n.* penalty ticket
记 ji⁴	*v.* write down, record

超 chao¹	*v.* exceed; pass
超速 chao¹su¹	*n.* speeding
尾 wei³	*n.* tail (opp. 头 tou²)
随 sui²	*v.* follow *prep.* (change) with
尾随过紧 wei³sui² guo⁴ jin³	tailgating
自 zi⁴	*pron.* oneself *adv.* by oneself
认 ren⁴	*v.* admit, acknowledge
倒霉 dao³mei²	*n.* bad luck (Cf. tone of 倒 in Passage 24.)
法院 fa³yuan⁴	*n.* court
法官 fa³guan¹	*n.* judge
还 huan²	*v.* return
公道 gong¹dao⁴	*n.* justice

Supplementary Vocabulary and Expressions

damage	损坏 (sun³huai⁴)
dent	坑 (keng¹)
drive	开车 (kai¹che¹)
driver's license	驾照 (jia⁴zhao⁴)
driving after drinking	酒后驾车 (jiu³hou⁴ jia⁴che¹)
hit and run	肇事后逃逸 (zhao⁴shi⁴ hou⁴ tao²yi⁴), 撞了就溜 (zhuang⁴ le jiu⁴ liu¹)
insurance card	保险单 (bao²xian³ dan¹)
lose control	失控 (shi¹kong⁴)
registration card	登记证 (deng¹ji⁴zheng⁴)
seat belt	安全带 (an¹quan²dai⁴)
speed limit	限速 (xian⁴su⁴)
steering wheel	方向盘 (fang¹xiang⁴pan²)
tire	轮胎 (lun²tai¹)

A kilometer is roughly 0.6 miles.
一公里约等于 0.6 英里.
(Yi⁴ gong¹li³ yue¹ deng³yu² ling² dian³ liu⁴ ying¹li³.)
We are restricted to a speed of 25 miles in built-up areas.
在闹区时速限制是二十五英里.
(Zai⁴ nao⁴ qu¹ shi²su⁴ xian⁴zhi⁴ shi⁴ er⁴shi²wu³ ying¹li³.)

36. Exercises

I. Tone Practice:

tui⁴ 退 back up   tui³ 颓 decadent   tui² 腿 leg   tui¹ 推 push
sui⁴ 岁 year   sui³ 髓 marrow   sui² 随 follow   sui¹ 虽 though

II. Fill in the blanks with words from the text:

1. 昨天我真倒 _____. 出了车祸.
2. 在六十五号公路上我紧 _____ 着一辆面包车.
3. 我的奔驰车 _____ 上了那辆面包车.
4. 面包车没坏, 奔驰的头给撞 _____ 了.
5. 车灯给撞_____ 了.
6. 水箱儿_____ 水了.
7. 车门儿也关不 _____ 了.
8. 我的车是全 _____ 的. 是上星期买的.
9. 在六十五号公路上经常出 _____.
10. 在那条号公路上, 车 _____ 至多 65 英里 (ying¹li³: mile).
11 在拐弯的地方不可以突然 _____ 车.
12. 当然, 也不可以 _____ 车.
13. 你知道他们 _____ 了我多少钱?
14. 还记了我十个 _____.
15. 我一定要上法院, 要法官还我 一个_____.

III. Translate the following sentences into Chinese, using 出:

1. What happened?
2. This occurred in 1977.
3. Lao Huang has something wrong with his stomach.
4. He has a big happy (喜 xi³) event in his family.
5. Drive carefully (小心 xiao³xin¹) to avoid any accident.

三十七. 快餐

A: 几位¹?

B: 两个人.

A: 请这儿坐. 您二位²想吃点儿什么?

B: 我们饿得慌³!你们有什么快餐?

A: 有盒饭,面条、饺子、还有蛋炒饭... 这是菜单儿.

B: 你等一等⁴. 我们看一下.

A: 好.你们慢慢儿看.
　　……

B: 来⁵一斤饺子、两瓶儿啤酒.

A: 好嘞!

B: 要等多久?

A: 不超过三分钟.

B: 好!比⁶麦当劳还快,这真叫快餐!
　　……
　　我要用一下厕所.你们厕所在哪儿?

A: 右边拐角的地方就是.

37. Kuai⁴can¹

A: Ji³ wei⁴?

B: Liang³ ge ren².

A: Qing³ zher⁴ zuo⁴. Nin² er⁴ wei⁴ xiang³ chi¹ diar³ shen²me?

B: Wo³men e⁴ de huang! Ni³men you³ shen²me kuai⁴can¹?

A: You³ he²fan⁴, mian⁴tiao², jiao³zi, hai²you³ dan⁴chao³fan⁴... Zhe⁴ shi cai⁴dar¹.

B: Ni² deng³yideng³. Wo³men kan⁴ yixia⁴.

A: Hao³. Ni³men man⁴mar kan⁴.
　　……
B: Lai² yi⁴ jin¹ jiao³zi, liang³ piãr² pi²jiu³.

A: Hao³lei!

B: Yao⁴ deng³ duo¹jiu³?

A: Bu⁴ cha¹guo⁴ san¹ fen¹zhong¹.

B: Hao³! Bi³ Mai⁴dang¹lao² hai² kuai⁴, zhe⁴ zhen¹ jiao⁴ kuai⁴can¹!
　　……
　　Wo³ yao⁴ yong⁴ yi²xia⁴ ce⁴suo³. Ni³men ce⁴suo³ zai⁴ nar³?

A: You⁴ bian guai²jiao³ de di⁴fang jiu⁴ shi⁴.

37. Fast Food

A: How many people?

B: Two.

A: Please come here. What will you like

to have?

B: We are starving! What fast food do you

have?

A: We have rice in boxes, noodles, jiaozi

and fried rice with eggs....

Here is the menu.

B: Just a moment. Let's take a look.

A: OK. Take your time.

......

B: A *jin* of jiaozi and two bottles of beer.

A: OK.

B: How long do we have to wait?

A: Three minutes or less.

B: Good. It's faster than McDonald's!

This truly *is* fast food!

......

I want to use the restroom. Where's it?

A: On the right at the corner.

37. Notes

1. 几 位? (Ji³ wei⁴?): How many of you? 位 (wei⁴) is a measure word for people, showing respect. (Cf. Passage 23.) Thus in answering a waiter's question "几 位? (Ji³ wei⁴?) ", the right response is "... 个 人 (... ge ren²)". You should not repeat the word 位 (wei⁴) just used by the waiter.

2. 您 二 位 (nin² er⁴ wei⁴): you two The expression is even more courteous than 你 们 两 位 (ni³men liang³ wei⁴).

3. 饿 得 慌 (o⁴ de huang): awfully hungry ...得 慌 (...de huang) denotes some extent that one cannot endure. It is a colloquial expression. Less colloquial is ...得 很 (...de hen³). 疼 **得 慌** (teng² **de huang**) unbearably painful, 累 **得 慌** (lei⁴ **de huang**) be tired out 我 心 里 闷 **得 慌**, 看 来 我 的 心 脏 病 要 犯 了. (Wo³ xin¹ li men¹ **de huang**, kan⁴lai wo³ de xin¹zang⁴ bing⁴ yao⁴ fan⁴ le.) I feel bored beyond endurance; perhaps I will have a heart attack. 得 慌 (de huang) is not stressed.

4. 等 一 等 (deng³yideng³): wait a bit, just a moment The structure "*v.* + 一 (yi¹) + same *v*" shows the action takes place only once or lasts very shortly. Eg. 看 一 看 (kan⁴yikan⁴) take a look, 笑 一 笑 (xiao⁴yixiao⁴) give a smile (in taking pictures = say cheese) The second verb can be changed to 下 (xia⁴) without changing the meaning. Eg. 看 一 看 (kan⁴yikan⁴) = 看 一 下 (kan⁴ yi²xia⁴) (See Note 3, Passage 13.)

5. 来 (lai²): This word is used to replace a verb according to the context. In ordering food at a restaurant it is often used to mean *give (me)*.... 给 我 **来** 个 糖 醋 鱼! (Gei² wo³ **lai²** ge tang² cu⁴ yu²!) I want a sweet and sour fish! 我 们 **来** 盘 棋 吧. (Wo³men **lai²** pan² qi² ba.) Let's play a game of chess. 你 **来** 个 笑 话 吧. (Ni³ **lai²** ge xiao⁴hua ba.) Tell us a joke.

6. 比 (bi³): than It is used in comparison. 我 **比** 他 大 几 岁. (Wo³ **bi³** ta¹ da⁴ ji³ sui⁴.) I am several years older than he. 他 汉 语 讲 得 **比** 我 好. (Ta¹ han⁴yu³ jiang³ de **bi²** wo² hao³.) He speaks Chinese better than I do.

146

37. Vocabulary

快 kuai^4 *a.*, *adv.* fast, soon (opp. 慢 man^4)

快餐 kuai^{4}can^1 *n.* fast food

这儿 zher^4 *adv.* here (opp. 那儿 nar^4)

饿 e^4 hungry (opp. 饱 bao^3)

慌 huang^1 *adv.* awfully

盒饭 he^{2}fan^4 *n.* rice in a box

饺子 jiao^{3}zi   *n.* boiled stuffed dumpling

蛋炒饭 dan^{4}chao^{3}fan^4 *n.* fried rice with eggs

菜单 cai^{4}dan^1 *n.* menu

斤 jin^1 *n.* unit of weight used in China (= 0.5 kg. = 1.1023 lb.)

瓶 ping^2 *meas.*, *n.* bottle

啤酒 pi^{2}jiu^3 *n.* beer

酒 jiu^3 *n.* wine; liquor (In China any alcoholic drink is called 酒 jiu^3.)

好嘞 hao^{3}lei   okay (used by waiters in response to customers' orders)

超过 chao^{1}guo^4 *v.* exceed, more than (opp. 不到 bu^{2}dao^4)

比 bi^3 *conj.*, *prep.* as, than; *v.* compare with

麦当劳 mai^{4}dang^{1}lao^2 *n.* McDonald's

厕所 ce^{4}suo^3 *n.* restroom

边 bian^3 *n.* side, edge; (glasses) frame

拐角 guai^{2}jiao^3 corner

Supplementary Vocabulary and Expressions

baozi	包子 (bao^{3}zi) (steamed stuffed bun)
buffet	自助餐 (zi^{4}zhu^{4}can^3)
guotier	锅贴儿 (guo^{1}tier^1) (pan-fried jiaozi)
hamburger	汉堡包 (han^{4}bao^{2}bao^3)
hot dog	热狗 (re^{4}gou^3)
junk food	垃圾食品 (la^{1}ji^1 shi^{2}pin^3)
mantou	馒头 (man^{2}tou) (steamed bun without stuffing)
salad	色拉 (se^{4}la^1), 沙拉 (sha^{1}la^1)
tangyuan	汤圆 (tang^{1}yuan^2), 元宵 (yuan^{2}xiao^1) (boiled round sweet dumpling)
wonton (soup)	馄饨 (hun^{2}tun^2)
zongzi	粽子 (zong^{4}zi) (boiled sticky rice wrapped in bamboo leaves)

Do you eat to live, or live to eat?
你是为了活才吃，还是为了吃才活?
(Ni^3 shi^4 wei^4 le huo^2 cai^2 chi^1, hai^{2}shi wei^4 le chi^1 cai^2 huo^2?)
Do you know what soup is the heaviest in the world?
你知道世界上最重的汤是什么汤?
(Ni^3 zhi^{1}dao shi^{4}jie^4 shang zui^4 zhong^4 de tang^1 shi shen^{2}me tang^1?)
Answer: *Wonton soup* (because it is one ton).

37. Exercises

I. Tone Practice:

jiao¹ 焦 charred   jiao² 嚼 chew   jiao³ 脚 foot   jiao⁴ 叫 yell

piao¹ 飘 float in air   piao² 嫖 go whoring   piao³ 瞟 look sidelong   piao⁴ 票 ticket

II. Give the Chinese equivalent of the following words:

hungry	fry	braking	car accident
cough	pollen	sign	bottle

III. Make questions to which the following sentences are the answers:

1. 是, 是上馆子了.
2. (一共) 两个人.
3. 和一个朋友.
4. 没有, 我们吃的是快餐.
5. 不是. 我们吃了中国快餐.
6. 吃了饺子.
7. 他们有盒饭.
8. 盒饭量太大, 我们吃不下.
9. 哦, 他们没有. 快餐店哪有鱼香肉丝?
10. 喝了点儿啤酒.
11. 当然不能. 我们是坐计程车 (ji⁴cheng²che¹: taxi) 回家的.
12. 我喜欢那家快餐店.

IV. Combine each pair of the following sentences into sentences of comparison, by using the word 比:

Example: Yesterday it rained heavily.   Today it rained more heavily.
           今天的雨比昨天还大.

1. I am 21.   My brother is 23.
2. I speak Chinese well.   Many people speak Chinese much better.
3. I ate a *jin* of *jiaozi*.   My wife ate half a *jin* of *jiaozi*.
4. McDonald's serves fast.   That Chinese fast food store is even faster.
   (serve: 供应 gong¹ying⁴)

三十八. 水果

A: 天气太热了, 老是出汗.

B: 要多喝水, 多吃水果. 我每天至
少喝五杯水, 再加三件水果.

A: 你最喜欢吃什么水果?

B: 什么水果我都[1]爱吃: 桃子、橙
子、草莓、香蕉, 梨…. 你呢?

A: 我什么水果都不喜欢, 除了
苹果以外[2].

B: 为什么?

A: 你知道, 每天吃个苹果, 医生
不会靠近你了!

B: 哦, 为了不让人靠近你! 那与其
吃苹果, 还不如[3]吃洋葱.

A: 什么意思?

B: 每天吃个生洋葱, 谁都不[4]敢靠
近你了!

38. Shui²guo³

A: Tian¹qi⁴ tai⁴ re⁴ le, lao³shi⁴ chu¹han⁴.

B: Yao⁴ duo¹ he¹ shui³, duo¹ chi¹
shui²guo³. Wo² mei³tian¹ zhi⁴shao³ he¹
wu³ bei¹ shui³, zai⁴ jia¹ san¹ jian⁴
shui²guo³.

A: Ni³ zui⁴ xi³huan chi¹ shen²me shui²guo³?

B: Shen²me shui²guo³ wo³ dou¹ ai⁴ chi¹:
tao²zi, cheng²zi, cao³mei², xiang¹jiao¹,
li²…. Ni³ ne?

A: Wo³ shen²me shui²guo³ dou¹ bu⁴
xi³huan, chu²le ping²guo³ yi³wai⁴.

B: Wei⁴ shen²me?

A: Ni³ zhi¹dao, mei³tian¹ chi¹ ge ping²guo³,
yi¹sheng¹ bu² hui⁴ kao⁴jin⁴ ni³ le!

B: O¹, wei⁴le bu² rang⁴ ren² kao⁴jin⁴ ni³!
Na⁴ yu³qi² chi¹ ping²guo³, hai² bu⁴ru²
chi¹ yan²cong¹.

A: Shen²me yi⁴si?

B: Mei³tian¹ chi¹ ge sheng¹ yang²cong¹,
shei² dou¹ bu⁴ gan³ kao⁴jin⁴ ni³ le!

38. Fruit

A: It's too hot. I am sweating all the time.

B: Drink more water and eat more fruit.

I drink at least five cups of water and

eat three pieces of fruit every day.

A: What is your favorite fruit?

B: I like any fruit: peaches, oranges,

strawberries, bananas, pears…. And

you?

A: I do not like any fruit, except apples.

B: Why?

A: You know, an apple a day keeps the

doctor away!

B: Oh, for keeping people away, you'd

better eat onions, rather than apples.

A: What do you mean?

B: A raw onion a day keeps *everybody*

away!

38. Notes

1. 什么 (…) 都 (shen^{2}me dou^1): whatever This structure shows that there is no exception of what is mentioned. 他 **什么 都** 知道. (Ta^1 **shen^{2}me dou^1** zhi^{1}dao.) He knows everything. (= 他 是 个 万 事 通. Ta^1 shi^4 ge wan^{4}shi^{4}tong^1. He is an encyclopedia.) 他 **什么 都** 想学. (Ta^1 **shen^{2}me dou^1** xiang^3 xue^2.) He wants to learn everything. The negative is 什么 (…) 都 不 (shen^{2}me dou^1 bu^4). 他 **什么 都 不** 怕. (Ta^1 **shen^{2}me dou^1 bu^2** pa^4.) He is afraid of nothing. 报 纸 上 讲 的 他 **什 么 都 不** 信. (Bao^{4}zhi^3 shang jiang^3 de ta^1 **shen^{2}me dou^1 bu^2** xin^4.) He doesn't believe anything the newspapers say.

2. 除 了… 以 外 (chu^{2}le… yi^{3}wai^4): with the exception of 除 了 你 **以 外**, 没 人 迟 到. (**Chu^{2}le** ni^2 **yi^{3}wai^4**, mei^{2}ren^2 chi^2 dao^4.) No one was late except you. **除 了** 星 期 天 **以 外**, 图 书 馆 每 天 开 门. (**Chu^{2}le** xing^{1}qi^{1}tian^1 **yi^{3}wai^4**, tu^{2}shu^{1}guan^3 mei^{3}tian^1 kai^{1}men^2.) The library is open every day except Sunday. This phrase also means *besides*. **除 了** 你 **以 外**, 他 也 迟 到 了. (**Chu^{2}le** ni^2 **yi^{3}wai^4**, ta^1 ye^3 chi^2 dao^4 le.) He was also late besides you. The meaning of 除 了… 以 外 (chu^{2}le… yi^{3}wai^4) can be determined according to the context. The words 以 外 (yi^{3}wai^4) can be omitted.

3. 与 其… 不 如 (yu^{3}qi^2…bu^{4}ru^2): better to… than… The thing that is not chosen is placed after 与 其 (yu^{3}qi^2). 你 **与 其** 看 电 视, **不 如** 打 乒 乓. (Ni^2 **yu^{3}qi^2** kan^3 dian^{4}shi^4, **bu^{4}ru^2** da^3 ping^{1}pang^1.) It's better for you to play ping pang than to watch TV.

4. 谁 都 不 (shei^2 dou^1 bu^4): no one = 没 人 (mei^2 ren^2) **谁 都 不** 知 道. (**Shei^2 dou^1 bu^4** zhi^{1}dao.) = 没 人 知 道. (**Mei^2 ren^2** zhi^{1}dao.) No one knows.

38. Vocabulary

出 汗 chu[1]han[4]	*v.* sweat
加 jia[1]	*v.* add
	prep. plus
	(opp. 减 jian[3])
件 jian[4]	*meas.* used with clothes, fruit, luggage, etc.
什 么…都 shen[2]me…dou[1]	whatever
桃 子 tao[2]zi	*n.* peach
橙 子 cheng[2]zi	*n.* orange
草 莓 cao[3]mei[2]	*n.* strawberry
香 蕉 xiang[1]jiao[1]	*n.* banana
梨 li[2]	*n.* pear
除 了…以 外 chu[2]le… yi[3]wai[4]	*prep.* except; besides
苹 果 ping[2]guo[3]	*n.* apple
靠 近 kao[4]jin[4]	*v.* come near, approach
近 jin[4]	*a., adv.* near (opp. 远 yuan[3])
为 了 wei[4]le	*conj.* in order that, *prep.* for, for the sake of
与 其…不 如 yu[3]qi[2]… bu[4]ru[2]	*conj.* …not as good as, rather than
洋 葱 yang[2]cong[1]	*n.* onion
敢 gan[3]	*v.* dare

apricot	杏 子 (xing[4]zi)
avocado	奶 油 果 (nai[2]you[3] guo[1])
cantaloupe	草 皮 瓜 (cao[3]pi[2] gua[1])
cherry	樱 桃 (ying[1]tao[2])
coconut	椰 子 (ye[1]zi)
durian	榴 莲 (liu[2]lian[2])
fig	无 花 果 (wu[2]hua[1]guo[3])
grape	葡 萄 (pu[2]tao)
grapefruit	葡 萄 柚 (pu[2]taoyou[4])
guava	芭 乐 (ba[1]le[4]), 番 石 榴 (fan[1]shi[2]liu)
honey dew melon	白 蜜 瓜 (bai[2]mi[4]gua[1])
kiwi	猕 猴 桃 (mi[2]hou[2]tao[2])
loquat	枇 杷 (pi[2]pa)
lychee	荔 枝 (li[4]zhi[1])
mango	芒 果 (mang[2]guo[3])
papaya	木 瓜 (mu[4]gua[1])
persimmon	柿 子 (shi[4]zi)
pineapple	菠 萝 (bo[1]luo[2]), 凤 梨 (feng[4]li[2])
plum	李 子 (li[3]zi)
pomegranate	石 榴 (shi[2]liu)
star fruit	洋 桃 (yang[2]tao[2])
tangerine	橘 子 (ju[2]zi)

Is a tomato a fruit?
西 红 柿 算 是 水 果 吗?
(Xi[1]hong[2]shi[4] suan[4] shi[4] shui[2]guo[3] ma?)

38. Exercises

I. Tone Practice:

kuan¹ 宽 wide   kuan² --   kuan³ 款 sum of money   kuan⁴ --
kuang¹ 筐 basket   kuang² 狂 mad   kuang³ 夼 low land   kuang⁴ 矿 mine

II. Give the Chinese equivalent of the following words:

near   dare   peach   handling
spirit   life   bedroom   soul

III. Rewrite the following sentences by using 什么 (...) 都:

     1. 她不爱吃水果.
     2. 每天吃个生洋葱, 谁都不敢靠近你了.
     3. 我去过北京的每一个地方.
     4. 书上讲的也不都对.
     5. 你这样的人, 没有一点儿用处 (yong⁴chu: use).
     6. 哪一种人我没见过?

IV. Learn the two different meanings of 除了...以外 and then answer the questions:

     Example: 除了你以外, 谁都没迟到. (You were the only one that was late.)
                   除了你以外, 小苹也迟到了. (Xiao Ping and you were late.)
     Hint: When 除了 is used together with 也 or 还有, it usually means *besides*,
         otherwise it means *except*.

     1. 除了星期六以外, 我都有空.
         Is he available on Tuesday?
     2. 除了星期六以外, 我星期四也不空.
         Is he available on Friday?
     3. 我不喜欢的水果除了苹果以外, 还有梨.
         Does he like apples?
     4. 除了草莓以外, 我什么水果都不喜欢.
         Does he like strawberries?
     5. 我喜欢的水果, 除了苹果以外, 还是苹果.
         Does he like strawberries?

V. Fill in the blanks with the words from the text:
     1. 天太热, 喝下的水都变成 _____ 了.
     2. 最近浑身不得劲儿. _____ 头昏脑涨, 腰酸背痛.
     3. 你与其坐火车去, 还 _____ 坐飞机去.
     4. 我 _____靠近你, 你吃了生洋葱了吧?

三十九. 找眼镜

A: 你在找什么? 东翻西翻[1].

B: 奇怪! 我的眼镜儿丢了.刚才还在这儿.

A: 什么样的眼镜儿?

B: 就是那副老光的.

A: 黑边的?

B: 是.

A: 你甭找了. 我给你找着[2]了.

B: 在哪儿? 在桌子上?

A: 不是.

B: 在椅子上?

A: 不是.

B: 那在哪儿找到的?

A: 好好儿[3]地在你头上搁着呢!

B: 喔,在这儿. 我糊涂了.

A: 老了! 我也常常丢三落四[4].

39. Zhao³ Yan³jing⁴

A: Ni³ zai⁴ zhao³ shen²me? Dong¹ fan¹ xi¹ fan¹.

B: Qi²guai⁴! Wo³de yan³jiə̃r⁴ diu¹ le. Gang¹cai² hai² zai⁴ zher⁴.

A: Shen²meyang⁴ de yan³jiə̃r⁴?

B: Jiu⁴shi⁴ na⁴ fu⁴ lao³guang¹ de.

A: Hei¹ bian¹ de?

B: Shi⁴.

A: Ni³ beng² zhao³ le. Wo³ gei² ni² zhao³zhao² le.

B: Zai⁴ nar³? Zai⁴ zhuo¹zi shang?

A: Bu² shi⁴.

B: Zai⁴ yi³zi shang?

A: Bu² shi⁴.

B: Na⁴ zai⁴ nar³ zhao³ dao⁴ de?

A: Hao²haor³ de zai⁴ ni³ tou² shang ge¹ zhe ne!

B: O¹, zai⁴ zher⁴. Wo³ hu²tu le.

A: Lao³ le! Wo² ye³ chang²chang diu¹san¹ la⁴si⁴.

39. Looking for Glasses

A: What are you looking for, rummaging here and there?

B: Strange! My glasses disappeared. They were here a moment ago.

A: What kind of glasses?

B: My reading glasses.

A: With a black frame?

B: Yeah.

A: Don't look for them any more. I have found them for you.

B: Where did you find them? On the table?

A: No.

B: On the chair?

A: No.

A: Then where were they?

A: They are sitting on your head.

B: Oh, here they are. I'm so disoriented.

A: It's the age! I am always distracted too.

39. Notes

1. 东 … 西 … (dong[1]…xi[1]…): here and there, everywhere 有 个 人 在 院 子 外 面 **东 看 西 看** (or **东 张 西 望**). (You[3] ge ren[2] zai[4] yuan[4]zi wai[4]mian **dong[1]** kan[4] **xi[1]** kan[4] [or **dong[1]** zhang[1] **xi[1]** wang[4]].) A man is peering around outside the court-yard. Other examples: **东 奔 西 跑** (**dong[1]** ben[1] **xi[1]** pao[2]): run around, **东 拉 西 扯** (**dong[1]** la[1] **xi[1]** che[3]): drag in all sorts of irrelevant matters, **东 一 个, 西 一 个** (**dong[1]** yi[1] ge[4], **xi[1]** yi[1] ge[4]): be scattered here and there, **东 一 句, 西 一 句** (**dong[1]** yi[1] ju[4], **xi[1]** yi[1] ju[4]): talk incoherently

2. 找 着 (zhao[3]zhao[2]): have found 着 (zhao[2]) following a verb indicates that some action, purpose, or results have been achieved. 她 睡 **着** 了. (Ta[1] shui[4] **zhao[2]** le.) She has fallen asleep. 你 见 **着** 她 了 吗? (Ni[3] jian[4] **zhao[2]** ta[1] le ma?) Did you get to see her? Note when 着 expresses a continuous action or condition, it is pronounced differently. Cf. Note 3, Passage 28.

3. 好 好 儿 (hao[2]haor[3]): in perfectly good condition 这 孩 子 今 天 上 午 还 是 **好 好 儿** 的, 怎 么 现 在 已 经 进 医 院 了 呢? (Zhe[4] hai[2]zi jin[1]tian[1] shang[4]wu[3] hai[2]shi **hao[2]haor[3]** de, zen[3]me xian[4]zai[4] yi[3]jing jin[4] yi[1]yuan[4] le ne?) The kid was all right this morning, how come he is in hospital now? Cf. the other meaning of 好 好 儿 (hao[2]haor[3]) in Note 6, Passage 11.

4. 丢 三 落 四 (diu[1]san[1]la[4]si[4]): forgetful, lose this and forget that Similar structure: 说 三 道 四 (shuo[1]san[1]dao[4]si[4]) make irresponsible remarks, wantonly criticize, 推 三 阻 四 (tui[1]san[1]zu[3]si[4]) decline with all sorts of excuses, 挑 三 拣 四 (tiao[1]san[1]jian[3]si[4]) be choosy, 不 三 不 四 (bu[4]san[1] bu[2]si[4]) neither fish nor fowl So 三 and 四 mean *this or that*.

39. Vocabulary

眼 镜 yan³jing⁴   *n.* glasses

东...西 dong¹...xi¹   *adv.* (in looking for sth.) everywhere

翻 fan¹   *v.* rummage

奇 怪 qi²guai⁴   *a.* strange

丢 diu¹   *v.* lose, be lost; drop

刚 才 gang¹cai²   *adv.* just now, a moment ago

什 么 样 的 shen²meyang⁴de   what kind of

样 yang⁴   *n.* kind

副 fu⁴   *meas.* used with things of a pair or a set

    a. vice, deputy; side (effect)

老 光 lao³guang¹   *a.* presbyopic

黑 hei¹   *a., n.* black (opp. 白 bai²)

甭 beng²   *v.* don't, needn't (a combined character of 不 and 用)

着 zhao²   *part.* showing some action has been achieved

桌 子 zhuo¹zi   *n.* table, desk

椅 子 yi³zi   *n.* chair

搁 ge¹   *v.* put, stay

糊 涂 hu²tu   *a.* muddled, confused (opp. 清 醒 qing¹xing³)

常 常 chang²chang   *adv.* often (same as 经 常 jing¹chang²)

丢 三 落 四 diu¹san¹la⁴si⁴   forgetful, scatter-brained

落 la⁴   *v.* leave out; leave behind, forget to bring

    luo⁴   *v.* fall, drop

Supplementary Vocabulary and Expressions

astigmatic	散 光 (san³guang¹)
bifocal	双 光 (shuan¹guang¹)
cataract	白 内 障 (bai²nei⁴zhang⁴)
contact lenses	隐 形 眼 镜 (yin³xing² yan³jing⁴)
detached retina	网 膜 剥 离 (wang³mo² bo¹li²)
glaucoma	青 光 眼 (qing¹guang¹yan³)
farsighted	远 视 (yuan³shi⁴)
have good (poor) eyesight	视 力 [不] 好 (shi⁴li⁴ [bu⁴] hao³)
multifocal	多 光 (duo¹guang¹)
nearsighted	近 视 (jin⁴shi⁴)
sight test	验 光 (yan⁴guang¹)
sunglasses	墨 镜 (mo⁴jing⁴)

The eyes are the windows of the heart.
眼 睛 是 心 灵 的 窗 户. (Yan³jing shi⁴ xin¹ling² de chuang¹hu.)

39. Exercises

I. Tone Practice:

min¹ --   min² 民 folk   min³ 敏 nimble   min⁴ --

ming¹ --   ming² 名 name   ming³ 酩 dead drunk ming⁴ 命 life

II. Give the Chinese equivalent of the following words:

    glasses   frame   muddled   strange   black

III. Translate the following sentences containing 着 into English:

1. 她一路走, 一路唱着歌儿 (ger¹: song).
2. 我看, 他吃着了甜头 (甜头 tian²tou: benefit), 还会再来.
3. 请你在外面等一等, 没看我正忙着呢!
4. 叫你猜着了!
5. 他在站着做梦呢!
6. 他美国梦算 (suan⁴: at last) 是做着了.
7. 你到北京去的票买着了吗?
8. 她刚才在看电视, 看着, 看着, 就睡着了.

IV. Translate the following sentences into Chinese, using 什么样:

1. We repair all kinds of cars.
2. What kind of cell phone did you buy?
3. What kind of people does he think we are?
4. It's only two years since I last saw her, but how aged she looks!
5. Whatever nonsense (废话 fei⁴hua⁴) the newspapers say, some people always believe it.

四十. 讨价还价[1]

A: 这条项链多少钱?

B: 五百.

A: 五百? 太贵了!

B: 您先别说贵. 先看看货. 您看, 每
颗珠子都是又圆又亮[2]的!

A: 隔壁店里同样的[3]只卖二百.

B: 他们的质量哪有我们的好? 我
们的都是一级品.

A: 二百五怎么样?

B: 二百五? 连本儿也不够![4]

A: 不行? 那我走了! 再见!

B: 您别走. 您再加点儿!

A: 不加了!

B. 二百五实在太少了. 二百八吧!

A: 不卖, 拉倒[5]吧.

B: 行! 卖给你!

A: Zhe⁴ tiao² xiang⁴lian⁴ duo¹shao qian²?

B: Wu² bai³.

A: Wu² bai³? Tai⁴ gui⁴ le!

B: Nin² xian¹ bie² shuo¹ gui⁴, xian¹ kan⁴kan
huo⁴. Nin² kan⁴, mei³ ke¹ zhu¹zi dou¹ shi
you⁴ yuan² you⁴ liang⁴ de.

A: Ge²bi⁴ dian⁴ li tong²yang⁴ de zhi³ mai⁴ er⁴
bai³.

B: Ta¹men de zhi⁴liang⁴ na²you³ wo³men de
hao³? Wo³men de dou¹ shi yi⁴ji² pin³.

A: Er⁴ bai² wu³ zen³me yang⁴?

B: Er⁴ bai² wu³? Lian² bər³ ye³ bu² gou⁴!

A: Bu⁴xing²? Na⁴ wo² zou³ le! Zai⁴jian⁴!

B: Nin² bie² zou³. Nin² zai⁴ jia¹ diar³!

A: Bu⁴ jia¹ le!

B: Er⁴ bai² wu³ shi²zai⁴ tai⁴ shao³ le. Er² bai²
ba¹ ba!

A: Bu² mai⁴, la¹dao³ ba.

B: Xing²! Mai⁴ gei³ ni!

40. Bargaining

A: How much is this necklace?

B: Five hundred bucks.

A: Five hundred? That's way too much!

B: Don't say "too much". Look at it first.

  You see, every pearl is so round and

  bright!

A: The same thing in the next store is for

  only 200.

B: Their quality is definitely not as good!

  Ours are all Grade A pearls.

A: How about 250?

B: 250? That's lower than my cost price!

A: Then, bye!

B: Don't go away. Just add a little more!

A: No.

B: 250 is really too little. How about 280?

A: Then, forget it!

B: Well, deal!

40. Notes

1. 讨价还价 (tao³jia⁴ huan²jia⁴): bargaining 讨价 (tao³jia⁴) = 要价 (yao⁴jia⁴) name a price, 还价 (huan²jia⁴) make a counter-offer 他**讨价**太高, 我没法**还价**. (Ta¹ **tao³jia⁴** tai⁴ gao¹, wo³ mei² fa³ **huan²jia⁴**.) He asked too much and I couldn't make a counter-bid.

2. 又 … 又… (you⁴…you⁴…): both… and … 那本书**又**有趣, **又**有教育意义. (Nei⁴ ben³ shu¹ **you⁴** you³qu⁴ **you⁴** you³ jiao⁴yu⁴ yi⁴yi⁴.) The book is both interesting and instructive all at once. 他的太太**又**漂亮, **又**有才华. (Ta¹de tai⁴tai **you⁴** piao⁴liang, **you⁴** you³ cai²hua².) His wife is both beautiful and gifted.

3. 的 (de): used to form a structure without the central noun The noun omitted can be inferred from the context. Here 同样**的** (tong²yang⁴ **de**) means the same necklace. Similarly, the first expression 我们**的** (wo³men **de**) below in this passage means 我们的质量 (wo³men de zhi⁴liang⁴) our quality, and the second 我们**的** (wo³mcn **de**) is 我们的项链 (wo³men de xiang⁴lian⁴) our necklaces. Other examples: 我们**的**比你们**的**大. (Wo³men **de** bi² ni³men **de** da⁴.) Ours is larger than yours. 吃香**的**, 喝辣**的**. (Chi¹ xiang³ **de**, he¹ la⁴ **de**.) Eat delicious food and drink tasty liquors. 你**的**就是你**的**, 我**的**就是我**的**. (Ni³**de** jiu⁴ shi⁴ ni³**de**, wo³**de**jiu⁴ shi⁴ wo³**de**.) What is yours is yours and what is mine is mine.

4. 连本儿也不够! (Lian² bər³ ye³ bu² gou⁴!) That cannot even cover the cost! 够本儿 (gou⁴bər³) is to make enough money to cover the cost, just break even.

5. 拉倒 (la¹dao³): Let's forget it. This is a colloquial expression. The less colloquial is 就算了 (jiu⁴ suan⁴ le).

158

40. Vocabulary

讨价 tao³jia⁴	*v.* demand as a price
还价 huan²jia⁴	*v.* make a counter offer
项链 xiang⁴lian⁴	*n.* necklace
货 huo⁴	*n.* commodity, goods
颗 ke¹	*meas.* used with small and round things
珠 zhu¹	*n.* (or 珠子 zhu¹zi, 珍珠 zhen¹zhu¹) pearl
又…又 you⁴…you⁴	*conj.* both…and
圆 yuan²	*a.* round (opp. 方 fang¹)
亮 liang⁴	*a.* bright (opp. 暗 an⁴)
隔壁 ge²bi⁴	*a.* next door *adv.* in the next house
同样 tong²yang⁴	*a.* same (opp. 不一样 bu⁴ yi²yang⁴)
卖 mai⁴	*v.* sell (opp. 买 mai³)
他们的 ta¹men de	*pron.* their, theirs
质量 zhi⁴liang⁴	*n.* quality
哪有 na²you³	how could… have (used in rhetorical questions)
我们的 wo³men de	*pron.* our, ours
一级品 yi⁴ji² pin³	*n.* grade A product
够 gou⁴	*a.* enough, sufficient
实在 shi²zai⁴	*adv.* really, indeed
拉倒 lao¹dao³	let's forget it
卖给你. Mai⁴ gei³ ni.	I'll sell it to you. It's a deal.

Supplementary Vocabulary and Expressions

agate	玛瑙 (ma²nao³)
bracelet	手镯 (shou³zhuo²)
buy one; get one free	买一送一 (mai³ yi¹ song⁴ yi¹)
clearance	清仓 (qing¹cang¹)
coral	珊瑚 (shan¹hu²)
coupon	折扣券 (zhe²kou⁴ quan⁴)
crystal	水晶 (shui³jing¹)
diamond	钻石 (zuan⁴shi²)
ear rings	耳环 (er³huan²)
jade	玉 (yu⁴)
jewelry	珠宝 (zhu¹bao³)
no bargaining	不还价 (bu⁴ huan²jia⁴)
on sale	减价 (jian³jia⁴)
ornament	装饰品 (zhuang¹shi⁴ pin³)
pendant	坠儿 (zhuər¹)
quality goods at a fair price	货真价实 (huo⁴zhen¹ jia⁴shi²)
sapphire	翡翠 (fei³cui⁴)
sterling silver	纯银 (chun²yin²)
two years' warranty	保修两年 (bao³xiu¹ liang³ nian²)

All our goods are clearly priced.
我们的货全部明码标价.
(Wo³men de huo⁴ quan²bu⁴ ming²ma³ biao³jia⁴.)
Do you have anything bigger (smaller, less expensive, better)?
有大(小, 便宜, 好) 一点儿的吗?
(You³ da⁴ [xiao³, pian²yi, hao³] yi⁴diar³ de ma?)
Make me an offer!
你开个价吧! (Ni³ kai¹ ge jia⁴ ba!)
Satisfaction guaranteed, or your money back.
包你满意, 不满意可退钱.
(Bao¹ ni² man³yi⁴, bu⁴ man³yi⁴, ke³ tui⁴qian².)
We are not afraid that our goods are compared with others; we are only afraid that the customer knows nothing about the goods.
不怕货比货, 只怕不识货.
(Bu² pa⁴ huo⁴ bi³ huo⁴, zhi³ pa⁴ bu⁴ shi² huo⁴.)

40. Exercises

I. Tone Practice:

tian⁴ 掭 tidy (a brush pen)   tian³ 舔 lick   tian² 甜 sweet   tian¹ 天 sky

tuo⁴ 唾 saliva   tuo³ 妥 proper   tuo² 鸵 ostrich   tuo¹ 脱 put off

II. Fill in each blank with the noun that is understood from the context:

1. 我的眼镜儿是白边的, 你的 (　　　　) 呢?
2. 楼上的办公室比楼下的 (　　　　) 大.
3. 骑自行车的人比走路的 (　　　　) 多.
4. 他说的 (　　　) 是不是真的?
5. 他爱吃甜 (tian²: sweet) 的 (　　　　), 我爱吃辣 (la⁴: hot) 的.
6. 这是我的 (　　　　), 那才是你的.
7. 他说他的 (　　　), 我干我的 (　　　).
8. 这些花儿里, 那红的 (　　　　) 我最爱.

III. Complete the following dialog:

1. A: 我想买条项链.
   B: _____? (What kind of necklace do you want to buy?)
2. A: 我想买一条珠项链.
   B: _____? (How about this one?)
3. A: 这条太短, 有长一点儿的吗?
   B: _____. (Yes, we do. How about this one then?)
4. A: 这条长短倒可以, 可珠子不够圆, 也不够亮.
   B: _____. (These are really Grade A pearls. You can hardly find anything better.)
5. A: 那我只好到隔壁店里去瞧瞧了.
   B: 好. _____. (Bye!)

160

四十一. 社会问题

A: 你认为美国最严重的社会问题是什么?

B: 我认为在美国青年人吸毒的太多, 中年人过肥的太多, 老年人过[1]着孤独生活的太多.

A: 我同意你的看法. 那么中国有什么社会问题呢?

B: 有两个大问题: 一是男女人口不平衡, 二是贫富悬殊.

A: 哪个[2]比较更严重?

B: 是人口问题. 据说,十年以后[3], 有百分之八的男青年会娶不到[4]老婆.

A: 那会儿,恐怕要恢复"一妻多夫制"了!

B: 你在胡说什么呀? 政府正在认真解决这个问题呢.

41. She⁴hui⁴ Wen⁴ti²

A: Ni³ ren⁴wei² mei³guo² zui⁴ yan²zhong⁴ de she⁴hui⁴ wen⁴ti² shi⁴ shen²me?

B: Wo³ ren⁴wei² zai⁴ mei³guo² qing¹nian² ren² xi¹du² de tai⁴ duo¹, zhong¹nian² ren² guo⁴fei² de tai⁴ duo¹, lao³nian²ren² guo⁴ zhe gu¹du² sheng¹huo² de tai⁴ duo¹.

A: Wo³ tong²yi⁴ ni³de kan⁴fa. Na⁴me zhong¹guo² you³ shen²me she⁴hui⁴ wen⁴ti² ne?

B: You² liang³ ge da⁴ wen⁴ti²: yi¹ shi⁴ nan²nü³ ren²kou³ bu⁴ ping²hen², er⁴ shi⁴ pin² fu⁴ xuan²shu¹.

A: Nei³ge bi³jiao⁴ geng⁴ yan²zhong⁴?

B: Shi⁴ ren²kou³ wen⁴ti². Ju⁴shuo¹, shi² nian² yi³hou⁴, you² bai³ fen¹ zhi¹ ba¹ de nan² qing¹nian² hui⁴ qu³ bu²dao⁴ lao³po.

A: Ne⁴huər⁴, kong³pa⁴ yao⁴ hui¹fu⁴ "Yi⁴ qi¹ duo¹ fu¹ zhi⁴" le!

B: Ni³ zai⁴ hu²shuo¹ shen²me ya? Zheng⁴fu³ zheng⁴zai⁴ ren⁴zhen¹ jie³jue² zhei⁴ ge wen⁴ti² ne.

41. Social Problems

A: In your mind what are the most serious social problems in the U.S.?

B: I think that in the United States too many young people take drugs, too many middle-aged people are overweight, and too many seniors are lonely.

A: I agree with you. And what do you think are the social problems in China?

B: There are two big ones: one is the unequal number of the male and female population; the other is the wide gap between the rich and the poor.

A: Which of the two is more serious?

B: The population problem is. It's reported that in ten years about 8% of young men will not be able to find wives.

A: At that time perhaps polygamy will be restored.

B: You're talking nonsense! The government is taking serious measures to solve the problem.

41. Notes

1. 过 (guo⁴): *v.* spend (time); live, get along 我在朋友家过夜. (Wo³ zai⁴ peng²you jia¹ **guo⁴**ye⁴.) I stayed overnight at a friend's house. 你周末过得怎么样? (Ni³ zhou¹mo⁴ **guo⁴** de zen³meyang⁴?) How did you spend the weekend? 他们过着幸福的生活. (Ta¹men **guo⁴** zhe xing⁴fu² de sheng¹huo².) They live a happy life. 没有手机, 这日子怎么过? (Mei²you³ shou³ji¹ zhe⁴ ri⁴zi zen³me **guo⁴**? Without cell phones how can we get along?

2. 哪个 (nei³ge): which one Cf. 哪 in Passage 7 for its pronunciations in different linguistic circumstances.

3. 以后 (yi³hou⁴): …later, after… Like 以前 (yi³quin²), 以后 (yi³hou⁴) is also used with time words or independently. (Cf. Note 5, Passage 24 and Note 1, Passage 31.) 几天以后他爷爷就去世了. (Ji³ tian¹ **yi³hou⁴** ta¹ ye²ye jiu⁴ qu⁴shi⁴ le.) A few days later his grandpa passed away. 以后你不可再迟到了. (**Yi³hou⁴** ni³ bu⁴ ke³ zai⁴ chi²dao⁴ le.) In the future you may not be late again.

4. 娶不到 (qu³ bu²dao⁴): unable to marry (a woman) *V.* + 不到 (bu²dao⁴) means unable to do sth. Eg. 买不到 (mai³ bu²dao⁴) nowhere to buy, 拿不到 (na² bu²dao⁴) cannot get 想不到他家乡的变化会这么大. (Xiang³ **bu²dao⁴** ta¹jia¹xiang¹ de bian⁴hua⁴ hui⁴ zhe⁴me da⁴.) I never expected that his village would have changed so much.

41. Vocabulary

社会 she⁴hui⁴   *n.* society

问题 wen⁴ti²   *n.* problem, issue; trouble; question

认为 ren⁴wei²   *v.* consider, believe

青年人 qing¹nian² ren²   *n.* youth (opp. 老年人 lao³nian² ren²)

吸毒 xi¹du²   *n.* drug taking

吸 xi¹   *v.* smoke, inhale (opp. 呼 hu¹)

毒 du²   *n.* poison; drug

中年人 zhong¹nian² ren²   *n.* middle-aged people

过肥 guo⁴fei²   *a.* overweight, obese (opp. 过瘦 guo⁴shou⁴)

老年人 lao³nian² ren²   *n.* old people

孤独 gu¹du²   *a.* lonely

同意 tong²yi⁴   *v.* agree

看法 kan⁴fa   *n.* view, opinion

平衡 ping²hen²   *n.* balance

贫富 pin² fu⁴   *n.* the poor and the rich, poverty and wealth

悬殊 xuan²shu¹   *v.* differ widely

哪个 nei³ge   *pron.* which one

比较 bi³jiao⁴   *v.* compare, *adv.* fairly, comparatively

更 geng⁴   *adv.* more, less

以后 yi³hou⁴   later, after (opp. …以前 yi³qian²)

娶 qu³   *v.* marry (a woman) (opp. 嫁 jia³)

老婆 lao³po   *n.* (colloq.) wife (opp. 老公 lao³gong¹)

那会儿 ne⁴huər⁴   *adv.* at that (past or future) time (opp. 这会儿 (zhei⁴huər⁴ at this time)

恐怕 kong³pa⁴   *adv.* maybe, perhaps

恢复 hui¹fu⁴   *v.* restore

一妻多夫 yi⁴qi¹ duo¹fu¹   *n.* polygamy

妻 qi¹   *n.* wife

夫 fu¹   *n.* husband

制 zhi⁴   *n.* system, practice

胡说 hu²shuo¹   *v.* talk nonsense

呀 ya   *int.* same as 啊 (a¹), used after words with vowel ending

政府 zheng⁴fu³   *n.* government

正在 zheng⁴zai⁴   *adv.* in process (used to indicate a progressive action)

认真 ren⁴zhen¹   *adv.* earnestly, seriously *v.* take sth. to heart

解决 jie³jue²   *v.* solve

Supplementary Vocabulary and Expressions

corruption and degeneration 贪污腐化 (tan¹wu¹ fu³hua⁴)

homosexual 同性恋 (tong²xing⁴lian⁴)

job opportunity 就业机会 (jiu⁴ye⁴ ji¹hui⁴)

jobless 失业 (shi¹ye⁴)

prostitution 娼妓 (chang¹ji⁴)

public security 治安 (zhi⁴an¹)

terrorism 恐怖主义 (kong³bu⁴ zhu³yi⁴)

unemployment rate 失业率 (shi¹ye⁴lü⁴)

Who will you depend on when you get old?
你老了将依靠谁呀?
(Ni² lao³ le jiang¹ yi¹kao⁴ shei³ ya?)

41. Exercises

I. Tone Practice:

hao⁴ 耗 consume   hao³ 好 good   hao² 壕 trench   hao¹ 蒿 a plant
nao⁴ 闹 make a noise   nao³ 脑 brain   nao² 挠 scratch   nao¹ 孬 bad

II. Give the Chinese equivalent of the following words:

society   lonely   balance   perhaps   talk nonsense
earnestly   not as good as   sneeze   pitiful   reason

III. Translate the following sentences into English, paying attention to the different meanings of 问题:

1. 我有两个问题要请问你.
2. 我的引擎出问题了.
3. 我们在谈论美国的肥胖 (fei²pong⁴: corpulence) 问题.
4. 她老是问问题.
5. 一路上没出问题.
6. 政府有好多问题要解决.

IV. Choose the words from this passage to fill the blanks:

1. 我的手机丢了. 没有手机怎么_____!
2. 我是说着玩儿的, 她就_____ 了.
3. 你 _____ 他说的是不是真的?
4. 你 _____ 他说的话吗?
5. 他爷爷健康已经_____ 了百分之九十了.
6. 老爷爷已经八十八了. 孙子 (sun¹zi: grandson) 才八岁. 将来孙子当什么, 他恐怕看_____ 了.

164

四十二. 中医

A: 你爷爷的病好¹了吗?

B: 好了! 最后还是²中医治好的.

A: 我也特别相信中医. 好多西医治不了³的病中医却⁴可以治好.

B: 对. 中医治病不是"头痛医头, 脚痛医脚", 而是把人看作一个阴阳结合的整体. 这样就不会治好了病, 却治死了人.

A: 是. 而且中药主要是草本植物, 不是化学品, 所以副作用小.

B: 你说得对.

A: 听说, 蝎子、蜈蚣、和眼镜蛇的毒液都可以入药.

B: 一点儿没错⁵儿. 有时侯"以毒攻毒"非常有效.

42. Zhong¹yi¹

A: Ni³ ye²ye de bing⁴ hao³ le ma?

B: Hao³ le! Zui⁴hou⁴ hai²shi zhong¹yi¹ zhi⁴ hao³ de.

A: Wo² ye³ te⁴bie² xiang¹xin⁴ zhong¹yi¹. Hao³duo¹ xi¹yi¹ zhi⁴bu⁴liao³ de bing⁴ zhong¹yi¹ que⁴ ke²yi³ zhi⁴ hao³.

B: Dui⁴. Zhong¹yi¹ zhi⁴ bing⁴ bu² shi⁴ "tou²tong⁴ yi¹ tou², jiao³tong⁴ yi¹jiao³", er² shi⁴ ba³ ren² kan⁴ zuo⁴ yi² ge yin¹ yang¹ jie²he² de zheng²ti³. Zhe⁴yang⁴ jiu⁴ bu²hui⁴ zhi⁴hao³ le bing⁴, que⁴ zhi⁴ si³ le ren².

A: Shi⁴. Er²qie³ zhong¹yao⁴ zhu³yao⁴ shi⁴ cao²ben³ zhi²wu⁴, bu² shi⁴ hua⁴xue²pin³, suo²yi³ fu⁴zuo⁴yong⁴ xiao³.

B: Ni³ shuo¹ de dui⁴.

A: Ting¹shuo¹, xie¹zi, wu²gong¹ he² yan³jing⁴she² de du²ye⁴ dou¹ ke²yi³ ru⁴ yao⁴.

B: Yi⁴diar³ mei²cuor⁴. You³shi²hou "yi³ du² gong¹ du²" fei¹chang² you³ xiao⁴.

165

42. Traditional Chinese Medicine

A: Has your grandpa recovered?

B: Yes. He was finally cured by traditional Chinese medicine.

A: I have a lot of faith in Chinese medicine. Many diseases that can't be cured by Western medicine can be cured by Chinese medicine.

B: Right. Chinese medicine treats a patient as a combined whole of *yin* and *yang*, instead of "treating the head when the head aches and treating the foot when the foot hurts", thus avoiding the possibility of "Cure the disease, kill the patient".

A: Yes. In addition, Chinese medicines are mostly herbs, not chemicals. They have few side effects.

B: You are right.

A: I have heard that scorpions, centipedes and cobra's venom can all be used as medicine.

B: Right. Sometimes "to combat poison with poison" is an effective therapy.

42. Notes

1. 好 (hao³): (of diseases) be cured, (of people) become well 他 在 慢 慢 儿 地 **好** 起 来 了. (Ta¹ zai⁴ man⁴mar de **hao²** qi³lai le.) He is slowly getting better. 我 拿 不 准 她 的 病 会 不 会 **好**. (Wo³ na¹ bu⁴ zhun³ ta¹de bing⁴ hui⁴buhui⁴ **hao³**.) I doubt if she will recover.

2. 还 是 (hai²shi): meaning *just this*, *not others* **还 是** 他 帮 了 我 的 忙. (**Hai²shi** ta¹ bang¹ le wo³de mang².) Finally it was he that helped me. **还 是** 你 在 行. (**Hai²shi** ni³ zai⁴hang².) It's you that knows your stuff. Cf. Note 4, Passage 1and Note 2, Passage 34 for other meanings.

3. ...不 了 (bu⁴liao³): unable to do sth. 了 (liao³) is put after "*v.* + 得 (de)" or "*v.* + 不 (bu⁴)" to show ability or inability. 这 么 多 东 西 我 吃 不 了. (Zhe⁴me duo¹ dong¹xi wo³ chi¹**bu⁴liao³**.) I can't eat so much food. 这 事 儿 只 有 他 办 **得** 了. (Zhe⁴ shər⁴ zhi²you³ ta¹ ban⁴**deliao³**.) Only he can do it. 他 来 **得 了**, 来 **不 了**? (Ta¹ lai²**deliao³**, lai²**buliao³**?) Can he come or not? 这 个 病 人 怕 活 **不 了** 了. (Zhei⁴ ge bing⁴ ren² pa⁴ huo³**bu⁴liao³** le.) Perhaps that patient can't survive. In this construction 了 is pronounced liao³.

4. 却 (que⁴): yet, while, indicating transition 他 的 话 很 短, **却** 很 有 说 服 力. (Ta¹de hua⁴ hen² duan³, **que⁴** hen² you³ shuo¹fu² li⁴.) His statement is short, but very convincing. 这 中 药 很 苦, **却** 有 利 于 病. (Zhe⁴ zhong¹ yao⁴ hen² ku³, **que⁴** you³li⁴ yu² bing⁴.) The Chinese medicine may be very bitter to the taste, but it will do good to the illness.

5. 一 点 儿 没 (yi⁴diar³ mei²): not in the least 今 儿 **一 点 儿 没** 风. (Jiər¹ **yi⁴diar³ mei²** feng¹.) There isn't the least bit of wind today. 这 事 儿 **一 点 儿 没** 关 系. (Zhe⁴ shər⁴ **yi⁴diar³ mei²** guan¹xi.) It doesn't matter in the least. 这 事 儿 我 可 一 点 儿 **没** 听 说. (Zhe⁴ shər⁴ wo³ ke³ **yi⁴diar³ mei²** ting¹shuo¹.) I haven't heard about it at all.

42. Vocabulary

中医 zhong¹yi¹   *n.* traditional Chinese medical doctor, traditional Chinese medical science (opp. 西医 xi¹yi¹)

最后 zui⁴hou⁴   *adv.* finally (opp. 最初 zui⁴chu¹)

治好 zhi⁴hao³   *v.* cure

特 te⁴   *adv.* especially

特别 te⁴bie²   *adv.* particularly

相信 xiang¹xin⁴   *v.* believe in, have faith in

西医 xi¹yi¹   *n.* western medicine

了 liao³   (following "*v.* + 得" or "*v.* + 不") showing ability or inability, possibility or impossibility

...不了 bu⁴liao³   unable (to do sth.)

却 que⁴   *adv.* but, while

脚 jiao³   *n.* foot (opp. 头 tou²)

把...看作 ba³...kan⁴ zuo⁴   look upon...as

阴 yin¹   *n.* (in Chinese philosophy) the negative principle in nature

阳 yang²   *n.* the positive principle in nature

结合 jie²he²   *v.* combine

整体 zheng²ti³   *n.* whole (opp. 部分 bu⁴fen)

这样 zhe⁴yang⁴   *adv.* in this way (opp. 那样 na⁴yang⁴)

治死 zhi⁴ si³   *v.* kill by maltreatment

死 si³   *v.* die

而且 er²qie³   *adv.* moreover

中药 zhong¹yao⁴   *n.* traditional Chinese medication (opp. 西药 xi¹yao⁴)

药 yao⁴   *n.* medicine

草本 cao²ben³   *n.* herbs

植物 zhi²wu⁴   *n.* plants

化学 hua⁴xue²   *n.* chemistry

化学品 hua⁴xue²pin³   *n.* chemicals

副作用 fu⁴zuo⁴yong⁴   *n.* side effect

蝎子 xie¹zi   *n.* scorpion

蜈蚣 wu²gong¹   *n.* centipede

眼镜蛇 yan³jing⁴she²   *n.* cobra

毒液 du²ye⁴   *n.* venom

入药 ru⁴ yao⁴   used as medicine

一点儿没 yi¹diar³ mei²   not a little bit

以 yi³   *v.* use, apply, take

攻 gong¹   *v.* combat, attack

以毒攻毒 yi³du² gong¹du²   use poison as an antidote for poison

非常 fei¹chang²   *adv.* extraordinarily

有效 you³ xiao⁴   *a.* effective

Supplementary Vocabulary and Expressions

acupoint   穴位 (xue²wei⁴)

acupuncture and moxibustion   针灸 (zhen¹jiu³)

cupping   拔火罐 (ba² huo³guan⁴)

jingluo   经络 (jing¹luo⁴) (the channels, as a network of passages, through which vital energy circulates)

massage   按摩 (an⁴mo²)

pulse condition   脉象 (mai⁴xiang⁴)

the eight principal syndromes   八纲: 阴阳, 表里, 寒热, 虚实 (Ba¹gang¹: yin¹ yang², biao² li³, han² re⁴, xu¹ shi²) (*yin* and *yang*, exterior and interior, cold and heat, hypofunction and hyperfunction)

the four methods of diagnosis   四诊: 望闻问切 (Si⁴zhen³: wang⁴, wen², wen⁴, qie⁴) observation, auscultation, interrogation, and pulse feeling

Can you imagine that small boys' urine is also a Chinese medicine?
你能想象童便也是中药吗? (Ni² neng² xiang³xiang⁴ tong²bian⁴ ye³ shi⁴ zhong¹yao⁴ ma?)

42. Exercises

I. Tone Practice:

fan² 烦 trouble   fan³ 反 opposite   fan¹ 翻 turn   fan⁴ 饭 rice
fang² 房 room   fang³ 访 visit   fang¹ 方 square   fang⁴ 放 put

II. Fill in he blanks with words that are used in this text:

1. 你给我这么多的菜, 我吃_____.
2. 他叫我们快去快去, 自己 _____ 坐着不动.
3. 我把你_____ 我的老师.
4. 这事儿容易, 我马上就办, _____ 问题!
5. 这种药没有什么_____.

III. Answer the following questions:

1. 他的爷爷现在还有病吗?

2. 他请西医治过吗?

3. 那么他的病是西医治好的, 还是中医治好的?

4. 西药是不是以化学品为主?

5. 中药呢?

6. 哪种药副作用大, 草本植物呢, 还是化学品?

7. 什么叫 "以毒攻毒" ?

8. 你相信中医吗?

IV. Guess according to ancient Chinese philosophy which of the following belong to
yang and which belong to *yin*:

sun	moon	girl	boy	day	night	dark	bright
hot	cold	electron	proton	cathode	anode	privacy	publicity
high	low	front	back	summer	winter	death	life
wet	dry	quick	slow	narrow	wide	open	shut
noisy	quiet	soft	hard	war	peace		

四十三. 电脑

A: 我上个月买了一台笔记本电脑. 是中国制造的.

B: 中国制造的? 质量可靠吗?

A: 好极了! 功能齐全, 真是物美价廉. 我每天上网, 买东西、查资料、听音乐, 和朋友聊天儿, 已经 "不可一日无此君"[1] 了.

B: 你不是[2] 早就[3] 有电脑了吗?

A: 是.

B: 那台老的电脑呢?

A: 给我儿子用了.

B: 你儿子才四岁! 已经会用电脑了?

A: 会! 不信? 来我家看看! 他不但用得很老练, 还[4] 在教他三岁的妹妹和电脑下棋呢!

43. Dian[4]nao[3]

A: Wo[3] shang[4] ge yue[4] mai[3] le yi[4] tai[2] bi[3]ji[4]ben[3] dian[4]nao[3]. Shi[4] zhong[1]guo[2] zhi[4]zao[4] de.

B: Zhong[1]guo[2] zhi[4]zao[4] de? Zhi[4]liang[4] ke[3]kao[4] ma?

A: Hao[3] ji[2]le! Gong[1]neng[2] qi[2]quan[2], zhen[1] shi[4] wu[4]mei[3] jia[4]lian[2]. Wo[2] mei[3]tian[1] shang[4]wang[3], mai[3] dong[1]xi, cha[2] zi[1]liao[4], ting[1] yin[1]yue[4], he[2] peng[2]you liao[2]tiar[1], yi[3]jing "bu[4]ke[3] yi[2]ri[4] wu[2] ci[3] jun[1]" le.

B: Ni[3] bu[2]shi[4] zao[3]jiu[4] you[3] dian[4]nao[3] le ma?

A: Shi[4].

B: Na[4] tai[2] lao[3] de dian[4]nao[3] ne?

A: Gei[2] wo[3] er[2]zi yong[4] le.

B: Ni[3] er[2]zi cai[2] si[4] sui[4]! Yi[3]jing hui[4] yong[4] dian[4]nao[3] le?

A: Hui[4]! Bu[2] xin[4]? Lai[2] wo[3] jia[1] kan[4]kan! Ta[1] bu[2]dan[4] yong[4] de hen[2] lao[3]lian[4], hai[2] zai[4] jiao[1] ta[1] san[1] sui[4] de mei[4]mei he[2] dian[4]nao[3] xia[4]qi[2] ne!

169

43. Computers

A: I bought a new laptop last month. It is made in China.

B: From China? Is it reliable?

A: Great! It has all the functions. The quality is good and the price is inexpensive. I use the Internet every day to make purchases, look for information, listen to music, and shoot the breeze with friends. Now I can't do without it.

B: Didn't you have a computer before?

A: Yes!

B: Then where is the old one?

A: I gave it to my son to use.

B: Your son is only four years old! He already knows how to use computers?

A: Yeah, he knows how to use it. If you don't believe me, come see yourself. Not only is he using it skillfully but he is teaching his three-year old sister to play chess with the computer.

43. Notes

1. 不可一日无此君 (bu⁴ke³ yi²ri⁴ wu² ci³ jun¹): cannot part with it even for a single day, a set phrase that indicates how important sth. is. The two negative words 不 (or 非 fei¹) and 无 (or 不) combined are more emphatic than a single affirmative. 不是你的东西不要拿. (**Bu²** shi⁴ ni³de dong¹xi **bu²** yao⁴ na².) Do not take anything if it does not belong to you. 我不可不去. (Wo³ **bu⁴** ke³ **bu²** qu⁴.), 我非去不可. (Wo³ fei¹ qu⁴ bu⁴ ke³.) or 我不去不行. (Wo³ **bu²** qu⁴ **bu⁴** xing².) I simply must go. 不见不散! (**Bu²** jian⁴ **bu²** san⁴.) You mustn't go away before we meet!

2. 不是…? (bu²shi⁴…?): Is it not that …? used in rhetorical questions 他们不是早就离婚了吗? (Ta¹men **bu²shi⁴** zao³jiu⁴ li²hun¹ le ma?) They divorced long ago, didn't they? 他不是说不来了吗? (Ta¹ **bu²shi⁴** shuo¹ bu⁴ lai² le ma?) Didn't he say that he wouldn't come?

3. 早就 (zao³jiu⁴): long ago 我早就知道了. (Wo² **zao³jiu⁴** zhi¹dao le.) I knew that long ago. 我早就去过那儿了, 所以不想再去了. (Wo³ **zao³jiu⁴** qu⁴ guo nar⁴ le, suo²yi³ bu⁴ xiang³ zai⁴ qu⁴ le.) I've been there already, so I don't want to go again.

4. 不但… 还 (bu²dan⁴…hai²): not only … but 他不但会讲日语, 还会讲汉语. (Ta¹ **bu²dan⁴** hui⁴ jiang³ ri⁴yu³, **hai²** hui⁴ jiang³ han⁴yu³.) He speaks Chinese as well as Japanese. 他不但认出我来了, 还记得我的名字. (Ta¹ **bu²dan⁴** ren⁴ chu¹ wo³ lai²le, **hai²** ji⁴de wo³de ming²zi⁴.) He not only recognized me, but also remembered my name. The word 还 (hai²) can be replaced by 而且 (er²qie³) or 而且还 (er²qie³ hai²).

170

43. Vocabulary

电脑 dian^{4}nao^3 — *n.* computer (lit. electric brain), or 计算机 (ji^{4}suan^{4}ji^1 lit. calculating machine)

上个月 shang^4 ge yue^4 — *n., adv.* last month (opp. 下个月 xia^4 ge yue^4)

台 tai^2 — *meas.* used with machines or equipment

笔记本 bi^{3}ji^{4}ben^3 — *n.* note book

制造 zhi^{4}zao^4 — *v.* make, manufacture

可靠 ke^{3}kao^4 — *a.* reliable

功能 gong^{1}neng^2 — *n.* function

齐全 qi^{2}quan^2 — *a.* complete (opp. 欠缺 qian^{4}que^1)

物美价廉 wu^{4}mei^3 jia^{4}lian^2 — or 价廉物美 (jia^{4}lian^2 wu^{4}mei^3) good quality, but low price

上网 shang^{4}wang^3 — *v.* surf the web, use the internet

查 cha^2 — *v.* look for, look up

资料 zi^{1}liao^4 — *n.* information, data, file

音乐 yin^{1}yue^4 — *n.* music

朋友 peng^{2}you — *n.* friend

聊天 liao^{2}tian^1 — *v.* have a chat

不可 bu^{4}ke^3 — *v.* cannot

一日 yi^{2}ri^4 — *adv.* for one day

无 wu^2 — *v.* not have / *prep.* without

此 ci^3 — *pron.* this

此君 ci^{3}jun^1 — *n.* this person

不是…? bu^{2}shi^4 — is it not that…?

不信 bu^2 xin^4 — *v.* not believe

不但…还 bu^{2}dan^4…hai^2 — *conj.* not only … but

老练 lao^{3}lian^4 — *a.* skillful / *adv.* skillfully (opp. 生疏 sheng^1 shu^1)

教 jiao^1 — *v.* teach, coach (opp. 学 xue^2)

下棋 xia^{4}qi^2 — *v.* play chess

Supplementary Vocabulary and Expressions

disc — 碟片 (die^{3}pian^4)
download — 下载 (xia^{4}zai^4)
e-mail — 电邮 (dian^{4}you^2)
fax — 传真 (chuan^{2}zhen^1)
hardware — 硬件 (ying^{4}jian^4)
key board — 键盘 (jian^{4}pan^2)
mouse — 滑鼠 (hua^{2}shu^1)
save — 存储 (cun^{2}chu^3)
scan — 扫描传送 (sao^{3}miao^2 chuan^{2}song^4)
software — 软件 (ruan^{3}jian^4)
web site — 网址 (wang^{2}zhi^3)
word processing — 文字处理 (wen^{2}zi^4 chu^{2}li^3)

It is the human brain that created the computers.
电脑是人脑制造出来的。
(Dian^{4}nao^3 shi^4 ren^{2}nao^3 zhi^{4}zao^4 chu^{1}lai de.)

43. Exercises

I. Tone Practice:

qie⁴ 妾 concubine	qie³ 且 just	qie² 茄 eggplant	qie¹ 切 cut
jie¹ 街 street	jie² 洁 clean	jie³ 姐 elder sister	jie⁴ 借 borrow
lou⁴ 漏 leak	lou³ 篓 basket	lou² 楼 story	lou¹ 搂 hold in arms
chou¹ 抽 draw	chou² 稠 thick	chou³ 丑 ugly	chou⁴ 臭 bad smell

II. Answer the following questions according to the text?

1. 你那台笔记本电脑是什么时候买的?
2. 是哪儿制造的?
3. 中国造的质量可靠吗?
4. 功能怎么样?
5. 价钱呢?
6. 你除了用它查资料、买东西以外, 还干些什么?
7. 那是不是一天没有电脑你就很难过日子了.
8. 你以前有过电脑吗?
9. 那你有了电脑, 为什么还要买新的?
10. 你儿子和女儿也用电脑查资料吗?

III. Rewrite the following sentences to make them more emphatic by using double negatives:

1. 每天都要用它.
2. 《红楼梦》这本儿书你哪能不看呢!
3. 有件事儿我一定要告诉你.
4. 说该说的话, 做该做的事.
5. 他是知道的, 但是他不肯说.
6. 他的话儿你要信, 但也不可全信.
7. 她是人见人爱. (见到她的人都喜欢她).
8. 他说要来, 就一定会来.

IV. Rewrite the following sentences by replacing 又 … 又 with 不 但 … 还 (而 且):

1. 那本书又有趣, 又有教育意义.
2. 他的太太又漂亮又有才华.
3. 这颗珠子又圆又亮.
4. 中国造的东西价又廉, 物又美.

172

四十四. 随天气换衣服

A: 钱小姐, 今儿个风特大. 你穿得这么单薄! 天变冷了, 多穿上点儿, 着了凉, 可不是玩儿的!

B: 谢谢你的关心! 我这条[1]裙子是有点儿薄. 明儿得[2]穿厚一点儿的裤子了.

A: 天气变化快, 衣服得勤换!

B: 是.

A: 在我的老家天气变化特快. 大伙儿"早穿棉袄午穿纱, 围着火炉吃西瓜[3]".

B: 家里暖气很好, 我只穿一件衬衣, 出门儿就穿上一件外套.

A: 我也是. 出门儿随身[4]带一件坎肩儿, 冷就穿上, 热就脱下, 很方便.

44. Sui² Tian¹qi⁴ Huan⁴ Yi¹fu

A: Qian² xiao³jie, jiər¹ge feng¹ te⁴ da⁴. Ni³ chuan¹ de zhe⁴me dan¹bo²! Tian¹ bian⁴ leng³ le, duo¹ chuan¹ shang⁴ diar³, zhao² le liang², ke³ bu² shi⁴ war² de!

B: Xie⁴xie ni³de guan¹xin¹! Wo³ zhei⁴ tiao² qun²zi shi⁴ you² diar³ bao². Miə̃r² dei³ chuan¹ hou⁴ yi⁴diar³ de ku⁴zi le.

A: Tian¹qi⁴ bian⁴hua⁴ kuai⁴, yi¹fu dei³ qin² huan⁴!

B: Shi⁴.

A. Zai⁴ wo³de lao³jia¹ tian¹qi⁴ bian⁴hua⁴ te⁴ kuai⁴. Da⁴huor³ "zao³ chuan¹ mian²ao³ wu³ chuan¹ sha¹, wei² zhe huo³lu² chi¹ xi¹gua¹".

B: Jia¹ li nuan³qi⁴ hen² hao³, wo² zhi³ chuan¹ yi² jian⁴ chen⁴ yi¹, chu¹mər² jiu⁴ chuan¹ shang⁴ yi² jian⁴ wai⁴tao⁴.

A: Wo² ye³ shi⁴. Chu¹mər² sui²shen¹ dai⁴ yi² jian⁴ kan³jiar¹. Leng³ jiu⁴ chuan¹ shang⁴, re⁴ jiu⁴ tuo¹ xia⁴, hen³ fang¹bian⁴.

44. Changing Clothes for the Weather

A: Miss Qian, There's a lot of wind today. You are wearing so little clothing. The weather is turning cold. Put on more clothes. It's no joke catching a cold!

B: Thank you for your concern. This skirt is really a little too thin. I'll wear thicker pants tomorrow.

A: The weather is changing quickly. You need to change clothes in time for the weather.

B: Yes.

A: In my native town the weather changes so fast that people wear cotton padded jackets in the morning and wear thin silks at noon and they eat watermelons around stoves.

B: The heating in my home is very good. I only wear a shirt at home and when I go out, I put on a jacket.

A: Me too. I always have a vest with me. I put it on when I'm cold and take it off when I'm hot. It comes in very handy.

44. Notes

1. 我这条… (wo^3 zhei^4 tiao^2): this…of mine
   In this structure personal pronouns precede demonstrative pronouns. 你这件衬衣 (**ni**^{3} **zhei**^{4} jian^4 chen^{4}yi^1) this shirt of yours, 他那个朋友 (**ta**^{1} **nei**^{4} ge peng^{2}you) that friend of his 我这个老公啊, 真不像话! (**Wo**^{3} **zhei**^{4} ge lao^{3}gong^1 a, zhen^1 bu^2 xiang^{4}hua^4!) This husband of mine is really shocking!

2. 得 (dei^3): have to, need
   A summary of the various uses and pronunciations of 得:
   a. (de) expressing result or degree (See Note 3, Passage 9.)
   b. (de^2) all right, expressing agreement (See Note 5, Passage 19.)
   c. (de^2) get, obtain (See Passage 28.)
   d. (dei^3) have to (See Note 4, Passage 19 and this passage.)
   e. forming phrases:
      i. (de^2) forming the phrase 值得 (zhi^{2}de^2) worth while (See Note 3, Passage 18.)
      ii. (de) forming the phrase …得很 (de hen^3) very much (See Note 2, Passage 19.)
      iii. (de^2) forming the phrase 难得 (nan^{2}de^2) seldom (See Passage 21.)
      iv. (de^2) forming the phrase 得劲 (de^{2}jin^4) feel energetic (See Passage 28.)
      v. (de) forming the phrase …得了 (deliao^3) be able to (See Note 3, Passage 42.)

3. 吃西瓜 (chi^1 xi^{1}gua^1): eat watermelons
   In China watermelons are available usually only in summer, so people eat watermelons only in hot summer days.

4. 随身 (sui^{2}shen^1): (take) with one
   别随身带太多现金. (Bie^2 **sui**^{2}**shen**^{1} dai^4 tai^4 duo^1 xian^{4}jin^1.) Don't take too much cash with you. 随身带的行李至多二十公斤. (**Sui**^{2}**shen**^{1} dai^4 de xing^{2}li zhi^{4}duo^1 er^{4}shi gong^{1}jin^1.) You are allowed to carry at most 20 kilos of luggage with you.

44. Vocabulary

衣服 yi¹fu — *n.* clothing

风 feng¹ — *n.* wind

穿 chuan¹ — *v.* put on, wear (opp. 脱 tuo¹)

单薄 dan¹bo² — *a.* (of clothing) thin (opp. 厚实 hou⁴shi²)

冷 leng³ — *a.* cold (opp. 热 re⁴ or 暖 nuan³)

着凉 zhao²liang² — *v.* catch a cold

不是玩儿的 bu² shi⁴ war² de — it's no joke doing sth.

玩 wan² — *v.* play

关心 guan¹xin¹ — *v.* be concerned with
n. consideration (for)

裙子 qun²zi — *n.* skirt

薄 bao² — *a.* thin (opp. 厚 hou⁴)

明儿 miãr² — *n.* tomorrow (colloq. for 明天 ming²tian¹)

厚 hou⁴ — *a.* thick

裤子 ku⁴zi — *n.* pants

勤 qin² — *adv.* frequently, diligently (opp. 懒 lan³)

大伙儿 da⁴huor³ — *n.* all the people

棉袄 mian²ao³ — *n.* cotton-padded jacket

纱 sha¹ — *n.* silk, gauze

围 wei² — *v.* surround

火炉 huo³lu² — *n.* stove

西瓜 xi¹gua¹ — *n.* watermelon

暖气 nuan³qi⁴ — *n.* heating (opp. 冷气 leng³qi⁴)

衬衣 chen⁴yi¹ — *n.* shirt

出门 chu¹men² — *v.* go out (opp. 在家 zai⁴jia¹)

外套 wai⁴tao⁴ — *n.* loose coat (opp. 内衣 nei⁴yi¹)

随身 sui²shen¹ — *adv.* (take) with one

坎肩 kan³jian¹ — *n.* vest (or 背心 bei⁴xin¹)

脱 tuo¹ — *v.* take off (opp. 穿 chuan¹)

方便 fang¹bian⁴ — *a.* convenient

Supplementary Vocabulary and Expressions

clothes for casual wear — 日常穿的衣服 (ri⁴chang² chuan¹ de yi¹fu)

dawn coat — 羽绒服 (yu³rong² fu²)

double-layered — 夹的 (jia² de)

fashionable clothes — 时装 (shi²zhuang¹)

fur — 皮草 (pi²cao³)

gorgeously dressed — 穿得花枝招展 (chuan¹ de hua¹zhi¹ zhao¹zhan³)

immaculately dressed — 衣冠楚楚 (yi¹guan¹ chu²chu³)

lining — 里子 (li³zi)

neatly dressed — 穿得整洁 (chuan¹ de zheng³jie²)

simply dressed — 穿着素净 (chuan¹zhuo² su⁴jing⁴)

sloppily dressed — 衣冠不整 (yi¹guan¹ bu⁴ zheng³)

unlined — 单的 (dan¹ de)

woolen — 羊毛的 (yang²mao² de)

She was decked out in her finest clothes.
她穿上了最好看的衣服，打扮得漂漂亮亮。(Ta¹ chuan¹ shang⁴ le zui⁴ hao³kan⁴ de yi¹fu, da³ban⁴ de piao⁴piao liang⁴liang.)

44. Exercises

I. Tone Practice:

niu² 牛 cow   niu¹ 妞 girl   niu⁴ 拗 stubborn   niu³ 扭 pinch, wrench
xue² 学 study   xue¹ 削 pare   xue⁴ 血 blood   xue³ 雪 snow

II. Connect the given words into sentences, using "personal *pron.* + demonstrative *pron.*":

1. 这个	总是	人	不听话	你	
2. 那条	喜欢	她	裙子	我	
3. 那位	喜欢	穿	太太	我	裙子
4. 那些	每天	老人	都	他们	锻炼身体

III. Answer the following questions according to the text:

1. 今天天气怎么样?
2. 钱小姐今天穿得很单薄还是很厚实?
3. 钱小姐今天穿了裤子还是裙子?
4. 她感冒了吗?
5. 衣服换得勤快的人是不是容易感冒?
6. "早穿棉袄午穿纱"是什么意思?
7. 出门随身带一件背心有什么好处 (hao³chu: benefit)?

IV. Read the following dialog and learn the two different meanings of 东西:

A: 上哪儿去?
B. 去买个手机. 我那个坏了. 没有手机日子怎么过?.
A: 一点儿也没错.
B: 我有三件东西是 "不可一日无此君" 的.
A: 哪三件?
B: 手机, 电脑, 和...
A: 和什么东西?
B: 和...和...我的先生.
A: 你怎么可以把你的先生和东西相提并论呢? (相提并论 xiang¹ti²bing⁴lun⁴: mention in the same breath) 你的先生是人. 他真不是个东西! (What a despicable creature he is! He's an absolute louse. Lit. Your husband is not a *thing*.)

V. Read the following sentence:

妞妞骑牛, 牛拗, 妞妞扭牛.

176

四十五. 喝酒

A: 酒是个坏东西, 也是个好东西.

B: 我不明白您的意思.

A: 少喝活血, 多喝伤身.

B: 您是说要掌握分寸?

A: 是. 我姥姥每顿饭都要喝三杯黄酒, 喝了三十多年了. 现在都[1]九十几了. 身子骨还特硬朗[2].

B: 有没有心脏病?

A: 没有.

B: 有没有高血压?

A: 没有.

B: 糖尿病?

A: 没有. 什么都没有. 每年做一次体检, 一切正常.

B: 那好啊, 可是每顿喝三杯茅台, 怕就受不了[3]了!

45. He[1] Jiu[3]

A: Jiu^3 shi^4 ge huai^4 dong^{1}xi, ye^3 shi^4 ge hao^3 dong^{1}xi.

B: Wo^3 bu^4 ming^{2}bai nin^{2}de yi^{4}si.

A: Shao^3 he^1 huo^{2}xue^4, duo^1 he^1 shang^{1}shen^1.

B: Nin^2 shi^4 shuo^1 yao^4 zhang^{3}wo^4 fen^{1}cun^4?

A: Shi^4. Wo^2 lao^{3}lao mei^3 dun^4 fan^4 dou^1 yao^4 he^1 san^1 bei^1 huang^2 jiu^3, he^1 le san^1 shi^2 duo^1 nian^2 le. Xian^{4}zai^4 dou^1 jiu^3 shi ji^3 le, shen^{1}zigu^3 hai^3 te^4 ying^{4}lang.

B: You^{3}mei^{2}you^3 xin^{1}zang^4 bing^4?

A: Mei^{2}you^3.

B: You^{3}mei^{2}you^3 gao^{1}xue^{4}ya^1?

A: Mei^{2}you^3.

B: Tang^{2}niao^4 bing^4?

A: Mei^{2}you^3. Shen^{2}me dou^1 mei^{2}you^3. Mei^3 nian^2 zuo^4 yi^{2}ci^4 ti^{2}jian^3, yi^{2}qie^4 zheng^{4}chang^2.

B: Na^4 hao^3 a, ke^{3}shi^4 mei^3 dun^4 he^1 san^1 bei^1 mao^{2}tai^2, pa^4 jiu^4 shou^{4}buliao^3 le!

45. Alcohol Drinking

A: Alcohol is both a good thing and a bad thing.

B: I don't see what you mean.

A: If you drink a little alcohol, it helps blood circulation; if you drink too much, it affects your health.

B: So, you mean the right quantity is important?

A: Yes. My grandma drinks three cups of yellow wine with her every meal. She has been drinking it for over thirty years and now she still stays healthy, even though she is over 90.

B: Does she have any heart diseases?

A: No.

B: High blood pressure?

A: No.

B: Diabetes?

A: No. She doesn't have any diseases. The annual checkup shows everything is normal.

B: That's good. But if she drinks three cups of *Maotai* with every meal, she probably can't bear it!

45. Notes

1. 都 (dou^1): already The usual meaning of 都 (dou^1) is *all*; here it means the same as 已经 (yi^{3}jing). 饭 **都** 凉 了, 快 吃 吧! (Fan^4 **dou**^{1} liang^2 le, kuai^4 chi^1 ba!) The food is already cold. Hurry up, eat it! **都** 十 点 了, 你 还 在 睡 觉? (**Dou**^{1} shi^2 dian^3 le, ni^3 hai^2 zai^4 shui^{4}jiao^4?) It's already ten and you are still sleeping?

2. 身 子 骨 还 特 硬 朗 (shen^{1}zigu^3 hai^3 te^4 ying^{4}lang): still stay very healthy This is a colloquial expression; the less colloquial is 身 体 还 很 健 康 (shen^{1}ti^3 hai^2 hen^3 jian^{4}kang^1), or simply 身 体 还 很 好 (shen^{1}ti^3 hai^2 hen^2 hao^3).

3. 受 不 了 (shou^{4}buliao^3): be unable to endure (Cf. Note 3, Passage 42.) 让 她 等 这 么 长 时 间 她 **受 不 了**. (Rang^4 ta deng^3 zhe^{4}me chang^2 shi^{2}jian^1 ta^1 shou^{4}buliao^3.) She can't stand being kept waiting so long. The positive form is 受 得 了 (shou^{4}de^{2}liao^3).
   A: 那 个 唠 叨 的 女 人 你 **受 得 了** 吗? (Na^3 ge lao^{2}dao de nü^{3}ren ni^3 **shou**^{4}**de**^{2}**liao**^{3} ma?) Can you endure that talkative woman?
   B: **受 不 了**! (**Shou**^{4}**bu**^{4}**liao**^{3}!) No. I can't!
   A phrase with similar meaning is 吃 不 消 (chi^{1}buxiao^1). 这 篇 文 章 又 长 又 臭, 真 让 看 的 人 **吃 不 消**. (Zhe^4 pian^1 wen^{2}zhang^1 you^4 chang^2 you^4 chou^4, zhen^1 rang^4 kan^4 de ren^2 **chi**^{1}**buxiao**^{1}.) No reader can put up with this long and lousy article.
   A: 每 顿 吃 八 块 大 肥 肉, 你 **吃 得 消** 吗? (Mei^3 dun^4 chi^1 ba^1 kuai^4 da^4 fei^2 rou^4, ni^3 **chi**^{1}**dexiao**^{1} ma?) Can you take it eating eight big pieces of fat meat for every meal?
   B: **吃 不 消**! (**Chi**^{1}**buxiao**^{1}!) No, impossible.

活 血 huo²xue⁴ — v. help blood circulation

伤 身 shang¹shen¹ — v. be harmful to health (opp. 健 身 jian⁴shen¹)

掌 握 zhang³wo⁴ — v. grasp, master, know well

分 寸 fen¹cun⁴ — n. proper limits, propriety

掌 握 分 寸 zhang³wo⁴ fen¹cun⁴ — exercise sound judgment, do sth. properly

姥 姥 lao³lao — n. grandma (mother's mother)

黄 酒 huang² jiu³ — n. yellow wine (made from rice, not very strong)

身 子 骨 shen¹zigu³ — n. health (Lit. body bone)

硬 朗 ying⁴lang — a. hale and hearty

血 压 xue⁴ya¹ — n. blood pressure

高 血 压 gao¹xue⁴ya¹ — n. high blood pressure

糖 尿 病 tang²niao⁴ bing⁴ — n. diabetes

一 次 yi²ci⁴ — adv. once (opp. 多 次 duo¹ci⁴)

体 检 ti² jian³ — n. physical examination (short for 体 格 检 查 ti³ge² jian³cha² 体 格 ti³ge²: physique, 检 查 jian³cha²: checkup)

一 切 yi²qie⁴ — n. everything, all

茅 台 mao²tai² — n. Maotai (powerful liquor produced in Guizhou Province in China, served at state banquet)

alcoholism	酗 酒 (xu⁴jiu³)
be too fond of drink	贪 杯 (tan¹bei¹)
brandy	白 兰 地 (bai²lan²di⁴)
get drunken	喝 醉 了(he¹ zui⁴ le)
gin	杜 松 子 酒 (du⁴ song¹zi jiu³)
great capacity for liquor	海 量 (hai³liang⁴)
half drunken	半 醉 (ban⁴zui⁴)
port wine	葡 萄 酒 (pu²taojiu³)
the older the mellower	越 陈 越 香 (yue⁴ chen² yue⁴ xiang¹)
vodka	伏 特 加 (fu²te⁴jia¹)
whisky	威 士 忌 (wei¹shi⁴ji⁴)
white (sorghum) spirit	白 干 (bai²gan¹) 高 粱 酒 (gao¹liang² jiu³)

To dispel misery and grief by drinking will only produce even more misery and grief.
借 酒 浇 愁 愁 更 愁.
(Jie⁴ jiu³ jiao¹ chou² chou² geng⁴ chou².)

45. Exercises

I. Read aloud each pair of the following words, paying attention to the tones:

台 太 　 填 天 　 玩 晚 　 想 香 　 坐 左 　 身 省 　 探 谈 　 无 乌 　 文 问
已 益

II. Fill in each of the following blanks with a right phrase from the list given below:

来得了　来不了　　受得了　　受不了　　治不了　　过不了　　死不了
省不了　算(suan⁴) 不了 (not be regarded as...)

1. A: 明天你 _____ 来不了?
2. B: 恐怕_____. 我要到医院去看我爸爸.
   A: 你爸爸什么病?
   B: 高血压、糖尿病, 还有肝也不太好.
3. A: 对老年人来说, 高血压和糖尿病_____ 什么大病.
4. B: 可我爸爸的血压和血糖都超过了二百五. 西医说已经 _____ 了. 他还
   说爸爸恐怕 _____ 圣诞节 (sheng⁴dan⁴jie²: Christmas). 我已经请了一
   位有名的 (you³ming² de: famous) 中医给他治了.
5. A: 那个西医胡说什么! 您老爸他身子骨这么硬朗, 又有好中医治疗, 他一
   定 _____!
6. B: 但愿如此. (Dan⁴yuan⁴ ru²ci³.: Let's keep our fingers crossed.)
   … …
   我给老爸治病花了不少钱. 有些 _____ 了.
7. A: 这些钱你是_____ 的. 谁叫你是他的儿子啊?
8. B: 你说得对._____ 我要受, 受不了我也要受. 他是我最亲爱的人哪!

III. Complete the following dialog:

A: 你姥姥喜欢_____吗?
B: 喜欢. 但是喝得 _____ .
A: 酒是一种_____ 身的药.
B: 是. 但要是喝得 _____ 量, 那就会_____ 身了.
A: 对. 做什么事都要 _____ 分寸.
B: 您姥姥都九十 _____ 了!
A: 不__.
B: 听说, 她每顿饭 _____ 要喝三杯茅台, 是吗?
A: 不是. 是三杯 _____.
B: 喔, 对. 要是 (yao⁴shi: if) 每顿喝三杯茅台, 她就活不 _____ 九十几了!

180

四十六. 破镜重圆¹

A: 我刚收到李小姐和麦当劳先生的请帖,他们下星期天结婚.

B: 他们不是去年刚离婚了吗?

A: 是啊. 去年离了婚²,今年再结婚.有什么不妥吗?

B: 没有,没有! 当然可以!

A: 他们离婚以后,双方都感到寂寞.李小姐想麦先生,麦先生也想李小姐.然后…

B: 然后,他们就重婚了?

A: 什么? 什么重婚?

B: 我是说他们又**重**新结**婚**了.

A: 这叫复婚,不叫重婚. "破镜重圆",是件好事儿!

46. Po⁴jing⁴ Chong² Yuan²

A: Wo³ gang¹ shou¹dao⁴ Li² xiao³jie he² Mai⁴dang¹lao² xian¹sheng de qing²tie³, ta¹men xia⁴ xing¹qi¹tian¹ jie²hun¹.

B: Ta¹men bu²shi⁴ qu⁴nian² gang¹ li²hun¹ le ma?

A: Shi⁴ a, qu⁴nian² li² le hun¹, jin¹nian² zai⁴ jie²hun¹. You³ shen²me bu⁴ tuo³ ma?

B: Mei²you³, mei²you³! Dang¹ran² ke²yi³!

A: Ta¹men li²hun¹ yi³hou⁴, shuang¹fang¹ dou¹ gan³dao⁴ ji⁴mo⁴. Li² xiao³jie xiang³ Mai⁴ xian¹sheng, Mai⁴ xian¹sheng ye² xiang³ Li² xiao³jie. Ran²hou⁴…

B: Ran²hou⁴ ta¹men jiu⁴ chong² hun¹ le?

A: Shen¹me? Shen¹me chong²hun¹?

B: Wo³ shi⁴ shuo¹ ta¹men you⁴ *chong²*xin¹ jie²*hun¹* le.

A: Zhe⁴ jiao⁴ fu⁴hun¹, bu² jiao⁴chong²hun¹. "Po⁴jing⁴ chong² yuan²", shi⁴ jian⁴ hao³shər⁴!

46. Broken Mirror Joined Together

A: I just got an invitation from Miss Li and Mr. McDonald. They're having their wedding next Sunday.

B: They just got divorced last year, didn't they?

A: Yes. They got divorced last year and want to get married again this year. Anything wrong?

B: Oh, no. Nothing wrong, of course.

A: After they got divorced, they felt very lonely. She missed him and he missed her. Then…

B: Then they will perform bigamy?

A: What? What bigamy?

B: I mean they will marry again.

A: This is marriage restored, not bigamy, a broken mirror rejoined together, something deserving praise.

46. Notes

1. 破镜重圆 (po^{4}jing^4 chong^2 yuan^2) a broken mirror rejoined together This expression is used to denote reunion of husband and wife after an enforced separation. In the past people used bronze discs as mirrors, so broken mirrors could be rejoined together and restored.

2. 离婚了 vs. 离了婚 (li^{2}hun^1 le vs. li^2 le hun^1) The former expresses an assertive fact, while the latter, in addition to an assertion, often suggests that there is some follow-up statement. A summary of some uses of 了 (le):

A. Used at the end of a sentence
   a. to show assertion:
      今天他喝酒了. (Jin^{1}tian^1 ta^1 he^{1}jiu^3 **le**.) He drank liquor today.
      她着凉了. (Ta^1 zhao^{2}liang^2 **le**.) She caught a cold.
      吃饭了! (Chi^1 fan^4 **le**!) Dinner time!
   b. to urge sb. to do sth.:
      走了, 走了! 快点儿走吧! (Zou^3 **le**, zou^3 **le**! Kuai^4 diar^3 zou^3 ba!) Let's go! Shake a leg!

B. Used after a v.
   a. to show an action (or a change) has been done or will have been done:
      我已经等了半天, 她还不来. (Wo^2 yi^{3}jing deng^3 **le** ban^{4}tian^1, ta^1 hai^2 bu^4 lai^2.) I've been waiting for a long time, but she still hasn't turned up.
   b. to suggest there is a follow-up statement:
      她着了凉, 就发烧了. (Ta^1 zhao^2 **le** liang^2, jiu^4 fa^{1}shao^1 le.) She caught a cold and had a fever. 他喝了酒, 然后开车, 就出车祸了. (Ta^1 he^2 **le** jiu^3, ran^{2}hou^4 kai^{1}che^1, jiu^4 chu^1 che^{1}huo^4 le.) He drank and drove and had an accident.
      吃了饭再走吧! (Chi^1 le fan^4 zai^4 zou^3 ba!) Stay till you have dinner here!

The addition of 了 sometimes may change the meaning of the previous words: 他**不在**, 刚出去. (Ta^1 **bu**^{2} **zai**^{4}, gang^1 chu^{1}qu^4.) He's not in. He just went out. 他**不在**了, 是去年去世的. (Ta^1 **bu**^{2}**zai**^{4} **le**, shi^4 qu^{4}nian^2 qu^{4}shi^4 de.) He is dead. He passed away last year. 他说**不行**, 我就没辙了. (Ta^1 shuo^1 **bu**^{4}**xing**^{2}, wo^3 jiu^4 mei^2 zhe^2 le.) He said no way, then I can't find any way out. 他老爸怕**不行**了. (Ta^1 lao^3 ba^4 pa^4 **bu**^{4}**xing**^{2} **le**.) His old father won't pull through, I'm afraid.

46. Vocabulary

镜 jing⁴   *n.* mirror

重 chong²   *adv.* again

收到 shou¹dao⁴   *v.* receive (opp. 发出 fa¹chu¹)

请帖 qing²tie³   *n.* invitation, invitation card

去年 qu⁴nian²   *n., adv.* last year (Lit. gone year)

离婚 li²hun¹   *n.* divorce
   v. get divorced

不妥 bu⁴tuo³   *a.* inappropriate 不妥 (bu⁴tuo³) is a little literary. The more straight-forward expression is 不合适 (bu⁴ he²shi⁴) or 不对 (bu²dui⁴).

妥 tuo³   *a.* proper, appropriate

双方 shuang¹ fang¹   *n.* both parties, both sides

感到 gan³dao⁴   *v.* feel

寂寞 ji⁴mo⁴   *a.* lonely

然后 ran²hou⁴   *adv.* then

重婚 chong²hun¹   *n.* bigamy
   v. perform bigamy

重新 chong²xin¹   *adv.* again, once more

复婚 fu⁴hun¹   *n.* marriage restored
   v. restore marriage

Supplementary Vocabulary and Expressions

marriageable age   可以结婚的年龄 (ke²yi³ jie¹hun¹ de nian²lin²)

remarry   再婚 (zai⁴hun¹)

remain a devoted couple to ripe old age   白头偕老 (bai²tou² xie²lao³)

wedding   婚礼 (hun¹li³)

Life is full of trials, little or big.
生活充满着考验, 大大小小的考验.
(Sheng¹huo² chong¹man³ zhe kao³yan⁴, da⁴da⁴ xiao²xiao³ de kao³yan⁴.)
The course of true love never runs smooth.
好事多磨. (Hao³ shi⁴ duo¹ mo².)

46. Exercises

I. Read aloud the following words, paying attention to the tones:

汁 治 之 直 脂 质 值　　烟 炎　因 印 阴　癌 爱　彩 菜 猜　白 百　带 呆　敢 干　钱 千 前　也 液

II. Turn the phonetic transcripts into Chinese characters and then translate them into English:

Example:　li²hun¹ → 离婚 → divorce

shuang¹fang¹　　zhao²liang²　qing²tie³　　　chen⁴yi¹　　dang¹ran²
liao²tian¹　　　ying⁴lang　　zhu⁴he⁴　　　ti²jian³　　tong²yi⁴

III. Choose the best answer for the following dialogues:

1. A: 你好!
   B: 你好! 我刚收到李小姐和麦先生的请帖, 他们马上要结婚了.
   A: _____ (a. 是吗? 那太好了. b. 结婚没什么不好. c. 他们为什么不结婚?)
2. A: 什么时候?
   B: _____ (a. 上星期四. b. 一年以后. c.下星期天).
3. A: 他们离过婚, 再结婚没有什么问题吧?
   B: _____ (a. 恐怕不妥. b. 你说有什么问题? c.问题大着呢!)
4. A: 他们离婚以后, 麦先生想李小姐吗?
   B: _____ (a. 李小姐感到很孤独. b.麦先生一直在想什么时候再结婚.
           c. 怎么不想? 想得都睡不着觉了.)
5. A: 那李小姐呢?
   B: _____ (a. 她当然也想. b. 她想要重婚. c. 她在想什么叫"破镜重圆".)
6. A: 那好啊! 他们应该结婚.
   B: _____ (a. 是. 不离婚不行. b. 是. 这是一件值得庆祝的事儿. c.是. 结婚
       总比离婚好.)

四十七. 老年痴呆

A: 你父母都健在吗?

B: 妈妈健在. 爸爸不在了. 去世了才三个月.

A: 是什么病?

B: 老年痴呆.

A: 我的舅舅也得了老年痴呆症. 这个病很难治.

B: 是. 我爸爸什么治疗都试过了, 都不管用[1].

A: 恐怕这种病要以预防为主[2].

B: 怎样预防?

A: 身体和头脑都需要活动, 尤其[3] 不能让脑细胞退化. 譬如每天下下棋, 或者打打桥牌对大脑很有帮助.

B: 天天打打麻将恐怕对大脑也很有好处!

A: 怎么的?[4] 你老是想打麻将!

47. Lao³nian² Chi¹dai¹

A: Ni³ fu⁴mu³ dou¹ jian⁴zai⁴ ma?

B: Ma¹ma jian⁴zai⁴, ba⁴ba bu²zai⁴ le. Qu⁴shi⁴ le cai² san¹ ge yue⁴.

A: Shi⁴ shen²me bing⁴?

B: Lao³nian² chi¹dai¹.

A: Wo³de jiu⁴jiu ye³ de² le lao³nian² chi¹dai¹ zheng⁴. Zhe⁴ ge bing⁴ hen³ nan² zhi⁴.

B: Shi⁴. Wo³ ba⁴ba shen²me zhi⁴liao² dou¹ shi⁴ guo le, dou¹ bu⁴ guan³yong⁴.

A: Kong³pa⁴ zhe⁴ zhong³ bing⁴ yao⁴ yi³ yu⁴fang² wei²zhu³.

B: Zen³yang⁴ yu⁴fang²?

A: Shen¹ti³ he² tou²nao³ dou¹ xu¹yao⁴ huo²dong⁴, you²qi² bu⁴ neng² rang⁴ nao³ xi⁴bao¹ tui⁴hua⁴. Pi⁴ru² mei³tian¹ xia⁴xia qi², huo⁴zhe³ da²da qiao²pai² dui⁴ da⁴nao³ hen² you³ bang¹zhu⁴.

B: Tian¹tian¹ da²da ma²jiang⁴ kong³pa⁴ dui⁴ da⁴nao³ ye² hen² you² hao³chu!

A: Zen³me de? Ni² lao³shi⁴ xiang² da³ ma²jiang⁴!

47. Alzheimer's Disease

A: Are your parents still healthy?

B: My mom is still healthy, but my dad passed away. He died only three months ago.

A: Of what disease?

B: Alzheimer's.

A: My uncle also got Alzheimer's. That disease is hard to cure.

B: Yes. My dad tried all sorts of cures, but nothing worked.

A: Maybe for this disease prevention should go first.

B: How do I prevent Alzheimer's?

A: Stay active physically and mentally; especially do not let your brain decline. For example, playing chess or bridge every day will give your brain a lot of help.

B: Playing *mahjong* every day may also help the brains function!

A: Why, you are always thinking of playing mahjong!

47. Notes

1. 管用 (guan³yong⁴): effective, same as 有效 (you³xiao⁴) 这药很**管用**.(Zhe⁴ yao⁴ hen² **guan³yong⁴**.) This medicine is very effective. 我们的劝告对她不**管用**. (Wo³men de quan⁴gao⁴ dui⁴ ta¹ bu⁴ **guan³yong⁴**.) Our advice has no effect on her.

2. 以... 为主 (yi³... wei²zhu³): give first place to, make…a priority 以我为主 (**yi² wo³ wei²zhu³**) be egoistic 她以素食为主. (Ta¹ **yi³** su⁴ shi² **wei²zhu³**.) Her main diet consists of vegetables. 中医治病, 以治本为主. (Zhong¹yi¹ zhi⁴bing⁴ **yi³** zhi⁴ben³ **wei²zhu³**.) The traditional Chinese medicine treats diseases by getting at the root of the diseases (instead of treating only the symptoms or bringing about only a temporary solution).

3. 尤其 (you²qi²): especially, in particular 她喜欢农村, **尤其**是春天的农村. (Ta¹ xi³huan nong²cun¹, **you²qi²** shi⁴ chun¹tian¹ de nong²cun¹.) She likes the country, especially in the spring. 每个人都努力学习, **尤其**是凯特 (Mei³ ge ren² dou¹ nu³li⁴ xue²xi², **you²qi²** shi⁴ Kai³te⁴.) Everyone studies hard, especially Kate. 尤其 (you²qi²) can be replaced by 特别 (te⁴bie²).

4. 怎么的? (Zen³me de?): How's that? What is the explanation of that? It's same as 怎么着? (Zen³mezhe?) or 怎么了?. (See Note 2, Passage 24.) **怎么的**? 今天你没上学? (**Zen³me de**? Jin¹tian¹ ni³ mei² shang⁴xue²?) What happened? You didn't go to school today?

47. Vocabulary

老年 lao^{3}nian^2 — *n.* senior (opp. 少年 shao^{4}nian^2 or 青年 qing^{1}nian^2)

痴呆 chi^{1}dai^1 — *a.* dull-witted *n.* dementia

老年痴呆 lao^{3}nian^2 chi^{1}dai^1 — *n.* Alzheimer's disease

父 fu^4 — *n.* (or 父亲 fu^{4}qin^1) father

母 mu^3 — *n.*(or 母亲 mu^{3}qin^1) mother

健在 jian^{4}zai^4 — *v.* (of a senior) be still alive and in good health

不在 bu^{2}zai^4 — *v.* be dead (usually with 了) be not in

去世 qu^{4}shi^4 — *v.* pass away

舅舅 jiu^{4}jiu — *n.* uncle (mother's brother)

治疗 zhi^{4}liao^2 — *n.* treatment *v.* treat

试 shi^4 — *v.* try

管用 guan^{3}yong^4 — *a.* effective, useful (opp. 无效 wu^{2}xiao^4)

种 zhong^3 — *n.* kind, type

以…为主 yi^3…wei^{2}zhu^3 — give first place to (opp. 以…为副 yi^3…wei^2 fu^4)

怎样 zen^{3}yang^4 — *adv.* how (same as 怎么 zen^{3}me or 怎么样 zen^{3}meyang^4)

头脑 tou^{2}nao^3 — *n.* brains, mind

尤其 you^{2}qi^2 — *adv.* especially

细胞 xi^{4}bao^1 — *n.* cell

退化 tui^{4}hua^4 — *v.* degenerate *n.* degeneration

大脑 da^{4}nao^3 — *n.* brain, cerebrum

譬如 pi^{4}ru^2 — (used to introduce illustrations or examples) as, like, for example

桥牌 qiao^{2}pai^2 — *n.* bridge (game)

帮助 bang^{1}zhu^4 — *n.*, *v.* help

好处 hao^{3}chu — *n.* benefit, advantage, good (opp. 坏处 huai^{4}chu)

Supplementary Vocabulary and Expressions

be in poor health	身体不好 (shen^{1}ti^3 bu^{4}hao^3)
diagnosis and therapy	诊断和治疗 (zhen^{3}duan^4 he^2 zhi^{4}liao^2)
in a coma	昏迷 (hun^{1}mi^2)
incontinence of feces	大便失禁 (da^{4}bian^4 shi^{1}jin^4)
osteoporosis	骨质疏松 (gu^{3}zhi^4 shu^{1}song^1)
Parkinson's disease	伯金森氏病 (bo^{2}jin^{1}sen^1 shi^4 bing^4)
prolong life	延年益寿 (yan^{2}nian^2 yi^{4}shou^4)
rehabilitation	复健 (fu^{4}jian^4)
urinary incontinence	小便失禁 (xiao^{3}bian^4 shi^{1}jin^4)

Prevention is better than treatment.
预防胜于治疗. (Yu^{4}fang^2 sheng^{4}yu^2 zhi^{4}liao^2.)

47. Exercises

I. Pronounce the following words correctly:

伤 资 查 质 娶 货 或 找 桃 换 恶 出 结 身 神
年 坏 拖 病 海

II. Give the opposite of the following words:

1. 去世　2. 无　3. 管用　4. 脑力　5. 薄　6. 教　7. 先　8. 上星期
9. 外套　10. 多次

III. Answer the following questions according to the text:

1. 他的妈妈是不是去世了?

2. 我没听说他爸爸已经不在了. 是什么时候去世的?

3. 是不是心脏病, 还是癌症?

4. 老年痴呆症是不是很容易治?

5. 他请中医治了没有?

6. 这个病是不是主要和心脏有关系?

7. 怎样可以让大脑不退化呢?

8. 我每天打太极 (tai⁴ji²: *Taiji* shadow-boxing), 这对脑细胞也有好处吗?

四十八. 彩票

A: 你美国梦实现了吗?

B: 实现了不到一半儿.

A: 此话怎讲[1]?

B: 车已经买了,房子还没有买....

A: 那你还得加把劲儿.

B: 我是在不断努力. 我每星期买
两张彩票, 已经买了八年了.

A: 你中过大奖了没有?

B: 还没有呢. 怕快了!

A: 彩票的大奖只不过[2]是"镜花
水月".

B: 不是总有人在不断地中大奖
吗?

A: 此话不假[3],可是有几个人中了
大奖了?

B: 就算[4]中大奖只不过是一场梦,
它还是一场值得一做的梦.

A: 那你就好好儿地去做你的梦吧!

48. Cai³piao⁴

A: Ni² mei³guo² meng⁴ shi²xian⁴ le ma?

B: Shi²xian⁴ le bu²dao⁴ yi²bar⁴.

A: Ci³ hua⁴ zen² jiang³?

B: Che¹ yi³jing mai³ le, fang²zi hai² mei²you²
mai³....

A: Na⁴ ni³ hai² dei³ jia¹ ba jiər⁴.

B: Wo³ shi⁴ zai⁴ bu²duan⁴ nu³li⁴. Wo² mei³
xing¹qi¹ mai² liang³ zhang¹ cai³piao⁴,
yi³jing mai³ le ba¹ nian² le.

A: Ni³ zhong⁴ guo da⁴ jiang³ le mei²you³?

B: Hai² mei²you³ ne. Pa⁴ kuai⁴ le!

A: Cai³piao⁴ de da⁴ jiang³ zhi³ bu²guo⁴ shi
"jing⁴hua¹ shui³yue⁴".

B: Bu²shi⁴ zong² you³ ren² zai⁴ bu²duan⁴ de
zhong⁴ da⁴ jiang³ ma?

A: Ci³ hua⁴ bu⁴ jia³, ke³shi⁴ you³ ji³ ge ren²
zhong⁴ le da⁴ jiang³ le?

B: Jiu⁴suan⁴ zhong⁴ da⁴ jiang³ zhi³ bu²guo⁴ shi
yi⁴ chang² meng⁴, ta¹ hai²shi yi⁴ chang²
zhi²de yi² zuo⁴ de meng⁴.

A: Na⁴ ni³ jiu⁴ hao²haor³ de qu⁴ zuo⁴ ni³de
meng⁴ ba!

48. Lottery

A: Have you realized the American dream?

B: I have realized less than half of the dream.

A: What do you mean?

B: I have bought a car but I do not own a house and….

A: Then you've got to keep working hard.

B: I do put my back into it: I buy two lottery tickets every week. I've been buying them for eight years.

A: Have you gotten any big prizes then?

B: Not yet so far, but I may get it soon!

A: The big money is only "a flower in the mirror" or "the moon in the water"!

B: But aren't there always big winners?

A: Yes, but *how many* people hit the jackpot?

B: If the jackpot is only a dream, it is still a dream worth dreaming.

A: Then go on pursuing your dream!

48. Notes

1. 此话怎讲? (Ci³ hua⁴ zen² jiang³?): What do you mean? This question is used when one wants the other party to give further explanation or elaboration. It is a little literary. The more colloquial form is 你这话什么意思? (Ni³ zhe⁴ hua⁴ shen³me yi⁴si?)

2. 只不过 (zhi³ bu²guo⁴): only, merely 我只不过是说个笑话儿. (Wo³ zhi³bu²guo⁴ shi shuo¹ ge xiao⁴huar.) I said it only as a joke. "世界是个大戏台, 世界上的男男女女只不过全是演戏的." (Shi⁴jie⁴ shi⁴ ge da⁴ xi⁴tai², shi⁴jie⁴ shang de nan²nan² nü²nü³ zhi³bu²guo⁴ quan² shi⁴ yan³xi⁴ de.) "All the world's a stage, and all the men and women merely players."
A summary of the multiple meanings of 过 (guo⁴) used in this book:
   a. *v. pass* Passage 25 (Note 4)
   b. *adv. too, over* Passage 35 (Note 1)
   c. *v. spend* (time) Passage 41 (Note 1)
   d. *part.* indicating a perfect action (neutral tone) Passage 24 (Note 6)
   e. used in the phrases: 不过 (bu²guo⁴) *but* Passage 10 (Note 5), 超过 (chao¹ guo⁴) *exceed* Passage 37, 只不过 (zhi³ bu²guo⁴) *only* Passage 48 (Note 2)

3. 此话不假. (Ci³ hua⁴ bu⁴ jia³.): That's true. (Lit. These words are not false.) More colloquial is 你说得不错. (Ni³ shuo¹ de bu²cuo⁴.)

4. 就算 (jiu⁴suan⁴): granted that, even if 就算有困难, 也不会太大. (Jiu⁴suan⁴ you³ kun⁴nan, ye bu² hui⁴ tai⁴ da⁴.) Granted that there are difficulties, they are not big ones. 就算你没错, 你也不该发火啊! (Jiu⁴suan⁴ ni³ mei²cuo⁴, ni² ye³ bu⁴ gai¹ fa¹huo³ a!) You shouldn't lose your temper even if you were right!

48. Vocabulary

彩票 cai^{3}piao^4 *n.* lottery

美国梦 mei^{3}guo^2 meng^4 *n.* American dream

实现 shi^{2}xian^4 *v.* realize, come true

...怎讲 zen^2 jiang^3 how to explain, what do you mean by

加劲 jia^{1}jin^4 *v.* make an extra effort

不断 bu^{2}duan^4 *adv.* continuously

努力 nu^{3}li^4 *v.* try hard, exert oneself

中 zhong^4 *v.* win (a prize in a lottery, etc.) Note its tone.

奖 jiang^3 *n.* prize

大奖 da^4 jiang^3 *n.* big prize, jackpot

就算 jiu^{4}suan^4 *conj.* granted that

只不过 zhi^{3}bu^{2}guo^4 *adv.* merely

镜花水月 jing^{4}hua^1 shui^{3}yue^4 flowers in a mirror and the moon in the water, sth. within sight but beyond reach, an illusion

Supplementary Vocabulary and Expressions

casino	赌场 (du^{2}chang^3)
drawing	抽奖 (chou^{1}jiang^3)
gambling	赌博 (du^{3}bo^2)
insatiable desire	贪 (tan^1)
odds	得奖机会 (de^{2}jiang^3 ji^{3}hui^4)
scratch-off	刮刮乐彩票 (gua^{1}gua^1 le^4 cai^{3}piao^4)
stake	下注 (xia^{4}zhu^4)
stop before going too far	适可而止 (shi^{4}ke^3 er^2 zhi^3)
try one's luck	碰运气 (peng^4 yun^{4}qi)

Cash or annuity?
一次拿现金, 还是每年领钱?
(Yi^{2}ci^4 na^2 xian^{4}jin^1, hai^{2}shi mei^{3}nian^2 ling^{3}qian^2?)

191

48. Exercises

I. Tone Practice:

yu^1 淤 silt up   nü^3 女 female   lü^3 铝 aluminum   ju^2 菊 mum   nüe^4 疟 malaria
ju^4 剧 drama   xu^1 虚 empty   lü^4 绿 green   qu^4 去 go   yun^4 晕 dizzy

II. Turn the phonetic spellings into Chinese characters and then translate them into English:

dao^{4}chu^4 bu^{2}duan^4 ce^{4}suo^3
yi^{2}ban^4 yu^{4}fang^2 pi^{4}ru^2
ji^{4}mo^4 bu^{4}ran^2 ke^{3}shi^4
lao^{3}lian^4 you^{2}qi^2 er^{2}qie^3

III. Fill in the blanks with words used in this text:

1. A: 酒是个坏东西, 也是个好东西.
   B: 此话 _____?
2. A: 只要肯 _____, 什么事都可以办到.
   B: 你说得对.
3. A: 她来了没有?
   B: 还没有呢. _____ 不来了.
4. A: 你经常买彩票. 中过奖没有?
   B: 没中过_____奖, 但小奖不断.
5. A: 你说大奖_____是 "镜花水月". "镜花水月"是什么意思?
   B: 镜中的花和水中的月你碰 (peng^4: touch) 得着吗? 拿 (na^2: obtain) 得到吗?
6. A: 你买彩票花了不少钱吧?
   B: 是. 但要是我不花钱, 我怎么 _____ 我的美国梦呢?
   A: 那祝你好运 (hao^{3}yun^4: good luck)!

192

四十九. 一个秘密

A: 花大嫂[1], 你这件衬衣真漂
亮!

B: 谢谢你!

A: 我喜欢上面的圆圈儿: 红、橙、
黄、绿、蓝、靛、紫. 像是一条
条[2]的彩虹!

B: 你猜, 什么颜色我最喜欢?

A: 红的?

B: 不对.

A: 紫的?

B: 不对. ... 金黄色. 你呢?

A: 我喜欢黑和白. 素净的衣服和
花衣服一样好看.

B: 对. 不过我还是爱好[3]彩色的.
...
告诉你一个秘密: 我的内衣、
内裤、胸罩都是五颜六色[4]的.

A: 你这是穿给你先生看的吧?

B: 别开玩笑[5]!

49. Yi² ge Mi⁴mi⁴

A: Hua¹ da⁴sao³, ni³ zhei⁴ jian⁴ chen⁴yi¹
zhen¹ piao⁴liang!

B: Xie⁴xie ni!

A: Wo² xi³huan shang⁴mian de yuan²quar¹:
hong², cheng², huang², lü⁴, lan², dian⁴,
zi³. Xiang⁴ shi yi⁴ tiao²tiao de
cai³hong².

B: Ni³ cai¹, shen²me yan²se⁴ wo³ zui⁴
xi³huan?

A: Hong² de?

B: Bu² dui⁴.

A: Zi³ de?

B: Bu² dui⁴. ... Jin¹ huang² se⁴. Ni³ ne?

A: Wo² xi³huan hei¹ he² bai². Su⁴jing⁴ de
yi¹fu he² hua¹ yi¹fu yi¹yang⁴ hao³kan⁴.

B: Dui⁴. Bu²guo⁴ wo³ hai²shi ai⁴hao⁴
cai³se⁴ de.... Gao⁴suo ni yi² ge mi⁴mi⁴:
wo³de nei⁴yi¹, nei⁴ku⁴, xiong¹zhao⁴ dou¹
shi⁴ wu³yan²liu⁴se⁴ de.

A: Ni³ zhe⁴ shi chuan¹ gei² ni³ xian¹sheng
kan⁴ de ba?

B: Bie² kai¹ wan²xiao⁴!

49. A Secret

A: Mrs. Hua. Your shirt is so beautiful!

B: Thank you.

A: I like the circles on it: red, orange, yellow, green, blue, indigo, and purple. They look like many rainbows.

B: Guess what my favorite color is!

A: Red?

B: No.

A: Purple?

B: No. … I like golden yellow most. How about you?

A: I like black and white. Quiet colored clothes are as beautiful as bright colored ones.

B: True, but I still prefer colorful clothes. … I'll tell you a secret: all my undershirts, underpants, and bras are very colorful.

A: That's for your husband to admire?

B: Stop joking!

49. Notes

1. 大嫂 (da^{4}sao^3): a polite form of address for a woman about one's own age If the woman is not married, use 大姐 (da^{4}jie^3). If she is about one's mother's age, use 大妈 (da^{4}ma^1) or 大娘 (da^{4}niang^2).

2. 一条条 (yi^4 tiao^{2}tiao): When two measure words are used together, they mean *a great number of*. Eg. 一朵朵鲜花儿 (yi^4 duo^{3}duo xian^1 huar^1) many fresh flowers, 一箱箱水果 (yi^4 xiang^{1}xiang shui^{2}guo^3) boxes and boxes of fruit The second measure word is usually unstressed.

3. 爱好 (ai^4 hao^4): be fond of When 好 (hao) is an adjective or adverb, it is 3rd tone; when it is a verb, it is 4th tone. 好客 (hao^{4}ke^4): be hospitable (Lit. be fond of guests), 好奇 (hao^4 qi^2): be curious (Lit. love novel things) 你好什么运动? (Ni^3 **hao^4** shen^{2}me yun^{4}dong^4?) What sports do you like?

4. 五颜六色 (wu^{3}yan^{2}liu^{4}se^4): of various colors, all the colors of rainbow (Lit. of five or six colors)

5. 开玩笑 (kai^1 wan^{2}xiao^4): crack a joke, make fun of 他老爱开玩笑. (Ta^1 lao^3 ai^4 **kai^1 wan^{2}xiao^4**.) He's always joking. 我是跟你开个玩笑, 你别当真. (Wo^3 shi^4 geng^1 ni^3 **kai^1** ge **wan^{2}xiao^4**, ni^2 bie^3 dang^4 zhen^1.) I was only joking. Don't take it seriously.

49. Vocabulary

秘密 mi⁴mi⁴   *n.* secret

大嫂 da⁴sao³   *n.* a polite form of address (Lit. big sister-in-law)

圆圈 yuan²quan¹   *n.* circle

蓝 lan²   *n., a.* blue

靛 dian⁴   *n., a.* indigo

紫 zi³   *n., a.* purple

像 xiang⁴   *v.* look like, resemble

彩虹 cai³hong²   *n.* rainbow

猜 cai¹   *v.* guess

颜色 yan²se⁴   *n.* color

金 jin¹   *n.* gold

     a. golden

素净 su⁴jing⁴   *a.* quiet (color), plain

好看 hao³kan⁴   *a.* good looking (opp. 难看 nan²kan⁴)

爱好 ai⁴hao⁴   *v.* love, be fond of (opp. 讨厌 tao³yan⁴)

彩色 cai³se⁴   *a.* colorful

内 nei⁴   *a.* inner, inside (opp. 外 wai⁴)

内衣 nei⁴yi¹   *n.* undershirt

内裤 nei⁴ku⁴   *n.* panties

胸 xiong¹   *n.* chest, breast

胸罩 xiong¹zhao⁴   *n.* bra (more colloq.: 奶罩 nai³zhao⁴, less colloq.: 文胸 wen²xiong¹)

开玩笑 kai¹ wan²xiao⁴   *v.* joke, make fun of

Supplementary Vocabulary and Expressions

dull coloring	色彩单调 (se⁴cai³ dan¹diao⁴)
flowery	花哨 (hua¹shao)
lingerie	女子内衣 (nü²zi³ nei⁴yi¹)

Hope everyone leads a colorful life.
愿每个人都过着丰富多彩的生活。
(Yuan⁴ mei³ ge ren² dou¹ guo⁴ zhe feng¹fu⁴ duo¹cai³ de sheng¹huo².)

49. Exercises

I. Pronounce the following words correctly:

衬 圈 像 罩 靛 痴 妥 耐 骑 箭
从 刷 栋 涨 该 层 却 齐 阴 内

II. Use the correct measure words with the following nouns:

一＿＿杂志 两＿＿ 水 三＿＿面包 四＿＿报纸 五＿＿电脑

III. Fill in the blanks with the appropriate words given below:
走走 够多 坐下 看了 开口 躺下 (tang³ xia⁴: lie down)

1. 别不好意思了, 你就 ＿＿＿＿＿＿ 吧! 她会同意的.
2. 别吃了, 你吃得 ＿＿＿＿＿＿ 的了.
3. 别老站着, ＿＿＿＿＿＿ 吧!
4. 别老坐着, ＿＿＿＿＿ 吧!
5. 别老躺着, 要躺出病来了. 出去＿＿＿＿＿＿吧.
6. 我的好太太! 都什么时候了, 还在看电视! 别＿＿＿＿＿＿, 上床睡觉吧!

IV. Complete the following four-character set phrases learned in this book:

物美 ＿＿＿＿ 破镜 ＿＿＿＿ 烟雾 ＿＿＿＿ 一箭 ＿＿＿＿ 一路 ＿＿＿＿
闭目 ＿＿＿＿ 四通 ＿＿＿＿ 男女 ＿＿＿＿ 丢三 ＿＿＿＿ 讨价 ＿＿＿＿

V. Answer the following questions according to the text:

1. 今天花大嫂穿的什么衬衣?

2. 她那件衬衣是条条的, 还是圈圈的?

3. 上面有几种颜色?

4. 花大嫂最喜欢什么颜色?

5. 你呢?

6. 素静的衣服和花衣服哪一种漂亮?

7. 花大嫂有一个什么秘密?

8. 你有没有什么秘密?

五十. 苦尽甘来

A: 什么事儿让你满面笑容¹的?

B: 我昨晚²和一个漂亮的中国姑娘约会了. 玩儿得真高兴!

A: 祝贺你!

B: 她就住在我家隔壁. 以前她说的话儿我不懂, 我说的话儿她也不懂. 我们只能隔着篱笆笑一笑. 昨儿我居然³可以用像样的汉语和她聊天儿了!

A: 没听说你会讲汉语!

B: 我下了一年的苦功, 把一本儿汉语会话书全部念完了.

A: 你学汉语就是为了要和那位中国姑娘谈恋爱吗?

B: 不, 不! 你可知道全世界有四分之一的人在说汉语. 学会⁴了中国话, 朋友遍天下!

A: 喔. 我现在明白了你为什么笑容满面.

50. Ku[3] Jin[4] Gan[1] Lai[2]

A: Shen[2]me shər[4] rang[4] ni[2] man[3]mian[4] xiao[4]rong[2] de?

B: Wo[3] zuo[2]wan[3] he[2] yi[2] ge piao[4]liang de zhong[1]guo[2] gu[1]niang yue[1]hui[4] le. War[2] de zhen[1] gao[1]xin[4]!

A: Zhu[4]he[4] ni!

B: Ta[1] jiu[4] zhu[4] zai[4] wo[3]jia[1] ge[2]bi[4]. Yi[3]qian[2] ta[1] shuo[1] de huar[4] wo[3] bu[4] dong[3], wo[3] shuo[1] de huar[4] ta[1] ye[3] bu[4] dong[3]. Wo[3]men zhi[3] neng[2] ge[2] zhe li[2]ba xiao[4] yi xiao[4]. Zuor[2] wo[3] ju[1]ran[2] ke[2]yi[3] yong[4] xiang[4]yang[4] de han[4]yu[3] he[2] ta[1] liao[2]tiar[1] le.

A: Mei[2] ting[1]shuo[2] ni[3] hui[4] jiang[3] han[4]yu[3]!

B: Wo[3] xia[4] le yi[4] nian[2] de ku[3]gong[1], ba[3] yi[4] bər[3] han[4]yu[3] hui[4]hua[4] shu[1] quan[2]bu[4] nian[4] wan[2] le.

A: Ni[3] xue[2] han[4]yu[3] jiu[4]shi[4] wei[4]le yao[4] he[2] nei[4] wei[4] zhong[1]guo[2] gu[1]niang tan[2] lian[4]ai[4] ma?

B: Bu[4], bu[4]! Ni[2] ke[3] zhi[1]dao quan[2] shi[4]jie[4] you[3] si[4] fen[1] zhi[1] yi[1] de ren[2] zai[4] shuo[1] han[4]yu[3]. Xue[2] hui[4] le zhong[1]guo[2] hua[4], peng[2]you bian[4] tian[1]xia[4]!

A: O[1]. Wo[3] xian[4]zai[4] ming[2]bai le ni[3] wei[4]shen[2]me xiao[4]rong[2] man[3]mian[4].

197

50. All's Well that Ends Well

A: What makes you all smiles?

B: Last evening I went out with a beautiful Chinese girl and had a really great time with her!

A: Congratulations!

B: She lives next door to me. Before, I didn't understand what she said and she didn't understand what I said. The only thing we could do was flash a smile at each other over the garden fence. But yesterday I was able to have a conversation with her *in perfect Chinese*!

A: I didn't know you speak Chinese!

B: In the past year I put a lot of time and effort into studying Chinese, and finally I finished a Chinese conversation book.

A: You studied Chinese just to date that Chinese girl?

B: Oh, no. You know, one fourth of the world population speaks Chinese. When I master Chinese I can make friends in every corner of the world!

A: Oh, now I understand why you are all smiles

50. Notes

1. 满面笑容 (man³mian⁴ xiao⁴rong²) or 笑容满面 (xiao⁴rong² man³mian⁴): be all smiles Opp. 满面愁容 (man³mian⁴ chou²rong²): looking extremely worried

2. 昨晚 (zuo² wan³): last night, short for 昨天晚上 (**zuo²**tian¹ **wan³**shang)

3. 居然 (ju¹ran²): unexpectedly 我很奇怪,他的梦想居然实现了. (Wo³ hen³ qi²guai⁴, ta¹de meng⁴xiang³ **ju¹ran²** shi²xian⁴ le.) To my surprise, his dream came true. 谁会想到他居然问出这种问题来? (Shei² hui⁴ xiang³ dao⁴ ta¹ **ju¹ran²** wen⁴chu¹ zhei¹ zhong³ wen⁴ti² lai²?) Who would have thought he would ask such a question? 没料到他居然在合同上签字了. (Mei³ liao⁴dao⁴ ta¹ **ju¹ran²** zai⁴ he²tong² shang qian¹ zi⁴ le.) Contrary to our expectation, he signed the contract. Another expression having the same meaning is 竟然 (jing⁴ran²). 那个鸟巢体育馆竟然只用了两年时间就建成了! (Nei⁴ ge niao³chao² ti³yu⁴quan³ **jing⁴ran²** zhi³ yong⁴ le liang³ nian² shi¹jian¹ jiu⁴ jian⁴ cheng² le.) Think that the Bird's Nest Stadium was completed in only two years!

4. 学会 (xue² hui⁴): learn, master 只要认真学,什么都能学会. (Zhi³yao⁴ ren⁴zhen¹ xue², shen²me dou¹ neng² **xue²hui⁴**.) If you study conscientiously, you can learn anything. 学会了中国话,就能实现中国梦. (**Xue²hui⁴** le zhong¹guo² hua⁴, jiu⁴ neng² shi²xian⁴ zhong¹guo² meng⁴.) Learn Chinese, and you will realize your Chinese dream. 她一学就会,但一会就忘. (Ta¹ yi⁴ **xue²** jiu⁴ **hui⁴**, dan⁴ yi² hui⁴ jiu⁴ wang⁴.) The moment she studies anything, she learns it, but the moment she learns it, she forgets it. The negative of 学会 (xue² hui⁴) is 学不会 (xue² bu² hui⁴). 他学了又学,就是学不会. (Ta¹ xue² le you⁴ xue², jiu⁴shi⁴ **xue² bu² hui⁴**.) He studied and studied, but could not learn it.

198

50. Vocabulary

尽 jin^4	*v.* finish
甘 gan^1	*n.* sweetness (opp. 苦 ku^3)
苦尽甘来 ku^3 jin^4 gan^1 lai^2	When bitterness is finished, sweetness begins. (Painstaking efforts are finally rewarded.)
满 man^3	*a.* full
笑 xiao^4	*v.* smile (opp. 哭 ku^1)
容 rong^2	*n.* appearance
约会 yue^{1}hui^4	*v.* date
高兴 gao^{1}xin^4	*a.* glad, happy (opp. 扫兴 sao^{3}xing^4)
祝贺 zhu^{4}he^4	*v.* congratulate
懂 dong^3	*v.* understand
隔 ge^2	*prep.* over, from the other side of
篱笆 li^{2}ba	*n.* fence
昨儿 zuor^2	*n., adv.* yesterday (colloq. of 昨天 zuo^{2}tian^1)
居然 ju^{1}ran^2	*adv.* unexpectedly
像样 xiang^{4}yang^4	*a.* presentable, decent
汉语 han^{4}yu^3	*n.* the Chinese language
讲 jiang^3	*v.* speak
苦功 ku^{2}gong^1	*n.* painstaking effort
会话 hui^{4}hua^4	*n.* conversation
全部 quan^{2}bu^4	*adv.* completely *a.* whole, entire
念 nian^4	*v.* read, study
谈恋爱 tan^2 lian^{4}ai^4	*v.* woo, show love
学会 xue^2 hui^4	*v.* learn
天下 tian^{1}xia^4	*n.* world (Lit. under heaven)

Supplementary Vocabulary and Expressions

lot by which people are brought together, synergy of conditions — 缘分 (yuan^{2}fen^4)

Contacts in the course of time bring about love.
日久生情. (Ri^{4}jiu^3 sheng^1 qing^2.)

May a man and a woman who have mutual affinity finally become husband and wife!
愿有情人终成眷属! (Yuan^4 you^3 qing^2 ren^2 zhong^1 cheng^2 juan^{4}shu^3!)

Smiles convey affection.
三笑留情. (San^1 xiao^4 liu^2 qing^2.)

Where there is a will there is a way. 有志者事竞成.
(You^3 zhi^4 zhe^3 shi^4 jing^4 cheng^2.)

You will feel high-spirited when you come upon a happy event.
人逢喜事精神爽.
(Ren^2 feng^2 xi^{3}shi^4 jing^{1}shen shuang^3.)

50. Exercises

I. Give the phonetic spellings of the following words and practice reading them:

粉　风　份　银　英　影　音　因　明　民　名　今　京　斤　经
进　镜　劲　平　贫　瓶　姓　心　新　信　行　幸　请　亲　情

II. Make sentences with the following words:

1. 高兴:
2. 居然:
3. 天下:
4. 不断:
5. 一切:
6. 恐怕:

III. Use the correct measure words with the following nouns:

六 ____ 狗　七 ____ 猫　八 ____ 客人　九 ____ 水果　十 ____ 房子

IV. Complete the following four-character phrases learned in this book:

____ 多夫　____ 攻毒　____ 医头　____ 医脚　____ 水月
____ 甘来　____ 满面　____ 脑涨　____ 六色　____ 背痛

V. Complete the following dialog according to the text:

1. A: 昨晚你和谁约会了?
   B:
2. A: 她长得怎么样?
   B:
3. A: 她住得离你家远吗?
   B:
4. A: 你对她是一见钟情, 还是三笑留情, 还是日久生情?
   B:
5. A: 你为什么不早一点和她约会?
   B:
6. A: 你中文学了多久了?
   B:
7. A: 你是为了要和她谈恋爱, 才学中文的吗?
   B:
8. A: 真是 "世上无难事, 只怕有心人"! 祝贺你!
   B:

练习参考答案
Key to Exercises

Passage 1

II. 1. 进 jin^4　2. 坐 zuo^4　　3. 谢谢 xie^{4}xie　4. 再见 zai^{4}jian^4　5. 喝 he^1

　6. 吧 ba　　7. 请 qing^3　8. 什么 shen^{2}me　9. 你好 ni^{2}hao^3　10. 橙汁儿 cheng^{2}zher^1

III. 1. a　　2. c　　　3. b　　　　4. a

Passage 2

I. yi^1 一　　diar^3 点儿　　shen^{2}me 什么　　hai^{2}shi 还是　　wo^3 我

II. 1. b　　　2. c　　　3. b　　　4. a

III. 1. 一杯水　2. 两杯咖啡　3. 八杯橙汁　4. 妈妈和爸爸　　5. 哥哥和妹妹

　6. 姐姐和弟弟　　　7. 她妈妈　　8. 他家　　　　9. 我有一个弟弟和一个

妹妹.　　　　10. 我家有四口人.

Passage 3

III 1. 你有没有空　2. 你有没有妹妹　3. 你有没有弟弟　4. 你有没有零钱

Passage 4

I. 1. yi^1　　2. yi^{2}ding^4　3. chi^1　　4. shuo^1　5. wan^{3}shang

　6. he^2　7. jiu^4　　8. gong^{1}fu　9. zhi^{1}dao　10. hai^{2}shi

II. Monday 星期一　　Tuesday 星期二　　Wednesday 星期三

　Thursday 星期四　　Friday 星期五　　Saturday 星期六

　Sunday 星期天 or 星期日

III. 1. 你是中国人吗? 我不是中国人.　　2. 你说普通话吗? 我不说普通话.

　3. 你们星期六有空儿吗? 我们没空.　　4. 普通话难学吗? 不难学.

　5. 你想喝水吗? 我不想.　　　　6. 她星期六一定等你吗? 不一定.

IV. 1. 他不是中国人.　　　　2. 广东话难学吗?

　3. 星期三她等我.　　　　4. 她星期二还是星期四来?

Passage 5

II 1. 几个　2. 多少　3. 多少　4. 几个 (If you choose 多少, what will the question

　imply?)

III. 1. 他还没有进来.　　2. 他们已经吃饭了.　3. 她已经结婚了, 但还没有孩子.

　4. 她还没有结婚, 所以还没有孩子.

IV. 1. 她一个孩子也没有.　2. 我一口茶也没喝.　3. 他一点儿空也没有.

V. 1. 我只要有空就来.　2. 只要你肯下功夫, 普通话就很容易学.

　3. 只要他来, 我就走.　4. 只要你想来, 你就来.

Passage 6

201

II. 1. 他不是中国人.　　2. 他没有儿子.　　　3. 那不是乌龙茶.　　4. 她不一定来.
　　5. 你没有女儿吗?　　6. 普通话不难学.　　7. 他爸爸没有癌症.　8. 他爸爸不知道喝茶可以预防癌症.

III. 1. 普通话还是广东话　　2. 有空还是没空　　3. 儿子还是女儿　　4. 好学还是不好学
　　(or 难学)　　5. 星期六还是星期天

IV. 1. 好, 谢谢!　　2. 很好. / 不错. / 不太好. / 很不好.　　3. (经常) 喝茶可以预防癌症.
　　4. 两个.

Passage 7

II. 1. 我叫…　　2. 我住在…　　3. (123) 456-7890　　4. 结了. / 还没有.　　5. 我没有孩子. /
我有 X 个孩子: X 个儿子, X 个女儿.

III 1. 一 三 五 七 九 yi¹ san³ wu³ qi¹ jiu³

　　2. 二 四 六 八 零 er² si⁴ liu⁴ ba¹ ling²

　　3. 七 九 四 零 三 二 六 八 一 五 qi¹ jiu³ si⁴ ling² san¹ er² liu⁴ ba¹ yi¹ wu³

IV. 1. 一三二五　　2. 七四八一　　3. 九八七二　　4. 一六八八六零
　　5. 九八零五三零八五四一七

Passage 8

II. 1. 七十　　2. 五十　　3. 六十四　　4. 四十二　　5. 八十一

III. 1. 你爸爸多大岁数了　　2. 你妹妹多大了　　3. 你小弟弟几岁　　4. 你多大了/ 你
　　呢

IV. 1. 我妈妈很好, 你妈妈呢?　　2. 黄小姐在办公室, 李小姐呢?
　　3. 你有三个男孩, 他呢?　　4. 我没有现钱, 你呢?
　　5. 你想吃好的, (你) 钱呢?　　6. 人呢? 我一个也没见!

Passage 9

III. 1. 可以. / 对不起, 我走不快. / 我已经走得很快了 (or 我已经走得够 gou⁴: enough
　　快的了), 不能再快了. / 我喜欢慢慢儿地 (慢慢儿地 man⁴mar de: slowly) 走.

　　2. 可以看了. / 还不能看. / 还不行 (不行 bu⁴xing²: no, won't do).

　　3. 可以. 我今年…. / 对不起, 我不能告诉你. / 这是我的秘密 (mi⁴mi⁴: secret) 我哪能
　　告诉你啊!

　　4. 可以. / 不能. / 我不知道.

IV. 1. 这么些书你一定看不完.

　　2. 你家有八口人, 家里哪能不热闹!

　　3. 他已经学了两年中文了, 中文哪能说不好?

　　4. 黄小姐有空, 她一定来!

Passage 10

II. 6:00 六点　　3:15 三点十五分 / 三点一刻　　8:30 八点半 / 八点三十分
　　7:45 七点三刻 / 七点四十五分 / 差一刻八点　　9:07 九点零七分 / 九点过七分
　　10:58 十点五十八分 / 差两分十一点　　4:39 四点三十九分
　　2:03 两点零三分 / 两点过三分

202

III. 1. 你每天几点睡觉?

    2. 你太太什么时候上班?

    3. 周末我十点才起床.

    4. 我太太每天晚上看电视, 所以睡得晚.

IV.1. 不过黄小姐还没有来   2. 可是我的中文还不太好   3. 可是一看电视就(要 / 会 / 想) 睡觉   4. 不过不知道他办公室的 (or 手机的) 电话号码

V. Sentences 2, 3, 4, 6, 8, and 10.

Passage 11

I. 总是 zong³shi   女 nü³   结婚 jie²hun¹   黄 huang²   对不起 dui⁴buqi³
   休息 xiu¹xi   大夫 dai⁴fu   舒服 shu¹fu   起床 qi³chuang²   睡觉 shui⁴jiao⁴

II. 1. A: 喂! X (李先生) 在吗?

    B: 他不在.

    A: 他去哪儿了?

    B: 他去看大夫了.

    A: 喔! 他哪儿 (or 有什么) 不舒服? / 他生病了? (生病 sheng¹bing⁴: be sick)

    B: 他发烧了.

  2. A: 喂! 小李在吗?

    B: 她在.

    A: 请她 听电话 .

    B: 好.

    C: 喂!

    A: 是小李吗?

    C: 是 / 我是 / 我就是 .

    A: 你好吗? 小李!

    C: 我很好, 谢谢!

III.1. 你爸爸每天什么时候睡觉?

    2. 他家是个大家庭.

    3. 我太太一看电视就睡觉.

    4. 我看了《红楼梦》, 可是还没有看《水浒》.

    5. 今天她可能不来.

Passage 12

II. 1.马上 2.好好儿 3.当然 4.可是 5.上班 6.理想 7.一...就 8.多半

III.1.什么信儿 / 什么事儿

    2.是, ... (sb.) 还没来 / 是, 我们要等 sb. 他一来, 就开会

    3.她哪儿不舒服 / 那你不来上班了

    4.你的中文已经不错了 / 所以你还得下功夫

Passage 13

III.1.我要买汉英词典. / 我要买英汉词典. / 我什么都不买. / 我不买词典,我要买....

    2.我先生姓张 / 他姓张 (李、王、黄...).

3. 可以了. / 说得很好. / 说得还不错. / 还不太好. / 还不太行.

4. … (两百五十, etc.) 块.

5. 不, 在中国, 女人结了婚, 不用先生的姓. / 不. 在中国结了婚的女人还用自己的
姓. (自己的 zi⁴ji³ de: one's own)

IV. 1. 再让我好好儿地想一下.

2. 对不起, 请您等一下.

3. 张先生没来, 不过张太太来了. / 张太太没来, 不过张先生来了.

4. 您一喝就知道味儿不错.

V. 他一学就 (会). 他一请就 (来). 他一去就(回). 他一回就(睡).

Passage 14

II. 1. 就 2. 陪 3. 咱们 4. 得 5. 有益

III. 1. 妈妈给小女儿买了水果.

2. 我要给我爸爸打电话.

3. 老黄给小黄捎了个信儿.

4. 李大夫给小张的妹妹瞧病.

5. 张先生给他们 (or 大伙儿 da⁴huor³: all the people) 说明了这本词典的用法.

IV. 1. There's a dictionary here and there's another over there.

2. If you still have anything to say, put it off until tomorrow.

3. One more person has not come yet.

4. There're two cups of tea there: one is oolong, and the other is also oolong.

5. He invited Lao Huang, Lao Li, Lao Zhang, and Xiao Wang as well.

Passage 15

III. 1. Today is Sunday.

2. She eats fish and vegetables every day.

3. It's getting late. I should go now. I'll come again tomorrow.

4. How many days do you need to finish that book?

5. I'd like to ask for a day's leave.

6. He stayed there for God knows how many days!

7. It has been raining every day these days.

8. You keep saying you would come to visit me, but when have you been here?

9. The weather forecast says it will rain in the day-time today, but look at the sky:
does it look like rain?

10. A: A rainy day is a day when a host puts up his guest for the night. So will you ask
me to stay?

B: When it rains, it may mean that God wants to put you up. But it is God, not me.

IV. 1. 好 2. 大 3. 慢 4. 快 5. 说 / 开口 6. 冷 7. 多 8. 吃

Passage 16

II. 1. 你词典买了没? 2. 他零钱给你了没? 3. 她走了没?

4. 你请了假没? 5. 他上纽约了没?

III. 1. 你买的是单程票还是来回票 2. 你下星期五上北京还是去纽约

3. 会上你用了中文, 还是英文 4. 你喜欢吃面包, 还是米饭

5. 天气预报说明天下雨还是不下雨

IV. 1. b   2. a   3. c   4. c   5. a

Passage 17

III. 1. 也   2. 都   3. 听   4. 有时候   5. 什么   6. 在   7. 成   8. 没

9. 贵   10. 不然

Passage 18

I. 哪儿 nar³   哪些 nei³xie¹   多少 duo¹shao   医院 yi¹yuan⁴   先生 xian¹sheng

孩子 hai²zi   咱们 zan²men   瞧 qiao²   来回 lai²hui²   哎哟 ai¹yo¹

II. 1. 月   2. 旅游   3. 准备   4. 值得   5. 祝

III. 1. 我们明年到中国去.   2. 你去哪儿吃饭?   3. 你到北京去吗?

4. 你想去纽约还是去上海?   5. 老黄到医院去了.

Passage 19

II. 1. 舒服   2. 休息   3. 来回   4. 块儿

III. 1. 好极了   2. 还好   3. 不太好   4. 好得很

IV. 1. 红烧鱼好吃得很.   2. 今天天气闷热得很.   3. 游泳池里的水凉得很啊!

4. 她睡觉晚得很.   5. 中国的家常饭菜脂肪少得很.

Passage 20

II. 1. 在纽约   2. 在家   3. 在飞机上   4. 在楼上   5. 在汽车下面 / 底下

6. 在回来的路上

III. 1. 十多个人   2. 三个多月   3. 八十多岁   4. 三十多天

IV. 1. 太好了   2. 好 / 行 / 干吧 / 这么办 / 好好儿干吧   3. 你不看病啦 / 你去哪儿

4. 就走吧 / 就得快点儿走   5. 就吃了

Passage 21

II. 1. 坏   2. 地   3. 下   4. 去   5. 有   6. 多   7. 小   8. 晚 / 迟   9. 早晨

10. 经常

III. 1. 书   2. 菜 / 水果 / 东西   3. 茶 / 果汁   4. 话   5. 人 / 客人

IV. 1. 他把我的汽车修好了.   2. 我把她叫"大姐".   3. 他把开会的时间忘了.

4. 把第一本学完了, 再学第二本.

V. 1. 上 / 去 / 下中国馆子了. / 到中国馆子去了.   2. 吃了三个菜. / 三个.   3. 没吃
鱼. 但我吃了鱼香肉丝, 肉丝里有鱼的香味儿.   4. 很喜欢. 我吃饭不可以没有肉.
/ 我每顿都要肉.   5. 吃了豆腐. 豆腐也算 (suan⁴: be regarded as) 蔬菜吧?.   6. 肉丝
儿和豆腐的味道好极了, 但是宫爆鸡丁儿的味道不怎么样.   7. 有点儿高.   8. 难得
吃吃, 有什么关系?

Passage 22

I. 大 (da⁴) 鱼   大 (dai⁴) 夫   觉 (jue²) 得   睡觉 (jiao⁴)
地 (di⁴) 方   好好地 (de)   生 (sheng¹) 小孩   张先生 (sheng)

III. 1. 至少   2. 至多   3. 至少   4. 至多   5. 至多   6. 至少

205

IV. 1. 不可以缺少　2. 小时　　3. 平时　　4. 节目　　5. 那　　　6. 只有

　　7. 再说　　　　8. 适合 / 合适

Passage 23

II. 1. 奶奶　　　　2. 爷爷　　　　3. 从　　　4. 时候　　　　5. 见面

III. 1. Hello!　　　2. fixed　　　3. several　　4. quite a while　　5. very

　　6. good　　　7. very　　　8. how many　9. a lot of　　　10. fine day

　　11. a little better 12. recovered　13. tasty　　　14. interesting　　15. OK

IV. 1. 我奶奶对我**可**好!

　　2. 昨儿夜里的雨下得**可**大!

　　3. 你**可**来了, 让我好等啊!

　　4. 你**可**知道李小姐要结婚了?

　　5. 这**可**不是我说的.

　　6. 我**可**没这么说.

Passage 24

II. 1. 牙齿越刷越白.　　2. 他每年都要到中国去探亲.　　3. 经常洗牙, 牙肉就不会出血了.　　4. 我半小时前吃过午饭了.　　5. 你才来, 让我好等啊!

III. 1. 至少两次. (最好每次吃完饭以后都刷牙.) 2. 可能感冒 (发烧)了. / 要吃头痛片吗?

　　3. 得去看大夫了. / 得去医院了. 4. 干吗不去看大夫啊? 5. 他多大岁数了? / 什么病?

IV. 1. 我没有想到她会来, 她**倒**来了. 2. 他病没有治好, 钱**倒**花了不少.　　3. 钱花得不多, 饭菜**倒**是很好吃. 4. 我奶奶大毛病**倒**没有, 就是小毛小病很多. 5. 他奶奶快九十了, 身体**倒**还健康.

Passage 25

II. 1. a　　2. c　　　3. a　　　4. c

III. 1. 南　2. 北　　3. 东　　4. 西　5. 东　　6. 北　7. 西

Passage 26

II. 1. 好　2. 晚 / 早　3. 早 / 晚　4. 多　5. 久　6. 大　7. 舒服　8. 贵

III. 1. 到处 (dao⁴chu⁴)　2. 喜欢 (xi³huan)　3. 友好 (you²hao³)　　　4. 值得 (zhi²de²)

　　5. 麻烦 (ma²fan)　6. 印象 (yin⁴xiang⁴) 7. 打电话 (da³dian⁴hua⁴)　8. 素菜 (su⁴cai⁴)

　　9. 简单 (jian³dan¹)　10. 探望 (tang⁴wang⁴)

IV. 1. 姑娘　2. 水果　3. 会议　4. 天气　5. 节目　6. 大鱼大肉

Passage 27

II. 1. 定 / 订 / 买　2. 游　3. 抽　4. 吃　5. 说 / 讲 / 学　6. 动

III. 1. 他把房间的钥匙给了我. 2. 她奶奶给了她她爷爷的相片儿. 3. 爷爷把一本最好看的书给了我. 4. 奶奶给她吃最好的菜.

IV. 1. 可以看一下您的相片儿吗? 2. 可以把您的词典给我用一下吗? /可以用一下您的词典吗? 3. 我可以定一个单人房间吗?　4. 我可以在这儿抽烟吗? 5. 您可以告诉我您今年多大吗? /您可以告诉我您的年龄 (or 岁数) 吗?

Passage 28

II. 1. 这事儿他还不知道. 要么给他打个电话, 要么请人给他捎个信儿.

2. 他要么不知道, 要么装糊涂.

3. 要么进来, 要么出去, 不要老站在门口.

4. 要么你跟我一起去, 要么你呆在家里. 你自己定.

III. 1. 站着　2. 听着　3. 开着　4. 走着　5. 瞧着

IV. 1. 看出　2. 听出　3. 闻出　4. 喝出　5. 摸出

Passage 29

II. 1. neutral (weak)　2. neutral　3. 3rd　4. 2nd　5. 2nd　6. 3rd

III. 1. 眼科 (小儿科 pediatrics, or 外科 surgery, etc.) 大夫

2. 睡得太多了

3. 她不爱我

4. 钱不够 / 没有钱 / 我太太不准我买

5. 当不了 / 进不了医科大学 / 学医时间太长了 / 没有钱交学费 / 我不是念大学的
料 (I am no college material.)

IV. 1. 你半夜两点才睡觉! 难怪你今天迟到了.

2. 难怪他这几天这么高兴, 他考上医科大学了.

3. 这几个月来, 他一直工作过度. 难怪他要病倒了.

4. 难怪找不到人, 都开会去了.

Passage 30

II. 1. 快乐　2. 平安　3. 长寿　4. ... (早日康复 kang¹fu⁴: recovered, be well again /
考上大学 / 好运 hao³yun⁴: good luck)

III. 1. 因为他有病.　2. 因为是我太太的生日.　3. 因为是天气预报说的 / 因为
我听了天气预报.　4. 因为医生挣的钱多.　5. 因为他老是浑身没劲儿.

6. 因为我家人多.

IV. 1. 进来　2. 好　3. 少　4. 好　5. 右　6. 休息　7. 好看 / 漂亮

8. 闷热　9. 睡觉　10. 难得

Passage 31

III. 1. 他的孙子**考上**了普林斯顿大学了.

2. 昨天他在街上**碰上**了她.

3. 他一见到她就**爱上**了她. (A set phrase is 一 见 钟 情 yi² jian⁴ zhong¹ qing².)

4. 我去晚了, 没**吃上**饭.

5. 她到农村去, **见上**了她二十年没见面的老奶奶.

6. 他学会了普通话, **交上**了好多中国朋友.

IV. 1. 不大　2. 大不　3. 不大　4. 大不　5. 不大　6. 不大　7. 不大/ 大不　8. 不大

Passage 32

II. 1. 不, 只有四号窗口可以换钱.

2. 可以. 可以用信用卡换钱.

207

3. 是. 人民币也可以换成美元.

4. 要填一张表, 要在上面签个名.

5. 汇率就是一个国家的钱可以换多少外国的钱.

6. 要. 银行要扣一些钱.

7. 这是手续费.

8. 不行. 只能取人民币.

III.1. 变成　2. 办成　3. 说成　4. 病成　5. 结成　6. 换成　7. 煮成　8. 磨成

Passage 33

II. 1. 问一问　2.看　看　3. 听一听　4. 摸一摸　5. 猜一猜　6. 想一想

7. 尝一尝　8. 闻一闻

III.1. 是误点了. 2. 布告牌上说的. 3. 问过了. 说那边 (na⁴bian¹: there) 天气不好. 4.
大约一个半小时. 5. 到登机口去等吧! 6. 我带了一本杂志, 可以消磨时间.

7. 你就闭目养神吧! / 到免税商店(mian³shui⁴ shang¹dian⁴: duty free stores) 去转转
(zhuan⁴zhuan: stroll) 吧! / 我的杂志借 (jie⁴: lend) 给你看. / 你去喝杯咖啡吧!

Passage 34

II. 1. 到处　2. 王国　3. 高原　4. 听说　5. 庆祝

6. 原因　7. 身份　8. 辛苦　9. 航空　10. 现在

III.1. 工具　2. 美国　3. 印象　4. 发展　5. 发达　6. 主要　7. 锻炼

8. 一箭

IV.1. 那匹 (pi³: *meas.* used with horse, donkey, etc.) 马又高有大. / 他的哥哥长得又高
又大. 2. 那位上海姑娘又聪明, 又漂亮. 3. 这事儿他办得又快又好.

4. 抽烟、喝酒又花钱, 又有害健康.

V. 1. Even his dad smiled. 2. She didn't answer cven my letter. 3. He went away
without even turning his head. 4. Even old people all came out to watch the
excitement. 5. Embarrassment flushed her face. 6. He was so absorbed in Mahjong
that he even ignored meals and sleep.

Passage 35

II. 1. 她唱得好得很. 2. 美国的交通很发达. 3. 你的意思我明白得很.

4. 老师挣的钱很少, 可是他们的工作重要得很. 5. 以前他们生活很苦.

III. 1. 过肥　2. 过谦　3. 过奖　4. 过快　5. 过量　6. 过高　7. 过早

IV. 1. 感冒　2. 过敏　3. 宠物/花生 (hua¹sheng¹: peanut)　4. 就　5. 严重

Passage 36

II. 1. 霉　2. 跟　3. 撞　4. 扁　5. 破　6. 漏　7. 上　8. 新　9. 车祸

10. 速　11. 刹　12. 超　13. 罚　14. 点　15. 公道

III.1. 出了什么事儿?　2.这事儿出在 1977 年. 3. 老黄的胃出了点儿毛病.

4. 他家里出了一件大喜事儿. 5. 小心开车, 别出车祸.

Passage 37

II. hungry 饿　　　fry 炒　　　car accident 车祸　　braking 刹车

cough 咳嗽   pollen 花粉   sign 签名   bottle 瓶

III.1. 你们昨天上馆子吃饭了吗?

2. 你们几个人去的?

3. 和谁一起去的?

4. 你们是不是点了好多菜?

5. 你们是在麦当劳吃的吗?

6. 你们吃了什么?

7. 他们也有盒饭吗?

8. 你们为什么不吃盒饭?

9. 他们有鱼香肉丝吗?

10. 你们喝了酒没有?

11. 你们喝了酒还能开车吗?

12. 你喜欢那家快餐店,还是喜欢麦当劳?

IV.1. 我哥哥比我大两岁. / 我比哥哥小两岁.

2. 好多人汉语讲得比我好得多.

3. 我比我爱人多吃了半斤饺子. /我太太比我少吃了半斤饺子.

4. 那家中国快餐店比麦当劳供应得还要快.

Passage 38

II. near 近   dare 敢   peach 桃子   handling 手续(费)

spirit 神   life 生活   bedroom 卧室 soul 灵魂

III.1. 她什么水果都不爱吃.

2. 每天吃个生洋葱, 什么人都不敢靠近你了.

3. 北京的什么地方我都去过.

4. 书上讲的也不是什么都对.

5. 你这样的人, 什么用处都没有.

6. 我什么样的人没见过?

IV.1. Yes. 2. Yes   3. No   4. Yes.   5. No

V. 1. 汗   2. 老是 3. 不如   4. 不敢

Passage 39

II. glasses 眼镜   frame 边   muddled 糊涂   strange 奇怪 black 黑

III.1. She walked along, singing.

2. I think he will come again, because he has got some benefit.

3. Please wait outside. Do you see I am busy now?

4. You guessed it right.

5. He is standing dreaming!

6. He has realized his American dream.

7. Have you got the ticket to Beijing?

8. She was watching TV and, watching and watching, fell asleep.

IV.1. 什么样的车我们都修.

2. 你买的是什么样的手机?

3. 他以为我们是什么样的人?

209

4. 没见她才两年. 瞧她老成什么样子了?

5. 不管报纸上说的是些什么样的废话, 有些人总会相信的.

Passage 40

II. 1. 眼镜　　2. 办公室　　3. 人　　4. 话 / 事儿

5. 东西 / 食品　6. … (anything)　7. 话儿; 事儿　8. 花儿

III.1. 您要什么样的项链?　2. 您看看, 这一条怎么样?　3. 有有有! 你再看看这条怎么样?　4. 这些可都是真的一级品. 恐怕你找不到再好的了.　5. 您慢走.

Passage 41

II. society 社会　　lonely 孤独, 寂寞　　balance 平衡　　　　perhaps 恐怕
talk nonsense 胡说　earnestly 认真　　not as good as 不如　　sneeze 打喷嚏
pitiful 可怜的　　reason 原因, 理由

III.1. I have two questions to ask you.

2. Something has gone wrong with my engine.

3. We are talking about the obesity problem in the U. S.

4. She is always asking questions.

5. The trip went off without mishap.

6. The government has a lot of problems to solve.

IV. 1. 过　2. 认真　3. 认为 / 说　4. 同意　5. 恢复　6. 不到

Passage 42

II. 1. 不了　　　　2. 却　　3. 看作　　　4. 一点儿没/没　5. 副作用/作用/用

III.1. 他的病好了.　2. 治过.　3. 是中医治好的.　4. 是的.　　　5. 中药以草本植物为主.

6. 化学品副作用大.　7. "以毒攻毒" 就是用毒的东西来治病.

8. 我很相信中医.

IV.*Yin*: moon, girl, night, dark, cold, electron, cathode, privacy, low, back, death, wet, slow, narrow, shut, quiet, soft, peace

Yang: sun, boy, day, bright, hot, proton, anode, publicity, high, front, life, dry, quick, wide, open, noisy, hard, war

Passage 43

II. 1. 上个月买的.　　2. 是中国制造的.　3. 质量很好 / 没问题.　4. 功能齐全.

5. 价钱也不贵.　6. 还用它买机票、定旅馆房间、看电影, 什么都要用上它.

7. 你说得对. 不可一日无此君!　　8. 有过.　9. 旧的给儿子和女儿用了.

10. 不. 他们查什么资料? 他们玩游戏 (you²xi⁴: games) 呢!

III.1. 没有一天不用它. 2.《红楼梦》这本书你不能不看. 3. 有件事我不能不告诉你.

4. 不该说的话不说, 不该做的事不做. / 不说不该说的话, 不做不该做的事.

5. 他不是不知道, 是不肯说. 6. 他的话你不可不信, 也不可全信.

7. 见到她的人没有一个不喜欢她. 8. 他说要来, 就不会不来.

IV.1. 那本书不但有趣, 还 (or 而且) 有教育意义.

2. 他的太太不但漂亮, 而且 (还) 有才华.

3. 这颗珠子不但圆而且亮.

4. 中国造的东西不但价廉, 而且物美.

Passage 44

II. 1. 你这个人总是不听话.
2. 我喜欢她那条裙子. / 她喜欢我那条裙子.
3. 我那位太太喜欢穿裙子.
4. 他们那些老人每天都锻炼身体.

III. 1. 很冷, 风很大. 2. 她穿得很单薄. 3. 裙子. 4. 没有. 5. 不容易感冒
6. 意思是早晨很冷, 中午很热. 天气变化很快. 7. 冷就穿上, 热就脱下. 这样就不容易感冒了.

Passage 45

I. 台 tai^2 太 tai^4 填 tian^2 天 tian^1 玩 wan^2 晚 wan^3 想 xiang^3 香 xiang^1
坐 zuo^4 左 zuo^3 生 sheng^1 省 sheng^2 探 tan^4 谈 tan^2 无 wu^2 乌 wu^1
文 wen^2 问 wen^4 已 yi^3 益 yi^4

II. 1. 来得了   2. 来不了   3. 算不了   4. 治不了; 过不了   5. 死不了   6. 受不了
7. 省不了   8. 受得了

III. A: 喝酒   B: 不多   A: 健   B: 过; 伤   A: 掌握   B: 几 / 多   A: 错   B: 都   A: 黄酒
B: 不到

Passage 46

I. 汁 zhi^1 治 zhi^4 之 zhi^1 直 zhi^2 脂 zhi^1 质 zhi^4 值 zhi^2 烟 yan^1
炎 yan^2 因 yin^1 印 yin^4 阴 yin^1 癌 ai^2 爱 ai^4 彩 cai^3 菜 cai^4
猜 cai^1 白 bai^2 百 bai^3 带 dai^4 呆 dai^1 敢 gan^3 干 gan^4 钱 qian^2
千 qian^1 前 qian^2 也 ye^3 液 ye^4

II. shuang^{1}fang^1 双方 two sides   zhao^{2}liang^2 着凉 catch a cold   qing^{2}tie^3 请帖 invitation card
chen^{4}yi^1 衬衣 shirt   dang^{1}ran^2 当然 certainly   liao^{2}tian^1 聊天 chat
ying^{4}lang^4 硬朗 healthy   zhu^{4}he^4 祝贺 congratulate   ti^{2}jian^3 体检 health checkup
tong^{2}yi^4 同意 agree

III. 1. a   2. c   3. b   4. c   5. a   6. b

Passage 47

I. 伤 shang^1 资 zi^1 查 cha^2 质 zhi^4 娶 qu^3 货 huo^4 或 huo^4 找 zhao^3 桃 tao^2
换 huan^4 恶 e^3 出 chu^1 结 jie^2 身 shen^1 神 shen^2 年 nian^2 坏 huai^4 拖 tuo^1
病 bing^4 海 hai^3

II. 1. 出生 / 健在   2. 有   3. 无效   4. 体力   5. 厚   6. 学   7. 后   8. 下星期
9. 内衣 10. 一次

III. 1. 他妈妈健在.   2. 三个月以前.   3. 都不是. 是老年痴呆症.   4. 不容易治.
5. 请了.   6. 主要和脑子有关系. 大脑衰退会引起 (ying^{2}qi^3 : lead to) 痴呆.
7. 平时要多用脑子, 不要让它退化.   8. 有好处. 对身心都有好处

Passage 48

211

II. dao^{4}chu^4 到处 everywhere   bu^{2}duan^4 不断 continuously   ce^{4}suo^3 厕所 rest room

yi^{2}ban^4 一半 half   yu^{4}fang^2 预防 prevent   pi^{4}ru^2 譬如 for instance

ji^{4}mo^4 寂寞 lonely   bu^{4}ran^3 不然 otherwise   ke^{3}shi^4 可是 but

lao^{3}lian^4 老练 skillful   you^{2}qi^2 尤其 especially   er^{2}qie^3 而且 moreover

III. 1. 怎讲　2. 努力　3. 怕　4. 大　5. 只不过　6. 实现

Passage 49

I. 衬 chen^4　圈 quan^1　像 xiang^4　罩 zhao^4　靛 dian^4　痴 chi^1　妥 tuo^3

耐 nai^4　骑 qi^2　箭 jian^4　从 cong^2　刷 shua^1　栋 dong^4　涨 zhang^4

该 gai^1　层 ceng^2　却 que^4　齐 qi^2　阴 yin^1　内 nei^2

II. 一本杂志　　两杯 / 瓶水　　三片 / 个面包　　四份报纸　五台电脑

III. 1. 开口　2. 够多　3. 坐下　4. 躺下　5. 走走　6. 看了

IV. 物美 价廉　破镜 重圆　烟雾 腾腾　一箭 双雕　一路 平安　闭目 养神

四通 八达　男女 老少　丢三 落四　讨价 还价

V. 1. 她穿了一件花花的衬衣.　　2. 圈圈的.　3. 七种.　4. 金黄色　5. 我喜欢黑和白.

6. 有时候一样漂亮.　　7. 她的内衣、内裤、胸罩全是彩色的.

8. 我没有什么秘密. / 谁没有一个两个秘密. / 当然有. 你想知道吗? 我明天告诉你.

Passage 50

I. 粉 fen^3　风 feng^1　份 fen^4　银 yin^2　英 ying^1　影 ying^3　音 yin^1　因 yin^1

明 ming^2　民 min^2　名 ming^2　今 jin^1　京 jing^1　斤 jin^1　经 jing^1　进 jin^4

镜 jing^4　劲 jin^4　平 ping^2　贫 pin^2　瓶 ping^2　姓 xing^4　心 xin^1　新 xin^1

信 xin^4　行 xing^2　幸 xing^4　请 qing^3　亲 qin^1　情 qing^2

III. 六条狗　　七只猫　　八位客人　　九件水果　　十栋房子

IV. 一妻 多夫　以毒 攻毒　头痛 医头　脚痛 医脚　镜花 水月

苦尽 甘来　笑容 满面　头昏 脑涨　五颜 六色　腰酸 背痛

V. 1. 和一个中国姑娘约会了.　2. 她长得美极了.　3. 就在隔壁.　4. 是三笑留情.

5. 我原来不会说中文. 心有余而力不足. (xin^1 you^3 yu^2 er^2 li^4 bu^4 zu^2: The spirit is willing but the flesh is weak.)　6. 学了一年.　7. 不是为了谈恋爱. 我喜欢中文, 我喜欢中国.

8. 谢谢!

词汇索引
Vocabulary Index

The number refers to the passage in which the word appears for the first time

215

fang²jian¹	房 间	27
fang²zi	房 子	25
fei¹chang²	非 常	42
fei⁴	肺	17
fei⁴	费	32
fen¹cun⁴	分 寸	45
fen¹zhong¹	分 钟	25
fen³	粉	35
fen⁴	份	33
feng¹	风	44
fu¹	夫	41
fu⁴	副	39
fu⁴	父	47
fu⁴hun¹	复 婚	46
fu⁴zuo⁴yong⁴	副 作 用	42

G

gai¹	该	1
gai³ge²	改 革	31
gan¹	干	10
gan¹	肝	28
gan¹	甘	50
gan¹yan²	肝 炎	28
gan³	敢	38
gan³dao⁴	感 到	46
gan³mao⁴	感 冒	11
gan⁴	干	10
gan⁴ma²	干 吗	23
gan⁴shen²me	干 什 么	10
gang¹	刚	19
gang¹cai²	刚 才	39
gao¹	高	21
gao¹xin⁴	高 兴	50
gao¹xue⁴ya¹	高 血 压	45
gao¹yuan²	高 原	34
gao⁴su	告 诉	8
ge	个	2
ge¹	搁	39
ge¹ge	哥 哥	2
ge²	隔	50
ge²bi⁴	隔 壁	40
gei³	给	12
geng¹	跟	36

geng⁴	更	41
gong¹	公	7
gong¹	宫	21
gong¹	攻	42
gong¹dao⁴	公 道	36
gong¹fu	功 夫	4
gong¹ju⁴	工 具	34
gong¹lu⁴	公 路	34
gong¹neng²	功 能	43
gong¹si¹	公 司	16
gong¹zuo⁴	工 作	29
gou³	狗	35
gou⁴	够	40
gu¹du²	孤 独	41
gu¹niang	姑 娘	23
gu⁴zhang⁴	故 障	20
guai²jiao³	拐 角	37
guai³	拐	25
guai⁴	怪	29
guan¹	关	36
guan¹xi	关 系	21
guan¹xin¹	关 心	44
guan³	馆	21
guan³…jiao⁴	管…叫…	35
guan³yong⁴	管 用	47
guan³zi	馆 子	21
Guang³dong¹	广 东	4
Guang³dong¹hua⁴	广 东 话	4
gui⁴	贵	16
guo	过	24
guo²	国	4
guo⁴	过	24
guo⁴fei²	过 肥	41
guo⁴min³	过 敏	35

H

hai²	还	1
hai²shi	还 是	1
hai²you³	还 有	13
hai³	海	18
hai²zi	孩 子	5
han⁴	汉	13
han⁴yu³	汉 语	50

216

hang²ban¹	航班	33
hang²kong¹	航空	16
Hang²zhou¹	杭州	26
hao² ji³ nian²	好几年	23
hao²haor³	好好儿	11
hao²jiu³	好久	15
hao³	好	1
hao³chu	好处	47
hao³duo¹	好多	30
hao³kan⁴	好看	49
hao³lei	好嘞	37
hao⁴	号	7
hao⁴ma³	号码	7
he¹	喝	1
he²	和	2
he²fan⁴	盒饭	37
hei¹	黑	39
hen³	很	2
hong²	红	9
hong²shao¹	红烧	14
hong²shao¹rou⁴	红烧肉	14
hong²lü⁴ deng¹	红绿灯	25
hou⁴	后	18
hou⁴	厚	44
hu²shuo¹	胡说	41
hu²tu	糊涂	39
hu³	浒	9
hua¹	花	35
hua¹fen³	花粉	35
hua⁴	话	4
hua⁴xue²	化学	42
hua⁴xue²pin³	化学品	42
huai⁴	坏	20
huan²	还	36
huan²jia⁴	还价	40
huan⁴	换	32
huan⁴cheng²	换成	32
huang¹	慌	37
huang²	黄	8
huang² jiu³	黄酒	45
hui¹fu⁴	恢复	41
hui²	回	16
hui²jia¹	回家	22
hui²lai²	回来	18
hui⁴	会	9

hui⁴hua⁴	会话	50
hui⁴lü⁴	汇率	32
hui⁴yi⁴	会议	12
hun¹	婚	5
hun¹	昏	28
hun²shen¹	浑身	28
huo²	活	28
huo²dong⁴	活动	28
huo²xue⁴	活血	45
huo³che¹	火车	34
huo³lu²	火炉	44
huo⁴	嚯	9
huo⁴	货	40

J

ji¹	机	7
ji¹	鸡	14
ji¹ding¹	鸡丁	21
ji¹piao⁴	机票	16
ji²	极	19
ji²dian³zhong¹	几点钟	10
ji²le	极了	19
ji³	几	2
ji⁴	记	36
ji⁴… you⁴	既…又	34
ji⁴mo⁴	寂寞	46
jia¹	家	2
jia¹	加	38
jia¹li	家里	7
jia¹ting²	家庭	2
jia²chang²	家常	14
jia³	假	11
jia⁴	假	11
jian³dan¹	简单	14
jian⁴	见	1
jian⁴	箭	34
jian⁴	件	38
jian⁴kang¹	健康	14
jian⁴mian⁴	见面	17
jian⁴zai⁴	健在	47
jiang²	江	26
jiang³	奖	48
jiang³	讲	50

217

jiang³jiu⁴	讲究	30
jiao¹	教	43
jiao¹tong¹	交通	34
jiao¹tong¹ gong¹ju⁴	交通工具	34
jiao³	脚	42
jiao³zi	饺子	37
jiao⁴	叫	7
jiər¹	今儿	11
jie¹	街	25
jie¹kou³	街口	25
jie²	结	5
jie²he²	结合	42
jie²hun¹	结婚	5
jie²mu⁴	节目	22
jie²shi²	结石	24
jie³jie	姐姐	2
jie³jue²	解决	41
jin¹	斤	37
jin¹	金	49
jin¹nian²	今年	8
jin¹tian¹	今天	15
jin³	紧	36
jin⁴	进	1
jin⁴	劲	28
jin⁴	近	38
jin⁴	尽	50
jing¹	京	18
jing¹chang²	经常	6
jing¹li³	经理	11
jing⁴	镜	46
jing⁴hua¹ shui³yue⁴	镜花水月	48
jiu³	九	7
jiu³	久	15
jiu³	酒	37
jiu⁴	就	4
jiu⁴	旧	13
jiu⁴	救	29
jiu⁴jiu	舅舅	47
jiu⁴suan⁴	就算	48
ju¹ran²	居然	50
jue²de	觉得	15

K

ka¹fei¹	咖啡	1

ka³	卡	27
kai¹	开	12
kai¹hui⁴	开会	12
kai¹shi³	开始	6
kai¹wan²xiao⁴	开玩笑	49
kan³jian¹	坎肩	44
kan⁴	看	9
kan⁴dao⁴	看到	25
kan⁴fa	看法	41
kao³	烤	14
kao⁴jin⁴	靠近	38
ke¹	科	29
ke¹	颗	40
ke²	咳	35
ke³	可	23
ke²sou	咳嗽	35
ke³yi³	可以	3
ke³kao⁴	可靠	43
ke³lian²	可怜	36
ke³neng²	可能	11
ke³shi⁴	可是	9
ke⁴	刻	10
ke⁴qi	客气	27
ke⁴ren²	客人	30
ken³	肯	4
kong¹	空	3
kong¹qi⁴	空气	34
kong³pa⁴	恐怕	41
kong⁴	空	3
kou³	口	2
kou⁴diao⁴	扣掉	32
ku³	苦	31
ku³gong¹	苦功	50
ku³jin⁴gan¹lai²	苦尽甘来	50
ku⁴zi	裤子	44
kuai⁴	块	13
kuai⁴	快	37
kuai⁴can¹	快餐	37
kuai⁴le⁴	快乐	30

L

la	啦	21
la¹dao³	拉倒	40

218

Pinyin	Chinese	Page
la^4	落	39
lai^2	来	3
lai^2 ren^2	来人	20
lai^{2}hui^2	来回	16
lan^2	蓝	49
lao^3	老	17
lao^{3}guang^1	老光	39
lao^{3}jia^1	老家	31
lao^{3}lao	姥姥	45
lao^{3}lian^4	老练	43
lao^{3}nian^2	老年	47
lao^{3}nian^2 chi^{1}dai^1	老年痴呆	47
lao^{3}nian^2 ren^2	老年人	41
lao^{3}po	老婆	41
lao^{3}shi^1	老师	29
lao^{3}shi^4	老是	28
le	了	1
leng^3	冷	44
li	里	7
li^2	梨	38
li^{2}ba	篱笆	50
li^{2}hun^1	离婚	46
li^{2}xiang^3	理想	5
Li^3	李	7
li^3	里	7
lian^2… ye^3	连…也	34
lian^{2}jia^4 piao^4	廉价票	16
liang^2	凉	15
liang^{2}kuai^4	凉快	15
liang^3	两	2
liang^4	辆	36
liang^4	亮	40
liao^{2}tian^1	聊天	43
liao^3	了	42
ling^2	零	7
ling^2	铃	11
ling^{2}hun^2	灵魂	29
ling^{2}qian^2	零钱	13
liu^{2}bi^{2}ti^4	流鼻涕	35
liu^4	六	3
long^2	龙	6
lou^2	楼	9
lou^4	漏	36
lü^{2}guan^3	旅馆	25
lü^{3}ke^4	旅客	27
lü^{3}you^2	旅游	18
lu^4	路	18
lü^4	绿	14
lü^{4}se^4 shu^{1}cai^4	绿色蔬菜	14
luan^4	乱	28
luo^4	落	39

M

Pinyin	Chinese	Page
ma	吗	4
ma^{1}ma	妈妈	2
ma^2	麻	21
ma^{2}fan	麻烦	25
ma^{2}fan nin^2	麻烦您	25
ma^{2}jiang^4	麻将	28
ma^{2}po^2	麻婆	21
ma^{3}shang^4	马上	10
mai^3	买	13
mai^4	卖	40
Mai^4 gei^3 ni.	卖给你.	40
Mai^{4}dang^{1}lao^2	麦当劳	37
man^3	满	50
man^4	慢	13
mang^2	忙	29
mao^1	猫	35
mao^2	毛	13
mao^{2}bing^4	毛病	20
mao^{2}cao^3	茅草	31
mao^{2}cao^{3}fang^2	茅草房	31
mao^{2}tai^2	茅台	45
mei^2	没	3
mei^{2}guan^{1}xi	没关系	21
mei^{2}you^3	没有	3
mei^3	每	10
mei^{3}ci^4	每次	24
mei^{3}guo^2	美国	34
mei^{3}guo^2 meng^4	美国梦	48
mei^{3}li^4	美丽	26
mei^{3}tian^1	每天	10
mei^{3}yuan^2	美元	32
mei^{4}mei	妹妹	2
men^{1}re^4	闷热	15
men	们	3
men^2	门	36

pi⁴ru²	譬如	47
pian⁴	片	14
piao⁴	票	16
piao⁴liang	漂亮	23
pin²fu⁴	贫富	41
ping¹an¹	平安	18
ping²	瓶	37
ping²guo³	苹果	38
ping²hen²	平衡	41
ping²shi²	平时	22
po²	婆	21
po⁴	破	36
pu³tong¹	普通	4
pu³tong¹hua⁴	普通话	4

Q

qi¹	七	7
qi¹	妻	41
qi²	骑	34
qi²guai⁴	奇怪	39
qi²quan²	齐全	43
qi³chuang²	起床	10
qi³fei¹	起飞	33
qi⁴che¹	汽车	20
qian¹	千	32
qian¹ming²	签名	32
qian²	钱	13
qian²	前	24
qian²mian	前面	36
qiao²	瞧	13
qiao²pai²	桥牌	47
qin¹ren²	亲人	23
qin²	勤	44
qing¹nian²ren²	青年人	41
qing²	情	36
qing²kuang⁴	情况	36
qing²tie³	请帖	46
qing³	请	1
qing³jia⁴	请假	11
qing⁴zhu⁴	庆祝	30
qu¹	区	31
qu³	取	32
qu³	娶	41

qu⁴	去	11
qu⁴nian²	去年	46
qu⁴shi⁴	去世	47
quan²	全	21
quan²bu⁴	全部	50
quan²xin¹	全新	36
que¹shao³	缺少	22
que⁴	却	42
qun²zi	裙子	44

R

ran²hou⁴	然后	46
rang⁴	让	12
re⁴	热	2
re⁴nao	热闹	2
ren²	人	2
ren²kou³	人口	2
ren²min²	人民	26
ren²min²bi⁴	人民币	32
ren²ren²	人人	26
ren⁴	认	36
ren⁴wei²	认为	41
ren⁴zhen¹	认真	41
ri⁴	日	30
rong²	容	50
rong²yi⁴	容易	4
rou⁴	肉	14
ru⁴ yao⁴	入药	42

S

san¹	三	3
se⁴	色	14
sha¹	纱	44
sha¹che¹	刹车	36
shan¹	山	31
shang	上	3
shang¹shen¹	伤身	45
shang⁴	上	3
shang⁴ge yue⁴	上个月	43
shang⁴ban¹	上班	10
Shang⁴hai³	上海	18
shang⁴wang³	上网	43

221

shang⁴wu³	上午	11
shao¹	烧	11
shao¹	捎	12
shao³	少	5
shao⁴	少	5
she⁴hui⁴	社会	41
shei²	谁	23
shen¹fen	身份	27
shen¹ti³	身体	21
shen¹zigu³	身子骨	45
shen²	神	33
shen²me	什么	1
shen²me...dou¹	什么...都	38
shen²meyang⁴de	什么样的	39
sheng¹	生	5
sheng¹huo²	生活	26
sheng¹ri	生日	30
sheng³	省	34
sheng³qian²	省钱	34
sheng⁴di⁴	胜地	15
shi¹mian²	失眠	28
shi²	十	8
shi²	实	29
shi²hou	时候	10
shi²ji³	十几	23
shi²jian¹	时间	10
shi²xian⁴	实现	48
shi²yong⁴	实用	13
shi²zai⁴	实在	40
shi⁴	是	1
shi⁴	室	7
shi⁴	事	12
shi⁴	试	47
shi⁴	世	34
shi⁴ shei²	是谁	23
shi⁴he²	适合	22
shi⁴jie⁴	世界	34
shou¹	收	13
shou¹dao⁴	收到	46
shou³	手	7
shou³ji¹	手机	7
shou³shu⁴	手术	17
shou³xu⁴	手续	32
shou⁴	受	35
shou⁴shang¹	受伤	36

shu¹	书	9
shu¹cai⁴	蔬菜	14
shu¹fu	舒服	11
shu⁴	术	17
shua¹ya²	刷牙	24
shuang¹fang¹	双方	46
shui²guo³	水果	14
shui³	水	1
shui³xiang¹	水箱	36
shui³jiao⁴	睡觉	10
shuo¹	说	4
shuo¹ shi²hua⁴	说实话	29
shuo¹ming¹	说明	13
si¹	丝	21
si³	死	42
si⁴	四	4
si⁴tong¹ ba¹da²	四通八达	34
song⁴	送	27
Su¹zhou¹	苏州	26
su⁴	速	34
su⁴cai⁴	素菜	25
su⁴jing⁴	素净	49
su⁴zao⁴	塑造	29
suan¹	酸	28
sui²	随	36
sui²shen¹	随身	44
sui⁴	岁	8
sui⁴shu	岁数	8
suo²yi³	所以	2

T

ta¹	他	8
ta¹	她	23
ta¹	它	35
ta¹men	他们	8
ta¹men	她们	35
ta¹men de	他们的	40
tai²	台	43
Tai²wan¹	台湾	23
tai⁴	太	3
tai⁴tai	太太	3
tan²lian⁴ai⁴	谈恋爱	50
tan⁴wang⁴	探望	23

223

225

zhao^3	找	13
zhao^4	罩	36
zhe	着	28
zhe^4 ji^3 tian^1	这几天	15
zhe^4	这	9
zhe^{4}me	这么	9
zhe^{4}mexie^1	这么些	9
zhe^{4}yang^4	这样	42
zhei^4	这	9
zhen^1	真	31
zheng^{2}ti^3	整体	42
zheng^{3}tian^1	整天	28
zheng^4	症	6
zheng^4	挣	29
zheng^4	正	33
zheng^{4}chang^2	正常	28
zheng^{4}fu^3	政府	41
zheng^{4}ming^2	证明	27
zheng^{4}qiao^3	正巧	33
zheng^{4}zai^4	正在	41
zher^4	这儿	37
zhi^1	汁	1
zhi^1	只	4
zhi^1	之	26
zhi^{1}dao	知道	3
zhi^{1}fang^2	脂肪	14
zhi^2 you^3	只有	22
zhi^{2}de	值得	18
zhi^{2}wu^4	植物	42
zhi^{2}ye^4	职业	29
zhi^3	只	4
zhi^{3}bu^{4}guo^4	只不过	48
zhi^{3}yao^4	只要	4
zhi^4	制	41
zhi^4	治	42
zhi^4 hao^3	治好	42
zhi^4 si^3	治死	42
zhi^{4}liang^4	质量	40
zhi^{4}liao^2	治疗	47
zhi^{4}shao^3	至少	22
zhi^{4}zao^4	制造	43
zhong^1	中	3
zhong^{1}guo^2	中国	4
zhong^{1}guo^{2}ren^2	中国人	4
zhong^{1}nian^{2}ren^2	中年人	41
zhong^{1}wen^2	中文	4
zhong^{1}wu^3	中午	3
zhong^{1}yang^1	中央	7
zhong^{1}yao^4	中药	42
zhong^{1}yi^1	中医	42
zhong^3	种	47
zhong^4	中	48
zhong^4	重	12
zhong^{4}yao^4	重要	12
zhou^1	周	10
zhou^{1}mo^4	周末	10
zhu^1	珠	40
zhu^{3}ya^4	主要	34
zhu^4	住	7
zhu^4	祝	18
zhu^{4}he^4	祝贺	50
zhuang^4	撞	36
zhun^{2}dian^3	准点	33
zhun^3	准	28
zhun^{3}bei^4	准备	18
zhuo^{1}zi	桌子	39
zi	子	5
zi^{1}liao^4	资料	43
zi^3	子	5
zi^3	紫	49
zi^4	自	36
zi^{4}xing^{2}che^1	自行车	34
zong^3	总	2
zong^{3}shi	总是	2
zou^3	走	1
zui^4	最	5
zui^{4}hou^4	最后	42
zui^{4}jin^4	最近	28
zuo^{2}tian^1	昨天	19
zuo^3	左	25
zuo^4	坐	1
zuo^4	作	10
zuo^4	做	30
zuo^{4}meng^4	做梦	28
zuor^2	昨儿	50

Appendix 1

汉 语 发 音
Chinese Pronunciation

A. Scheme for Chinese Phonetic Alphabet 汉 语 拼 音 方 案

Alphabet

a as a in f**a**ther	**b** as p in s**p**y	**c** as ts in i**ts**	**d** as t in s**t**udy
e as u in circ**u**s	**f** as f in **f**un	**g** as k in s**k**y	**h** as h in **h**at
i as ee in m**ee**t	**j** as j in **j**ob	**k** as k in in**k**	**l** as l in **l**ot
m as m in **m**ill	**n** as n in **n**ote	**o** as o in g**o**	**p** as p in **p**ost
q as ch in **ch**eck	**r** as r in **r**ut	**s** as s in **s**un	**t** as t in **t**ar
u as oo in f**oo**d	**v** as v in **v**ote	**w** as w in **w**atch	**x** as sh in fi**sh**
y as s in plea**s**ure	**z** as ds in wor**ds**		

Consonants

b	p	m	f	d	t	n	l	g	k	h
j	q	x	zh	h	sh	r	z	c	s	

Vowels

1	2	3	4	5	6	7
a	e	i	o	u	ü	er

ai	ei	ia	ou	ua	üe
ao	en	ie	ong	uo	üan
an	eng	iao		uai	ün
ang		iou		uei	
		ian		uan	
		in		uen	
		iang		uang	
		ing		ueng	
		iong			

1. When **zh**, **ch**, **sh**, **r**, **z**, **c**, or **s** forms a syllable, use vowel **i** after them, that is, they are written as **zhi**, **chi**, **shi**, **ri**, **zi**, **ci**, and **si**.
2. When the vowel **er** is used at the end of a word, but does not form a separate syllable, write **r** only.
3. When there is no consonant before the vowel **i** or any of the compound vowels beginning with **i** (in the third column above), the vowel is written as **yi**, **ya**, **ye**, **yao**, **you**, **yan**, **yin**, **yang**, **ying**, or **yong**.
4. When there is no consonant before the vowel **u** or any of the compound vowels beginning with **u** (in the fifth column above), the vowel is written as **wu**, **wa**, **wo**, **wai**, **wei**, **wan**, **wen**, **wang**, or **weng**.

227

5. When there is no consonant before the vowel **ü** or any of the compound vowels beginning with **ü** (in the sixth column above), add **y** in writing and omit the two dots above **u**, that is, they are written as **yu**, **yue**, **yuan**, and **yun**.

6. When the vowel **ü** or any of the compound vowels beginning with **ü** (in the sixth column above) is spelt with the consonant **j**, **q**, or **x**, the two dots above **u** are dropped; that is, they are written as **ju**, **qu**, and **xu**. When they are spelt with the consonant **n** or **l**, the two dots are not dropped; that is, they are written as **nü** and **lü**.

7. When the vowel **iou**, **uei**, or **uen** is preceded by a consonant, it is written as **iu**, **ui**, or **un**, that is, the middle **o** or **e** is dropped. Eg. **niu**, **gui**, **lun**.

B. The Four Tones of Chinese Pronunciation 四声

With the exception of some words that are always neutral (unstressed), every Chinese character has four tones.

1st tone: 阴平 (yin^{1}ping^1) high and flat

2nd tone: 阳平 (yang^{2}ping^1) high and rising

3rd tone: 上声 (shang^{3}sheng^1) falling and then rising

4th tone: 去声 (qu^{4}sheng^1) falling

In this book superscripts 1, 2, 3, 4 are used at the end of each syllable to denote the tone of the preceding syllable, for example, ba^1 (1st tone), ba^2 (2nd tone), ba^3 (3rd tone), ba^4 (4th tone). If the tone is neutral, no numbers are marked. In some books the following symbols are put above the vowels to show the tones:

First tone: (¯)

Second tone: (/)

Third tone: (ˇ)

Fourth tone: (\ )

Tones are important because different tones of the same sound may represent different characters and different meanings.

ma^1 妈 mom	ma^2 麻 flax	ma^3 马 horse	ma^4 骂 swear at	ma 吗 (a *part.*)
ba^1 疤 scar	ba^2 拔 pull up	ba^3 把 hold	ba^4 爸 dad	ba 吧 (a *part.*)
ji^1 鸡 chicken	ji^2 急 impatient	ji^3 挤 squeeze	ji^4 寄 mail	

C. Shift of Tones 声调转移

When two tones are closely linked together, usually there is tonal modification.

1. Third tone to second tone:
    When a syllable of a third tone is followed by another syllable of third tone, the first syllable will usually change into second tone.

你好!	Hello!	ni^{3}hao^3 → ni^{2}hao^3 (3-3 to 2-3)
我喜欢	I like	wo^3 xi^{3}huan → wo^2 xi^{3}huan (3-3-0 to 2-3-0)
很简单	very simple	hen^3 jian^{3}dan^1 → hen^2 jian^{3}dan^1 (3-3-1 to 2-3-1)

也得来　should also come　　ye^3 dei^3 lai^2 → ye^2 dei^3 lai^2 (3-3-2 to 2-3-2)

五哩路　five miles' distance　wu^3 li^3 lu^4 → wu^2 li^3 lu^4 (3-3-4 to 2-3-4)

我也好　I am also well.　　　wo^3 ye^3 hao^3 → wo^2 ye^2 hao^3 (3-3-3 to 2-2-3)

In the last example above the third tone word 也 (ye^3) is changed into the second tone because it is influenced by the following third tone word 好 (hao^3). Now although the third tone 我 (wo^3) is followed by a changed second tone word 也 (ye^2), it is still influenced by the original third tone of the word 也 and changes into second tone.

2. Shift of tones of "一" (yi), "七" (qi), "八" (ba), and "不" (bu):

一 (yi) one:

1st. tone (in isolation or at the end of a group of words):

一、二、三　(yi^1, er^4, san^1) one, two, three (in counting)

第一　(di^{4}yi^1) first

意见不一　(yi^{4}jian^4 bu^{4}yi^1) (opinions differ)

2nd. tone (before a fourth tone):

一半　(yi^{2}ban^4) half

一定　(yi^{2}ding^4) surely

一块钱 (yi^2 kuai^4 qian^2) one *yuan*

4th. tone (before a 1st., 2nd., or 3rd. tone):

一些　(yi^{4}xie^1) some

一回　(yi^{4}hui^2) once

一起　(yi^{4}qi^3) together

七 (qi) seven

1st. tone (regular tone)

七夕 (qi^{1}xi^1) the seventh evening of the seventh moon

2nd. tone (before a 4th. tone)

七月 (qi^{2}yue^4) July

八 (ba) eight:

1st. tone (regular tone)

八成 (ba^{1}cheng^2) eighty per cent

八方 (ba^{1}fang^1) the eight points on the compass, that is, the four directions, north, south, east, west, plus the directions between each of them

2nd. tone (before a 4th. tone)

八月 (ba^{2}yue^4) August

八卦 (ba^{2}gua^4) the Eight Diagrams (formed by whole and broken lines formerly used in divination)

十八岁 (shi^{1}ba^{2}sui^4) eighteen years old

不 (bu) no, not:

4th. tone　(in isolation or before a 1st., 2nd., or 3rd. tone):

　不, 我不明白. (Bu⁴, wo³ bu⁴ ming²bai.) No, I don't understand.

　不安 (bu⁴an¹) restless

　不得了 (bu⁴de²liao³) desperately serious

　不久 (bu⁴jiu³) before long

2nd. tone　(before a 4th. tone):

　不是 (bu² shi⁴) no

　不客气 (bu² ke⁴qi) you are welcome

D. Examples of Words and Expressions with Neutral Tones

轻 声 的 词 语 示 例

In normal or rapid speed speech many words are pronounced with a neutral tone.

A. People 人：

姑娘 (gu¹niang) girl　　　　大夫 (dai⁴fu) doctor

朋友 (peng²you) friend　　　学生 (xue²sheng) student

小姐 (xiao³jie) miss　　　　护士 (hu⁴shi) nurse

B. Family members and relatives 家人、亲戚：

妈妈 (ma¹ma) mom　　　　　爸爸 (ba¹ba) dad

太太 (tai⁴tai) wife　　　　　妹妹 (mei⁴mei) younger sister

姐姐 (jie³jie) elder sister　　夫人 (fu¹ren) wife

弟弟 (di⁴di) younger brother　哥哥 (ge¹ge) elder brother

先生 (xian¹sheng) husband　　丈夫 (zhang⁴fu) husband

爷爷 (ye²ye) father's father　　奶奶 (nai³nai) father's mother

姥姥 (lao³lao) mother's mother　叔叔 (shu¹shu) father's younger brother

舅舅 (jiu⁴jiu) mother's brother　伯伯 (bo²bo) father's elder brother

C. Fruit 水果：

葡萄 (pu²tao) grape　　　　　核桃 (he²tao) walnut

枇杷 (pi²pa) loquat　　　　　石榴 (shi²liu) pomegranate

D. Organs or parts of the body 器官或身体的部分：

舌头 (she²tou) tongue　　　　屁股 (pi⁴gu) buttocks

头发 (tou²fa) hair　　　　　　眼睛 (yan³jing) eye

耳朵 (er³duo) ear　　　　　　胳臂 (ge²bei) arm

眉毛 (mei²mao) eyebrow　　　嘴巴 (zui³ba）mouth

E. Vegetables 蔬菜：

蘑菇 (mo²gu) mushroom　　　胡萝卜 (hu²lu²bo) carrot

F. Food 食品：

豆腐 (dou⁴fu) bean curd　　　伙食 (huo³shi) mess

点心 (dian³xin) snack　　　　高粱 (gao¹liang) sorghum

G. Heavenly bodies 天体:

星星 (xing^1<u>xing</u>) stars 月亮 (yue^4<u>liang</u>) moon

H. Animals 动物:

狐狸 (hu^2<u>li</u>) fox 猩猩 (xing^1<u>xing</u>) orangutan

骆驼 (luo^4<u>tuo</u>) camel 喜鹊 (xi^3<u>que</u>) magpie

I. Time 时间:

晚上 (wan^3<u>shang</u>) night 时候 (shi^2<u>hou</u>) time

早上 (zao^3<u>shang</u>) morning 五月 (wu^3<u>yue</u>) May

J. Positions 位置:

前面 (qian^2<u>mian</u>) front 后面 (hou^4<u>mian</u>) back

下面 (xia^4<u>mian</u>) below 里边 (li^3<u>bian</u>) inside

那里 (na^4<u>li</u>) there 这里 (zhe^4<u>li</u>) here

墙上 (qiang^2<u>shang</u>) on the wall

K. Objects 物品:

东西 (dong^1<u>xi</u>) thing 钥匙 (yao^4<u>shi</u>) key

衣服 (yi^1<u>fu</u>) clothing 行李 (xing^2<u>li</u>) luggage

首饰 (shou^3<u>shi</u>) jewelry 玻璃 (bo^1<u>li</u>) glass

扫帚 (sao^4<u>zhou</u>) broom 簸箕 (bo^4<u>ji</u>) dustpan

喇叭 (la^3<u>ba</u>) trumpet 风筝 (feng^1<u>zheng</u>) kite

篱笆 (li^2<u>ba</u>) fence 窗户 (chuang^1<u>hu</u>) window

琵琶 (pi^2<u>pa</u>) *pipa* (a musical instrument)

L. Verbs 动词:

看见 (kan^4<u>jian</u>) see 知道 (zhi^1<u>dao</u>) know

认识 (ren^4<u>shi</u>) know 照顾 (zhao^4<u>gu</u>) attend to

明白 (ming^2<u>bai</u>) understand 佩服 (pei^4<u>fu</u>) admire

咳嗽 (ke^2<u>sou</u>) cough 打听 (da^2<u>ting</u>) ask about

喜欢 (xi^3<u>huan</u>) like 休息 (xiu^1<u>xi</u>) rest

嘱咐 (zhu^3<u>fu</u>) enjoin 罗嗦 (luo^1<u>suo</u>) long-winded

哆嗦 (duo^1<u>suo</u>) tremble 觉得 (jue^2<u>de</u>) feel

唠叨 (la^2<u>dao</u>) be garrulous 答应 (da^1<u>ying</u>) agree

收拾 (shou^1<u>shi</u>) tidy up 打发 (da^3<u>fa</u>) send

看看 (kan^4<u>kan</u>) take a look 谈谈 (tan^2<u>tan</u>) have a chat

谢谢 (xie^4<u>xie</u>) thanks 是 (<u>shi</u>) be, as equational verb (in rapid speech)

M. Adjectives or adverbs 形容词或副词:

聪明 (cong^1<u>ming</u>) intelligent 清楚 (qing^1<u>chu</u>) clear

老实 (lao^3<u>shi</u>) honest 便宜 (pian^2<u>yi</u>) inexpensive

漂亮 (piao^4<u>liang</u>) beautiful 暖和 (nuan^3<u>huo</u>) warm

活泼 (huo^2<u>po</u>) lively 糊涂 (hu^2<u>tu</u>) muddleheaded

热闹 (re^4<u>nao</u>) lively 舒服 (shu^1<u>fu</u>) comfortable

客气 (ke^4<u>qi</u>) courteous 多少 (duo^1<u>shao</u>) how many

已经 (yi^3<u>jing</u>) already 扎实 (zha^1<u>shi</u>) solid

N. Abstract ideas 抽象概念:

看法 (kan⁴fa) view   说法 (shuo¹fa) statement

想法 (xiang³fa) idea   任务 (ren⁴wu) (task)

知识 (zhi¹shi) (knowledge)   找头 (zhao³tou) change (from money paid)

意思 (yi⁴si) meaning   消息 (xiao¹xi) news

味道 (wei⁴dao) taste   部分 (bu⁴fen) portion

用处 (yong⁴chu) use   难处 (nan²chu) difficulty

麻烦 (ma²fan) trouble   功夫 (gong¹fu) kung fu

关系 (guan¹xi) relationship   困难 (kun⁴nan) difficulty

力气 (li⁴qi) strength   故事 (gu⁴shi) story

疙瘩 (ge¹da) knot in heart   短处 (duan³chu) weakness

长处 (chang²chu) strong points

O. Pronouns (in object positions): 代词 (在宾格位置)

谢谢你 (xie⁴xie ni) thank you

给我写信 (gei³ wo xie³ xin⁴) write letters to me

P. Connectives 连词:

要是 (yao⁴shi) if   要么 (yao⁴me) either...or

还是 (hai²shi) or   要不是 (yao⁴bushi) if it were not for

Q. Numerals 数词:

二十六 (er⁴ shi liu⁴) twenty six

三十五 (san¹ shi wu³) thirty five

坐一坐 (zuo⁴ yi zuo⁴) be seated for a while

等一等 (deng³ yi deng³) wait a bit

R. Particles 助词:

子 (zi):   盘子 (pan¹zi) plate   橙子 (cheng²zi) orange

        嗓子 (sang³zi) (throat)   房子 (fang²zi) house

        乱子（luan⁴zi）disturbance   饺子 (jiao³zi) dumpling with stuffing

头 (tou):   馒头 (man²tou) steamed bun   甜头 (tian²tou) benefit

        看头 (kan⁴tou) something worth seeing

们 (men):   我们 (wo³men) we   朋友们 (peng²you men) friends

        孩子们 (hai²zi men) children   咱们 (zan²men) we

的 (de):   你的 (ni³de) your   我的 (wo³de) my

        别的 (bie²de) other   好的 (hao³ de) good

        看过的书 (kan⁴guo de shu¹) books that have been read

        是我打破的. (Shi⁴ wo² da³po⁴ de.) It's me who broke it.

了 (le):   去了 (qu⁴ le) be gone   太好了 (tai⁴ hao³ le) excellent

吗 (ma):   是吗? (Shi⁴ ma?) Really?   你好吗? (Ni² hao³ ma?) How are you?

嘛 (ma):   就是嘛. (Jiu⁴shi⁴ ma.) Exactly.

        你就对他直说嘛. (Ni³ jiu⁴ dui⁴ ta zhi²shuo¹ ma.) Just speak frankly to him.

呢 (ne):   你呢? (Ni³ ne?) And you?

他在找你呢! (Ta^1 zai^4 zhao^3 ni $\underline{ne}$!) He is looking for you!

吧 (ba): 咱们走吧. (Zan^{2}men zou^3 $\underline{ba}$.) Let's go.

喝点儿水吧. (He^1 diar^3 shui^3 $\underline{ba}$.) Just drink some water.

她来不了了吧? (Ta^1 lai^2 buliao^3 le $\underline{ba}$?) She can't come, can she?

过 (guo): 吃过 (chi^1 $\underline{guo}$) have eaten 　来过 (lai^2 $\underline{guo}$) have been here

个 (ge): 一个 (yi^2 $\underline{ge}$) one 　　三个 (san^1 $\underline{ge}$) three 　　这个 (zhe^4 $\underline{ge}$) this

着 (zhe): 别站着. (Bie^2 zhan^4 $\underline{zhe}$.) Don't just stand there.

你听着. (Ni^3 ting^1 $\underline{zhe}$.) Listen.

么 (me): 这么 (zhe^4 $\underline{me}$) so 　　那么 (na^4$\underline{me}$) in that way, then

什么 (shen^2$\underline{me}$) what 　　多么 (duo^1$\underline{me}$) how

地 (de): 好好地 (hao^{2}hao^3 $\underline{de}$) nicely 　健康地 (jian^{4}kang^1 $\underline{de}$) healthily

得 (de): 好得很 (hao^3$\underline{de}$hen^3) very good

走得快 (zou^3 $\underline{de}$ kuai^4) walk fast

看得起 (kan^4$\underline{de}$qi^3) think highly of

吃得消 (chi^1$\underline{de}$xiao^1) be able to bear

不 (bu): 对不起 (dui^4$\underline{bu}$qi^3) sorry

说不定 (shuo^1$\underline{bu}$ding^4) perhaps

差不多 (cha^4$\underline{bu}$duo^2) almost

要不得 (yao^4$\underline{bu}$de) no good

看不起 (kan^4$\underline{bu}$qi^3) look down upon

来不来 (lai^2$\underline{bu}$lai^2) come or not

吃不消 (chi^1$\underline{bu}$xiao^1) be unable to endure

听不见 (ting^1$\underline{bu}$jian^4) be unable to hear

走不快 (zou^3 $\underline{bu}$ kuai^4) cannot walk fast

不得 (bude): 马虎不得 (ma^{3}hu $\underline{bude}$) must not be careless

见不得人 (jian^4 $\underline{bude}$ ren^2) shameful to see people

到 (dao): 提到 (ti^2$\underline{dao}$) mention 　　见到 (jian^4$\underline{dao}$) see

来 (lai): 过来 (guo^4$\underline{lai}$) come over

说来话长. (Shuo^1$\underline{lai}$ hua^{4}chang^2.) It's a long story.

去 (qu): 过去 (guo^4$\underline{qu}$) go over 　　出去 (chu^1$\underline{qu}$) go out

让她说去! (Rang^4 ta shuo^1$\underline{qu}$!) Let her say what she likes!

起来 (qilai): 看起来 (kan^4$\underline{qilai}$) it looks

组织起来 (zu^{3}zhi^1 $\underline{qilai}$) get organized

冷起来了. (Leng^2 $\underline{qilai}$ le.) It's getting cold.

过来 (guolai): 走过来 (zou^3 $\underline{guolai}$) come over

转过来 (zhuan^4 $\underline{guolai}$) turn round

醒过来 (xing^3 $\underline{guolai}$) wake up

过去 (guoqu): 飞过去 (fei^1 $\underline{guoqu}$) fly past

晕过去了 (yun^4 $\underline{guoqu}$ le) have fainted

E. Suffixation of R 儿化

Suffixation of a non-syllabic *r* to nouns and sometimes verbs causes a retroflexion of the preceding vowel.

非成节音 *r* 可作后缀, 加于某些名词或动词之后, 使其前一元音成为卷舌音.

1. Suffixed *r* with final *a, e, o, u* and *ü*:

Final letter(s)	Endings with R Suffixation	Examples	Notes
a → (ia, ua)	ar	马 (ma^3 → mar^3) horse 匣 (xia^2 → xiar^2) box 花 (hua^1 → huar^1) flower	Add r.
e → (ie, üe)	er	歌 (ge^1 → ger^1) song 碟 (die^2 → dier^4) small plate 月 (yue^4 › yucr) moon	
o → (ao, iao, uo)	or	婆 (po^2 → por^3) woman's mother-in-law 包 (bao^1 → baor^1) bag 条 (tiao^2 → tiaor^2) twig 火 (huo^3 → huor^3) fire	
u → (ou, iou)	ur	兔 (tu^4 → tur^4) rabbit 狗 (gou^3 → gour^3) dog 球 (qiu^2 → qiur) ball	
ü →	üer	鱼 (yu^2 → yuər^2) fish	Add ər. (ər is a retroflexed central vowel.)

2. Suffixed *r* with final *i*:

Final letter(s)	Endings with R Suffixation	Examples	Notes
i →	iər	皮 (pi^2 → piər) skin	Add ər.
(z, c, s, r, zh, ch, sh +) i →	ər	事 (shi^4 → shər^4) matter	Drop i and add ər. (The vowel i after z, c, s, r, zh, ch, and sh is an apical; after retroflexion it becomes ər.)
ei → (uei)		辈 (bei^4 → bər^4) generation 味 (wei^4 → wər^4) taste	Drop ei and add ər.
ai → (uai)	ar	孩 (hai^2 → har^2) child 块 (kuai^4 → kuar^4) piece	Drop i and add r.

234

3. Suffixed *r* with final *n*:

an → (ian, uan, üan)	ar	盘 (pan^2 → par^2) plate 馅 (xian^4 → xiar^4) stuffing 玩 (wan^2 → war^2) play 远 (yuan^3 → yuar^3) far	Drop n and add r.
en → (uen)	ər	根 (gen^1 → gər^1) root 吻 (wen^3 → wər^3) kiss	Drop en and add ər.
in →	iər	心 (xin^1 → xiər^1) heart	Drop n and add ər.
ün →	üər	裙 (qun^2 → quər^2) skirt	

4. Suffixed *r* with final *ng*:

ang → (iang, uang)	ãr	缸 (gang^1 → gãr^1) vat 秧 (yang^1 → yãr^1) seedling 晃 (huang^3 → huãr^3) flash past	Drop ng and add r. Since ng denotes nasal sound, after it is dropped, the vowel originally before it still retains the nasal sound, which is marked with a tilde sign ~ above the vowel.
ong → (iong)	õr	弓 (gong^1 → gõr^1) bow 熊 (xiong^2 → xiõr^2) bear	
eng → (ueng)	ə̃r	灯 (deng^1 → də̃r^1) lamp 瓮 (weng^4 → wə̃r^4) urn	Drop eng and add ə̃r.
ing →	iə̃r	瓶 (ping^2 → piə̃r^2) bottle	Drop ng and add ə̃r

235

Appendix 2

本书课文所用量词及其连用的名词
Measure Words and Nouns Used with Them in the Text

Measure Words: **Nouns Used with Them:**

杯 (bei^1):   牛奶 (niu^{2}nai^3) milk   水 (shui^1) water
           酒 (jiu^3) wine, liquor

家 (jia^1):   公司 (gong^{1}si^1) company   医院 (yi^{1}yuan^4) hospital
           银行 (yin^{2}hang^2) bank

口 (kou^3):   人 (ren^2) person

个 (ge):   人 (ren^2) person   哥哥 (ge^{1}ge) elder brother
           妹妹 (mei^{4}mei) younger sister   公司 (gong^{1}si^1) company
           孩子 (hai^{2}zi) child   儿子 (er^{2}zi) son
           信 (xin^4) message   鸡蛋 (ji^{1}dan^4) egg
           农村 (nong^{2}cun^1) village   卧房 (wo^{4}fang^2) bedroom
           卫生间 (wei^{4}sheng^{1}jian^1) bathroom
           地方(di^{4}fang) place   小时 (xiao^{3}shi^2) hour
           菜 (cai^4) dish, course   房间 (fang^{2}jian^1) room
           节目 (jie^{1}mu^2) program   月 (yue^4) month
           街口 (jie^{1}kou^3) intersection   印象 (yin^{4}xiang^4) impression
           学校 (xue^{2}xiao^4) school   星期 (xing^{1}qi^1) week
           苹果 (ping^{2}guo^3) apple   点 (dian^3) point
           整体 (zheng^{2}ti^3) whole   晚上 (wan^{3}shang) night

只 (zhi^1):   猫 (mao^1) cat

张 (zhang^1):   单子 (dan^{1}zi) form   彩票 (cai^{3}piao^4) lottery ticket
           表 (biao^3) form   罚单 (fa^{2}dan^1) traffic violation
                                       ticket

本 (ben^3):   书 (shu^1) book   词典 (ci^{2}dian^3) dictionary
           小说 (xiao^{3}shuo^1) novel   杂志 (za^{2}zhi^4) magazine

片 (pian^4):   面包 (mian^{4}bao^1) bread

场(chang^2):   雨 (yu^3) rain   梦 (meng^4) dream

场(chang^3):   电影 (dian^{4}ying^3) movie

部 (bu^4):   电影片 (dian^{4}ying^{3}pian^4) film

把 (ba^3):   劲 (jin^4) spurt of energy

顿 (dun^4):   饭 (fan^4) meal

位 (wei^4):   姑娘 (gu^{1}niang) girl

栋 (dong^4):   房子 (fang^{2}zi) building

份 (fen^4):   报纸 (bao^{4}zhi^3) newspaper

条 (tiao^2):   狗 (gou^3) dog   项链 (xiang^{4}liang^4) necklace

彩虹 (cai^3hong^2) rainbow

辆 ($liang^4$):　　　面包车 ($mian^4bao^1che^1$) mini-bus

瓶 ($ping^2$):　　　啤酒 (pi^2jiu^3) beer

件 ($jian^4$):　　　水果 ($shui^3guo^3$) fruit　　　衬衣 ($chen^4yi^1$) shirt

　　　　　　　　　外套 (wai^4tao^4) coat　　　好事 (hao^3shi^4) good thing

副 (fu^4):　　　眼镜 (yan^3jing^4) glasses

颗 (ke^1):　　　珠子 (zhu^1zi) pearl

台 (tai^2):　　　电脑 ($dian^4nao^3$) computer　　　电视机 ($dian^4shi^4ji^1$) TV set

Appendix 3

数 词 Numerals

Cardinal:

一 (yi^1)	one
二 (er^4)	two
三 (san^1)	three
四 (si^4)	four
五 (wu^3)	five
六 (liu^4)	six
七 (qi^1)	seven
八 (ba^1)	eight
九 (jiu^3)	nine
十 (shi^2)	ten
十一 (shi^2 yi^1)	eleven
十二 (shi^2 er^4)	twelve
十九 (shi^2 jiu^3)	nineteen
二十 (er^4 shi^2)	twenty
二十三 (er^4 shi^2 san^1)	twenty three
三十 (san^1 shi^2)	thirty
四十 (si^4 shi^2)	forty
五十 (wu^3 shi^2)	fifty
六十 (liu^4 shi^2)	sixty
七十 (qi^1 shi^2)	seventy
八十 (ba^1 shi^2)	eighty
九十 (jiu^3 shi^2)	ninety
百 (bai^3)	hundred
一百 (yi^1 bai^3)	one hundred
千 (qian^1)	thousand
两千 (liang^3 qian^1)	two thousand
万 (wan^4)	ten thousand
三万 (san^1 wan^4)	thirty thousand
一百万 (yi^1 bai^3 wan^4)	million
七百万 (qi^1 bai^3 wan^4)	seven million
亿 (yi^4)	hundred million
兆（zhao^4)	trillion, thousand billion

Ordinal: Ordinal numbers are formed by adding the word 第 (di^4) before cardinal numbers.

第一 (di^4 yi^1)	first
第三 (di^4 san^1)	third
第一百 (di^4 yi bai^3)	hundredth

238

Appendix 4

表示时间的词 Time Words

秒 (miao^3) second
分 (fen^1) minute
小时 (xiao^{3}shi^2) hour
天 (tian^1) day
星期 (xing^{1}qi^1) week
月 (yue^4) month
季 (ji^4) season
年 (nian^2) year
世纪 (shi^{4}ji^4) century

3:00	三点钟 (san^1 dian^3 zhong^1)	three o'clock
2:15	两点一刻 (liang^2 dian^3 yi^1 ke^4) or	quarter after two
	两点十五分 (liang^2 dian^3 shi^2 wu^3 fen^1)	two fifteen
3:45	三点三刻 (san^1 dian^3 san^1 ke^4) or	quarter before four
	三点四十五分 (san^1 dian^3 si^4 shi^2 wu^3 fen^1)	three forty five
4:30	四点半 (si^4 dian^3 ban^4)	four thirty
4:54	五点差六分 (wu^2 dian^3 cha^4 liu^4 fen^4)	six minutes before five
7:08	七点零八分 (qi^1 dian^3 ling^2 ba^1 fen^1) or	eight minutes after seven
	七点过八分 (qi^1 dian^3 guo^4 ba^1 fen^1)	

清晨	(qing^{1}chen^2)	early morning
早晨	(zao^{3}chen^2)	(early) morning
上午	(shang^{4}wu^3)	A.M.
中午	(zhong^{1}wu^3)	noon
下午	(xia^{4}wu^3)	P.M.
傍晚	(bang^{4}wan^3)	toward evening, at dusk
晚上	(wan^{3}shang)	evening, night
夜间	(ye^{4}jian^1)	night
半夜	(ban^{4}ye^4)	midnight
深夜	(shen^{1}ye^4)	late at night

前年	(qian^{2}nian^2)	the year before last
去年	(qu^{4}nian^2)	last year
四天(以)前	(si^4 tian^1 (yi^3) qian^2)	four days ago
大前天	(da^{4}qian^{2}tian^1)	three days ago
前天	(qian^{2}tian^1)	day before yesterday
昨天	(zuo^{2}tian^1)	yesterday

今 天 (jin¹tian¹)   today
明 天 (ming²tian¹)   tomorrow
后 天 (hou⁴tian¹)   day after tomorrow
大 后 天 (da⁴hou⁴tian¹)   three days from today
四 天 以 后 (si⁴ tian¹ yi³hou⁴)   four days from today
明 年 (ming²nian²)   next year
后 年 (hou⁴nian²)   the year after next

星 期 天 (xing¹qi¹ tian¹) or
星 期 日 (xing¹qi¹ ri⁴)   Sunday
星 期 一 (xing¹qi¹ yi¹)   Monday
星 期 二 (xing¹qi¹ er⁴)   Tuesday
星 期 三 (xing¹qi¹ san¹)   Wednesday
星 期 四 (xing¹qi¹ si⁴)   Thursday
星 期 五 (xing¹qi¹ wu³)   Friday
星 期 六 (xing¹qi¹ liu⁴)   Saturday

一 月 (yi² yue⁴)   January
二 月 (er⁴ yue⁴)   February
三 月 (san¹ yue⁴)   March
四 月 (si⁴ yue⁴)   April
五 月 (wu³ yue⁴)   May
六 月 (liu⁴ yue⁴)   June
七 月 (qi² yue⁴)   July
八 月 (ba² yue⁴)   August
九 月 (jiu³ yue⁴)   September
十 月 (shi² yue⁴)   October
十 一 月 (shi² yi² yue⁴)   November
十 二 月 (shi² er⁴ yue⁴)   December

七 月 四 号 (qi² yue⁴ si⁴ hao⁴)   July the fourth
十 月 一 号 (shi² yue⁴ yi² hao⁴)   October the first
十 二 月 二 十 五 号 (shi² er⁴ yue⁴   25th of December
          er⁴ shi² wu³ hao⁴)
春 天 (chun¹ tian¹)   spring
夏 天 (xia⁴ tian¹)   summer
秋 天 (qiu¹ tian¹)   fall
冬 天 (dong¹ tian¹)   winter

Appendix 5

常用北京俚语

Frequently Heard Slang in Beijing Dialect

WORDS	MEANINGS	EXAMPLES
ao^{2}tour 熬头儿	烦心 (fan^{2}xin^1) annoying, annoyed	今年流年不利, 受气**熬头**儿的事儿特多. (Jin^{1}nian^2 liu^{2}nian^2 bu^2 li^4, shou^{4}qi^4 **ao^{2}tour** de shər^4 te^4 duo^1.) This is an unlucky year. There are so many things that make me annoyed.
ba^{2}jiaor^3 把角儿	路口拐角儿的地方 (lu^{4}kou^3 guai^{2}jiaor^3 de di^{4}fang) street corner	胡同**把角**儿有家卖大碗儿茶的. (Hu^{2}tong^4 **ba^{2}jiaor^3** you^3 jia^1 mai^4 da^{4}war^3 cha^1 de.) There is a store at the street corner selling big bowls of tea.
bai^{2}pur^3 摆谱儿	摆架子 (bai^2 jiao^{4}zi) put on airs	他有了几个钱, 就爱**摆个谱**儿. (Ta^1 you^3 le ji^3 ge qian^2, jiu^4 ai^4 **bai^2** ge **pur^3**.) He likes to put on airs just because he has a little money.
ban^{1}gang^4 搬杠	无谓的争辩 (wu^{2}wei^4 de zheng^{1}bian^4) argue for the sake of arguing	我不跟你**搬**什么**杠**. (Wo^3 bu^4 gen^1 ni^3 **ban^1** shen^{2}me **gang^4**.) I won't bicker with you.
ban^{4}la^3 半拉	一半 (yi^{2}ban^4) half	她一个苹果都吃不了, 还分给妹妹**半拉**呢. (Ta^2 yi^4 ge ping^{2}guo^3 dou^1 chi^1 bu^{4}liao^3, hai^2 fen^1 gei^3 mei^{4}mei **ban^{4}la^3** ne.) She could not even finish an apple; she gave half of it to her sister.
ban^{4}shang^3 半晌	半天 (ban^{4}tian^1) a long time	她**半晌**说不出话儿来. (Ta^3 **ban^{4}shang^3** shuo^1 bu chu^1 huar^4 lai^2.) She couldn't utter a word for some while.
bei^{4}xing^4 背兴	倒霉 (dao^{3}mei^2) have bad luck	真**背兴**, 煮熟的鸭子飞了. (Zhen^1 **bei^{4}xing^4**, zhu^3 shou^2 de ya^{1}zi fei^1 le.) What lousy luck, a boiled duck flew away. (meaning some expected benefit is unexpectedly lost)

bər⁴ 倍 儿	分外 (fen⁴wai⁴) particularly	这 鸭 子 浇 上 了 酱 油, 颜 色 **倍 儿** 好 看. (Zhe⁴ ya¹zi jiao¹ shang⁴ le jiang⁴you², yan²se⁴ **bər⁴** hao³kan⁴.) When poured with soy sauce, the duck looks particularly beautiful.
bie²jie 别 介	不 必 (bu²bi⁴) do not do that	您 **别 介**! 我 来 办. (Nin² **bie²jie**! Wo³ lai² ban⁴.) No need for you to do that. Let me do it.
bie³du²zi 瘪 犊 子	窝 囊 废 (wo¹nangfei⁴) useless and worthless wretch	这 个 **瘪 犊 子** 不 靠 准 儿. (Zhe⁴ ge **bie³ du²zi** bu² kao⁴zhuər³.) This worthless wretch is not reliable.
bu² shi⁴ shan⁴char² 不 是 善 茬 儿	霸 道 (ba⁴dao⁴) masterful	她 从 小 就 **不 是 个 善 茬** 儿. (Ta¹ cong² xiao³ jiu⁴ **bu² shi⁴** ge **shan⁴char²**.) She has been very overbearing since she was a child.
cər⁴tou² 刺 儿 头	好 刁 难、不 易 对 付 的 人 (hao⁴ diao¹nan⁴, bu² yi⁴ dui⁴fu de ren²) person who deliberately creates difficulties and hence is hard to deal with	真 倒 霉, 碰 到 了 个 **刺 儿 头**. (Zhen¹ dao³mei², peng⁴ dao le ge **cər⁴tou²**.) What bad luck! The person I met with deliberately raised difficulties for me.
che³ xian²piar¹ 扯 闲 篇 儿	闲 扯 (xian²che³) engage in chitchat	没 功 夫 跟 你 **扯 闲 篇** 儿. (Mei² gong¹fu gen¹ ni² **che³ xian²piar¹**.) I have no time to engage in chitchat with you.
che³dan⁴ 扯 淡	胡 扯 (hu²che³) talk nonsense	别 **扯 淡**, 说 正 经 的. (Bie² **che³dan⁴**, shuo¹ zheng⁴jing de) Don't talk nonsense. Let's stick to the point.
chen¹ 抻	拖 延 (tuo¹yan²) play for time	靠 **抻** 日 子 不 济 事, 还 得 从 根 本 上 想 辙. (Kao⁴ **chen¹** ri⁴zi bu² ji⁴shi⁴, hai² de³ cong² gen¹ben³ shang xiang³ zhe².) To play for time is no help. We have to get at the root.
chi¹buliao³, dou¹zhe zou³ 吃 不 了, 兜 着 走	承 担 严 重 后 果 (cheng²dan¹ yan¹zhong⁴ hou⁴guo³) land oneself in serious trouble	出 了 事 儿, 叫 你 **吃 不 了, 兜 着 走**. (Chu¹ le shər⁴, jiao⁴ ni² **chi¹buliao³, dou¹zhe zou³**.) If anything goes wrong, you will get more than you bargained for.

chi^{1}xin^1 吃 心	用 功 (yong^{4}gong^1) study or work diligently	就冲他这个**吃心**劲儿, 奶奶不愁他考不上哈佛. (Jiu^4 chong^4 ta^1 zhe^4 ge **chi^{1}xin^1** jiər^4, nai^{3}nai bu^4 chou^2 ta^1 kao^1 bu^2 shang^4 Ha^{1}fo^2.) With his steady effort in study, grandma is not concerned about his being admitted to Harvard.
chou^3 瞅	看 (kan^4) take a look	我**瞅**了一眼, 没**瞅**出什么. (Wo^3 **chou^3** le yi^{4}yan^3, mei^2 **chou^3** chu^1 shen^{2}me.) I took a look, but I did not see anything wrong.
chu^1 men^{2}zi 出 门 子	出 嫁 (ch^{1}jia^4) (of women) marry	她两个女儿都早就**出门子**了. (Ta^3 liang^3 ge nü̃er^2 dou^1 zao^3 jiu^4 **chu^1 men^{2}zi** le.) Her two daughters got married and left her long ago.
chui^{1}hu^{2}zi deng^{4}yan^3 吹 胡 子 瞪 眼	发脾气 (fa^1 pi^{2}qi) vent one's spleen on sb.	他老对我**吹胡子瞪眼**的. (Ta^1 lao^3 dui^4 wo^3 **chui^{1}hu^{2}zi deng^{4}yan^3** de.) He always gets angry with me.
chuo^{1}ji^{3}lianggu^3 戳 脊 梁 骨	在背后指责 (zai^4 bei^{4}hou^4 zhi^{3}ze^2) criticize behind sb's back	这么做,不让人**戳**我**脊梁骨**吗? (Zhe^{4}me zuo^4, bu^2 rang^4 ren^2 **chuo^1** wo^3 **ji^{3}lianggu^3** ma?) If I do like this, will people not criticize me behind my back?
ci^{2}shi 瓷 实	扎实 (zha^{1}shi) solid	他天天锻炼,身体很**瓷实**. (Ta^1 tian^{1}tian^1 duan^{4}lian^4, shen^{1}ti^3 hen^3 **ci^{2}shi**.) He exercises every day and is of very solid build.
cou^{4}zhə̃r^3 凑 整 儿	凑成整数 (cou^{4}cheng^2 zheng^{3}shu^4) make a round number	总计二十八块四, 再加一点儿, **凑**个**整**儿吧. (Zong^{3}ji^4 er^{4}shi ba^2 kuai^4 si^4, zai^4 jia^1 yi^{4}diar^3, **cou^4** ge **zhə̃r^3** ba.) The total sum is \$28.4. Add a little more to make it a round number.
cun^4 寸	巧 (qiao^3) opportunely, as luck would have it	你来得真**寸**. 饭刚做好. (Ni^3 lai^2 de zhen^1 **cun^4**. Fan^4 gang^1 zuo^4 hao^3.) You arrived at a most opportune moment. Dinner is just ready.

da²yan³ 打眼 (or 招眼 zhao¹yan³)	引人注意 (yin³ ren² zhu⁴yi⁴) attract attention	你这身打扮多**打眼**啊! (Ni³ zhe⁴ shen¹ da³ban duo¹ **da²yan³** a!) The dress you are wearing is so conspicuous!
da³ zhao⁴miar⁴ 打照面儿	面对面相遇 (mian⁴ dui⁴ mian⁴ xiang¹yu⁴) come face to face with	他和我们**打**了个**照面**儿, 就走了. (Ta¹ he wo³men **da³** le ge **zhao⁴miar⁴**, jiu⁴ zou³ le.) He met us face to face and left right away.
da³ 打	从 (cong²) from	**打**哪儿说起呢? (**Da²** nar³ shuo¹ qi³ ne?) From where should I start?
dai⁴ ge haor³ 带个好儿	问候 (wen⁴hou⁴) say hello to sb.	见到她, 给我**带个好**儿. (Jian⁴ dao ta¹, gei² wo³ **dai⁴ ge haor³**.) Give her my greetings when you see her.
dan¹dai⁴ 担待	1. 担当责任 (dan¹dang¹ ze²ren⁴) bear responsibility 2. 原谅 (yuan²liang⁴) excuse	1. 他们都不在, 你就多**担待**些吧! (Ta¹men dou¹ bu²zai⁴, ni³ jiu⁴ duo¹ **dan¹dai⁴** xie ba!) They are all not here. Please take on more responsibilities! 2. 孩子小, 不懂事, 您多**担待**! (Hai²zi xiao³, bu⁴ dong³shi⁴, nin² duo¹ **dan¹dai⁴**!) The child is small and thoughtless. Please excuse him.
dang¹jiar⁴ 当间儿	中间 (zhong¹jıan¹) middle	照片儿左边儿是爸爸, 右边儿是妈妈, **当间**儿是我. (Zhao⁴piar⁴ zuo³biar¹ shi⁴ ba⁴ba, you⁴biar¹ shi⁴ ma¹ma, **dang¹jiar⁴** shi⁴ wo³.) In this picture on the left is papa, on the right is mom, and I am in the middle.
dang⁴zi 档子	件 (jian⁴) (a measure word)	这**档子**事儿我管不了. (Zhe⁴ **dang⁴zi** shər⁴ wo³ guan³ bu⁴liao³.) Such a thing is not my business.
dao²chi 倒饬	修饰 (xiu¹shi⁴) make up, dress up	您这副长相, 要不好好儿**倒饬倒饬**, 谁会黑上您哪? (Nin² zhe⁴ fu zhang³xiang⁴, yao⁴ bu⁴ hao²haor³ **dao²chi dao²chi**, shei² hui⁴ hei¹ shang⁴ nin² na?) With your features, if you are not decked all out, who will take a fancy to you?
dao⁴daor 道道儿	主意 (zhu³yi) idea	你脑袋里是有点儿**道道**儿. (Ni³ nao³dai⁴ li³ shi⁴ you² diar³ **dao⁴daor**.)

		There are really some ideas in your head.
de^{2}rər^2 得人儿	得人心 (de^2 ren^{2}xin^1) have the support of people	大伙儿都选她. 她**得人**儿. (Da^{4}huor^3 dou^1 xuan^3 ta^1. Ta^1 **de^{2}rər^2**.) Everyone elected her. She enjoys popular support.
de^{2}yãr^4 得样儿	得体 (de^{2}ti^3) appropriate	你穿了这身儿绿色的衣服真**得样**儿. (Ni^3 chuan^1 le zhei^4 shen^1 lü^{4}se^4 de yi^{1}fu zhen^1 **de^{2}yãr^4**.) You are very good looking in this green dress.
dei^3 得	舒服 (shu^{1}fu) comfortable	丈母娘看到了新女婿, 甭提她心眼儿里多**得**了. (Zhang^{4}mu^{3}niang^2 kan^4 dao^4 le xin^1 nü^{3}xu, beng^{2}ti^2 ta xin^{1}yar^3 li duo^1 **dei^3** le.) It warms the corners of her heart to see her new son-in-law.
ding^{1}diar^3 丁点儿	一点儿 (yi^{1}diar^3) a tiny bit	没一**丁点**儿麻烦. (Mei^2 yi^4 **ding^{1}diar^3** ma^{2}fan.) There isn't the slightest trouble.
dong^4 zhen^{1}ge^2 动真格	认真干 (ren^{4}zhen^1 gan^4) start in real earnest	这回他们要**动真格**了. (Zhe^{4}hui^2 ta^{1}men yao^4 **dong^4 zhen^{1}ge^2** le.) This time they will start in real earnest.
dou^{3}lou 抖搂	全部说出 (quan^{2}bu^4 shuo^{1}chu^1) expose	他喝多了, 把老婆的包袱底儿一股脑儿全**抖搂**出来了. (Ta^1 he^1 duo^1 le, ba^2 lao^{3}po^2 de bao^{1}fudiər^3 yi^{4}gu^{2}naor^3 quan^2 **dou^{3}lou** chu^{1}lai le.) He drank a lot and brought all his wife's secrets to light.
dou^{4}men^{1}zi 逗闷子	打趣 (da^{3}qu^4), 寻开心 (xun^2 kai^{1}xin) provoke laughter, make fun of	**逗闷子**得看对象, 这个母老虎是好惹的吗? (**Dou^{4}men^{1}zi** dei^3 kan^4 dui^{4}xiang^4, zhe^4 ge mu^2 lao^{3}hu shi^4 hao^3 re^3 de ma?) You cannot make fun without considering the target. Is that vixen a woman to be trifled with?
dou^{4}gər^2 逗哏儿	逗乐儿 (dou^{4}ler^4) amusing, humorous	他讲的真**逗哏**儿. (Ta^1 jiang^3 de zhen^1 **dou^{4}gər^2**.) What he said is really amusing.
duo^{1}zan 多咱	几时 (ji^{3}shi^1) what time	咱们**多咱**走? Zan^{3}men **duo^{1}zan** zou^3?)

245

		When are we leaving?
fər⁴ 份儿	地步 (di⁴bu) extent, stage	闹到这**份**儿上了, 她还当没事儿呢. (Nao⁴ dao zhe⁴ **fər⁴** shang⁴ le, ta¹ hai² dang⁴ mei²shər⁴ ne.) She got into such a mess, but still thinks everything is all right.
fu²ruar³ 服软儿	道歉 (dao⁴qian⁴) apologize	你去**服**个**软**儿, 不就结了吗? (Ni³ qu⁴ **fu²** ge **ruar³**, bu² jiu⁴ jie¹ le ma?) Just go make an apology, and the problem will be settled.
gan³qing 敢情	1. 原来是 (yuan²lai² shi⁴) so 2. 当然 (dang¹ran²) of course	1. 地上这么湿, **敢情**是昨晚下过雨了. (Di⁴shang zhe⁴me shi¹, **gan³qing** shi zuo² wan³ xia⁴ guo yu³ le.) The ground is wet, so it rained last night. 2. 你有大门子, 那**敢情**好. (Ni² you³ da⁴ men²zi, na⁴ **gan³qing** hao³.) You have a strong pull. That will be certainly wonderful.
gan³tãr⁴ 赶趟儿 (or gen¹tãr 跟趟儿)	来得及 (lai²deji²) be in time	你麻利些吧! 不马上走可就**赶**不上**趟**儿了. (Ni³ ma²li xie ba! Bu⁴ ma³shang⁴ zou³ ke³ jiu⁴ **gan³** bu²shang⁴ **tãr⁴** le.) Be quick! We'll be late if we don't leave at once.
ger⁴ 个儿	对手 (dui⁴shou³) match, competitor	他练过拳击, 就是三五个人也休想傍边儿, 哪是他的**个**儿! (Ta¹ lian⁴ guo quan³qi¹; jiu⁴shi⁴ san¹ wu⁵ ge ren² ye³ xiu¹ xiang³ bang⁴biar¹, na³ shi⁴ ta¹de **ger⁴**!) He practiced boxing; even three or five people cannot get close. They are no match for him!
guo⁴jier² 过节儿	心结 (xin¹jie²) grudge	他跟你有什么**过节**儿啊? (Ta¹ gen¹ ni³ you³ shen²me **guo⁴jier²** a?) What kind of animosity is there between you and him?
guo⁴xin¹ 过心	多心 (duo¹xin¹) suspicious, oversensitive	我不是说你, 你别**过心**. (Wo³ bu²shi⁴ shuo¹ ni³, ni³ bie² **guo⁴xin¹**.) I don't mean you. Don't be

246

		oversensitive.
han^{2}chen 寒碜 (or 寒伧)	1. 丢脸 (diu^{1}lian^3) be ashamed 2. 讥笑 (ji^{1}xiao^4) ridicule	1. 我**寒碜**, 没钱救灾. (Wo^3 **han^{2}chen**, mei^2 qian^2 jiu^4 zai^1.) I feel rather mean for not being able to donate for the disaster. 2. 你绕着弯儿**寒碜**我. (Ni^3 rao^3 zhe war^1 **han^{2}chen** wo^3.) You are making fun of me in a roundabout way.
hao^{3}shuo^1 好说	1. 好商量 (hao^3 shang^{1}liang) that can be talked over 2. 不敢当 (bu^{4}gan^{3}dang^1) not deserve it	1. 这事**好说**. (Zhe^4 shi^4 **hao^{3}shuo^1**.) This can be discussed. 2. **好说**! 你过奖了. (**Hao^{3}shuo^1**! Ni^3 guo^{4}jiang^3 le.) It's very good of you to say so. You flatter me.
he^{1}yi^{4}hu^2 喝一壶	受苦 (shou^{4}ku^3) suffer	在他上司前奏一本, 就够他**喝一壶**的. (Zai^4 ta^1 shang^{4}si^1 qian^2 zou^4 yi^{4}ben^3, jiu^4 gou^4 ta^1 **he^{1}yi^{4}hu^2** de.) If his conduct is reported to his superior, he will suffer.
hu^{2}zhou^1 胡诌	瞎编造 (xia^4 bian^{3}zao^4) fabricate	别**胡诌**了. 家走歇歇吧. (Bie^2 **hu^{2}zhou^1** le. Jia^1 zou^3 xie^{1}xie ba.) Stop making up wild stories. Go home and take a rest.
huai^{4}shuər^3 坏水儿	坏主意 (huai^4 zhu^{3}yi) dirty tricks	她一肚子**坏水**儿. (Ta^1 yi^{2}du^{4}zi **huai^{4}shuər^3**.) She is full of evil intention.
ji^{1}li ga^{1}lar^2 叽里旮旯儿	每个角落 (mei^3 ge jia^{3}luo^4) out-of-the-way place	叽里**旮旯**儿都找过了. (**Ji^{1}li ga^{1}lar^2** dou^1 zhao^3 guo le.) Every nook and cranny has been searched.
ji^{3}dui^4 挤对	压服 (ya^{1}fu^2) force sb. to yield	别再**挤对**你老公了. 让他喘口气吧. (Bie^2 zai^4 **ji^{3}dui^4** ni^2 lao^{3}gong^1 le. Rang^4 ta^1 chuan^2 kou^3 qi^4 ba.) Stop forcing your husband to yield. Let him have a breathing space.
jian^{3}lou^4 拣漏	得到意外的好处 (de^{2}dao^4 yi^{4}wai^4 de hao^{3}chu) pick up a good bargain, gain extra	花了一百块买了这个瓷瓶, 真让你**拣**到大**漏**了. (Hua^{1}le yi^{4}bai^3 kuai^4 mai^3 le zhei^4 ge ci^2 ping^1, zhen^1 rang^4 ni^2 **jian^3** dao^4 da^4 **lou^4** le.)

247

	unexpected advantage	You Paid $100 for that porcelain vase? You really picked up a good bargain.
jie^{1}char^2 接茬儿	接腔 (jie^{1}qiang^1) pick up the thread of a conversation and take part in it	他说了半天,没一个**接**他**茬**儿.的. (Ta^1 shuo^1 le ban^{4}tian^1, mei^2 yi^{2}ge **jie^1** ta^1 **char^2** de.) He talked for a long time, but nobody responded.
jie^{3}qi^4 解气	出气 (chu^{1}qi^4) work off one's anger	今天真**解气**. (Jin^{1}tian^1 zhen^1 **jie^{3}qi^4**.) Today I really felt avenged.
jie^4 yi^{2}bu^4 借一步	挪个地方 (nuo^2 ge di^{4}fang) change a place to do sth.	**借一步**说话. (**Jie^4 yi^{2}bu^4** shuo^{1}hua^4.) Let's change a place to talk.
jie^{4}guang^1 借光	劳驾 (lao^{2}jia^4) excuse me	**借光**, 请让让路. (**Jie^{4}guang^1**, qing^3 rang^{4}rang lu^4.) Excuse me, let me pass.
kai^{1}shuan^4 开涮	耍弄 (shua^{1}nong^4) make fun of	谁把我**开涮**了? (Shei^2 ba^2 wo^3 **kai^{1}shuan^4** le?) Who has tricked me?
kang^2 扛	撑 (cheng^1) sustain	他**扛**不住了. (Ta^1 **kang^2** bu^{2}zhu^4 le.) He can't last any longer.
ke^{3}xin^1 可心	合意 (he^{2}yi^4) be to one's liking	他娶了个**可心**的老婆. (Ta^1 qu^3 lc gc **ke^{3}xin^1** dc lao^{3}po^2.) He married a woman who met his wishes.
kou^{3}zhong^4 口重	1. 咸 (xian^2) salty 2. 爱吃咸的饮食 (ai^4 chi^1 xian^2 de yin^{3}shi^2) be fond of salty food	1. 我血压高,不能吃**口重**的. (Wo^3 xue^{4}ya^1 gao^1, bu^4 neng^2 chi^1 **kou^{3}zhong^4** de.) I have high blood pressure; I can't eat salty things. 2. 我**口重**. (Wo^2 **kou^{3}zhong^4**.) I like salty food.
lai^{2}zhe ...来着	(表示曾发生过某事) (biao^{3}shi^4 ceng^2 fa^{1}shen^1 guo mou^3 shi^4) (indicating sth. has happened)	你刚才说什么**来着**? (Ni^3 gang^{1}cai^2 shuo^1 shen^{2}me **lai^{2}zhe**?) What were you saying just then?
lao^{3}bi^{2}zi le 老鼻子了	多极了 (duo^1 ji^{2}le) plentiful	这种花天南地北**老鼻子了**. (Zhe^4 zhong^3 hua^1 tian^{1}nan^{3}di^{4}bai^3 **lao^{3}bi^{2}zi le**.)

		This flower is very abundant all over the country.
le⁴he 乐和	作乐（zuo⁴le⁴） seek pleasure and make merry	人老了,还能指着谁啊? 能**乐和**一天就**乐和**一天吧! Ren² lao³ le, hai² neng² zhi³ zhe shei³ a? Neng¹ **le⁴he** yi⁴tian¹ jiu⁴ **le⁴he** yi⁴tian¹ ba!) When one gets old, who can he depend on? He should, if possible, seek pleasure everyday.
leng⁴ 愣	1. 发呆 (fa¹dai¹) fall into a trance 2. 偏偏 (pian¹pian¹) in a firm manner	1. 你打什么**愣**儿? (Ni³ da³ shen²me **lə̃r⁴**?) Why are you in a daze? 2. 我好说歹说,他**愣**不答应. (Wo³ hao³shuo¹ dai³shuo¹, ta¹ **leng⁴** bu⁴ da¹ying.) I tried every possible way to persuade him, but he wouldn't agree.
lia³ 俩	两个 (liang³ge) two	一共五个,我吃了**俩**,她吃了仨. (Yi²gong⁴ wu³ ge, wo³ chi¹ le **lia³**, ta¹ chi¹ le sa¹.) There were altogether five. I ate two and she ate three.
liang²kou³zi 两口子	夫妻俩 (fu¹qi¹lia³) husband and wife	**两口子** 三天两头儿吵架. (**Liang²kou³zi** san¹ tian¹ liang³ tour² chao³jia⁴.) The couple quarrels almost every day.
liã⁴亮儿	灯火 (deng¹huo²) light	这黑灯瞎火的,拿个**亮**儿来吧. (Zhe⁴ hei¹deng¹xia⁴huo³ de, na¹ ge **liã⁴** lai² ba.) It's so dark. Bring me a light.
lin²liaor³ 临了儿	到最后 (dao⁴ zui⁴hou⁴) in the end	**临了**儿中国队进了个球. (**Lin²liaor³** zhong¹guo² dui⁴ jin⁴ le ge qiu².) The Chinese team kicked a goal in the end.
liu¹mər² 溜门儿	偷偷进门行窃 (tou¹tou¹ jin⁴men² xing² qie⁴) break into a house to steal	这阵儿**溜门**儿橇锁的特多. (Zhe⁴ zhər⁴ **liu¹mər²** qiao⁴suo³ de te⁴ duo⁴.) There have been numerous burglaries recently.
liu⁴war¹ 遛弯儿	散步 (san⁴bu⁴) take a walk	我刚才在花园里**遛**了个**弯**儿. (Wo³ gang¹cai² zai⁴ hua¹yuan² li **liu⁴** le ge¹ **war¹**.)

		I was taking a walk in the garden just then.
lou⁴dou¹ 漏兜	说漏了嘴 (shuo¹ lou⁴ le zui³) blurt sth. out	她话说得太多了. 说**漏兜**啦. (Ta¹ hua⁴ shuo¹ de tai⁴ duo¹ le. Shuo¹ **lou⁴dou¹** la.) She talked too much and thoughtlessly blurted something out.
lou⁴qie⁴ 露祛	出洋相 (chu¹ yang²xiang⁴) make an exhibition of oneself	那个老赶在城里到处**露祛**. (Nei⁴ ge lao²gan³ zai⁴ cheng² li dao⁴chu⁴ **lou⁴qie⁴**.) Everywhere in the city the country bumpkin made an exhibition of himself.
luo⁴haor³ 落好儿	得到称赞 (de²dao⁴ cheng¹zan⁴) win praise	他们的私事儿, 你去瞎搀和! 费了工夫, 还不**落好**儿. (Ta¹men de si¹shər⁴, ni³ qu⁴ xia¹ chan¹huo! Fei⁴ le gong¹fu, hai² bu² **luo⁴haor³**.) You participated in their private affair! You put in a lot of time, but was rewarded a thankless result.
mang²huo 忙活	忙碌 (mang²lu⁴) be busy	他成天价瞎**忙活**. (Ta¹ cheng²tian¹ jie xia¹ **mang²huo**.) He is busy for nothing all day long.
mei²yãr⁴ 没样儿	没规矩 (mei³ gui¹ju) badly-behaved	这孩子被大人惯得真**没样**儿了. (Zhe⁴ hai²zi bei⁴ da⁴ren² guan⁴ de zhen¹ **mei²yãr⁴** le.) The child who is spoiled by his parents behaves really badly.
mei²yiə̃r³ 没影儿	没根据 (mei² gen¹ju⁴) fictitious, groundless	她尽说些**没影**儿的事. (Ta¹jin⁴ shuo¹ xie¹ **mei²yiə̃r³** de shi⁴.) She is always talking about fictitious things.
mei²zhuər³ 没准儿	不一定 (bu⁴ yi²ding⁴) not definite	她来不来还**没个准**儿呢. (Ta¹ lai²bulai² hai² **mei² ge zhuər³** ne.) It's not clear whether she will come or not.
mi²deng 迷瞪	糊涂 (hu²tu) confused	你越讲我越**迷瞪**. (Ni³ yue⁴ jiang³ wo³ yue⁴ **mi²deng**.) The more you talk, the more confused I am.
mo²zui³pi²zi 磨嘴皮子	多费口舌 (duo¹ fei⁴ kou³she²) do a lot of idle talking	没时间和你**磨嘴皮子**. (Mei² shi²jian¹ he² ni³ **mo²zui³pi²zi**.) I have no time to waste my breath with you.

250

na²shi²hou 拿时候	解饱 (jie²bao³) delay the feeling of hungry	我不饿, 早上吃 的蛋炒饭**拿时候**. (Wo³ bu² e⁴, zao³shang chi¹ de dan⁴chao³fan⁴ **na²shi²hou**.) I am not hungry. The rice fried with eggs I ate this morning keeps me full.
na²tang² 拿糖	拿乔 (na²qiao¹), 故意表示为难 (gu⁴yi⁴ biao³shi⁴ wei²nan²) purposely express that there are difficulties in order to gain advantage	有什么条件直说吧.别**拿糖**了. (You³ shen²me tiao²jian⁴ zhi²shuo¹ ba. Bie² **na²tang²** le.) Say outright what conditions you want. Don't invent any excuse of having difficulties.
nai³men²zi 哪门子	什么 (表示不存在) (shen²me, biao³shi⁴ bu⁴ cun³zai⁴) what (showing there is really not such a thing)	你说的是**哪门子**事儿啊? (Ni³ shuo¹de shi **nai³men²zi** shər⁴ a?) What the hell are you talking about?
ning⁴ 拧	倔强 (jue²jiang⁴) pigheaded	你这个孬种可怎么这么**拧**呢? (Ni³ zhe⁴ ge nao¹zhong³ ke² zen³me zhe⁴me **ning⁴** ne?) You bad egg! Why are you so stubborn?
pao⁴niur¹ 泡妞儿	和女孩子一起吃喝玩乐 (he² nü³ hai²zi yi⁴qi³ chi¹he¹wan³le⁴) idle away one's time in pleasure-seeking with girls	他整天就是**泡妞**儿. (Ta² zheng³tian¹ jiu⁴ shi **pao⁴niur¹**.) He idles away all his time in pleasure-seeking with girls.
qiao²ni³shuo¹de 瞧你说的	哪里 (用于否定对方的话) (na³li) (yong⁴yu² fou³ding⁴ dui⁴fang¹ de hua⁴) not as what you said	**瞧你说的**! 我哪有你说的那么好 啊? (**Qiao²ni³shuo¹de**! Wo² na³you²ni³ shuo¹ de ne⁴me hao³ a?) What are you saying? Am I as good as what you said?
qu⁴le …去了	非常 (fei¹chang²) very, much	他到过的地方多得**去了**. (Ta¹ dao⁴ guo de di⁴fang duo¹de **qu⁴ le**.) He has been to so many places.
rao⁴bo²zi 绕脖子	转弯抹角 (zhuan³wan¹ mo⁴ jiao⁴) talk in a roundabout way	有话直说吧, 不要跟我**绕脖子** 啦. (You³ hua⁴ zhi²shuo¹ ba, bu² yao⁴ gen¹ wo³ **rao⁴bo²zi** la.)

251

		If you have anything to say, say it. Don't beat about the bush.
shang⁴huor³ 上火儿	生气 (sheng¹qi⁴) get angry	别**上火儿**,有话儿慢慢儿说. (Bie² **shang⁴huor³**, you³ huar⁴ man⁴mar shuo¹.) Don't be angry; take your time to say what you want to say.
shi²duo 拾掇	整理 (zhen²li³) tidy up	她从来就不**拾掇**屋子. (Ta¹ cong²lai² jiu⁴ bu⁴ **shi²duo** wu¹zi.) She never cleans her room.
shi³huai⁴ 使坏	出坏主意 (chu¹ huai⁴ chu³yi) suggest a bad idea	是她**使**的**坏**. (Shi⁴ ta¹ **shi³** de **huai⁴**.) It was she that suggested the evil idea.
shou⁴kan⁴ 受看	好看 (hao³kan⁴) good looking	武家的二郎比大郎**受看**. (Wu³ jia¹ de er⁴ long² bi³ da⁴ long² **shou⁴kan⁴**.) The second son in the Wu family is better looking than the first son.
sou¹ zhu³yi 馊主意	不高明的想法 (bu⁴ gao¹ming² de xiang³fa) rotten idea	你一准儿又有什么**馊主意**了. (Ni³ yi⁴zhuər³ you⁴ you³ shen²me **sou¹ zhu³yi** le.) I'm sure that a rotten idea has occurred to you.
sun³ 损	1.用尖刻的话挖苦人 (yong⁴ jian¹ke⁴ de hua⁴ wa¹ku ren²) make caustic remarks against sb. 2.刻薄 (ke⁴bo²), 恶毒 (e⁴du³) mean, shabby	1. 您这是夸我还是**损**我啊? (Nin² zhe⁴ shi⁴ kua¹ wo³ hai²shi **sun³** wo³ a'?) Are you saying it to praise me or to insult me? 2. 你这招不是忒**损**了吧? (Ni³ zhe⁴ zhao¹ bu² shi⁴ tei¹ **sun³** le ba?) Is that trick of yours not mean enough?
tao²huan 淘换	寻觅 (xun²mi⁴) seek	我没地跟你**淘换**去. (Wo³ mei² di⁴ gen¹ ni³ **tao²huan** qu.) Nowhere can I find it for you.
tao⁴jin⁴hu 套近乎	拉关系 (la¹ guan¹xi⁴) ingratiate oneself with	他想跟我女儿**套近乎**. 没门儿! (Ta¹ xiang³ gen¹ wo² nü³er² **tao⁴jin⁴hu**. Mei²mər².) He wants to make advances to my daughter. Not a chance!
tian¹du³ 添堵	让人心烦 (rang⁴ ren² xin¹fan²) annoy	他成心跟我**添堵**. (Ta¹ cheng²xin¹ gen¹ wo³ **tian¹du³**.) He deliberately upset me.

tiao^{1}yan^3 挑眼	多方挑剔 (duo^{1}fang^1 tiao^{1}ti^1) be fastidious, find fault in many ways	你干吗横挑鼻子竖**挑眼**的? (Ni^3 gan^{4}ma^2 heng^2 tiao^1 bi^{2}zi shu^4 **tiao^{1}yan^3** de?) Why on earth are you so hypercritical?
ting^{1}chuang^{2}hugər^1 听窗户根儿	偷听 (tou^{1}ting^1) eavesdrop	她喜欢**听窗户根**儿. (Ta^1 xi^{3}huan **ting^1 chuang^{2}hugər^1**.) She likes to eavesdrop.
tong^3 lou^{2}zi 捅娄子	惹祸 (re^{3}huo^4) start trouble	你**捅**大**娄子**啦. (Ni^2 **tong^3** da^4 **lou^{2}zi** la.) You've started big trouble.
wan^{2}yiər^4 玩意儿	东西 (dong^{1}xi^1) thing	什么新鲜**玩意**儿? (Shen^{2}me xin^{1}xian^1 **wan^{2}yiər^4**?) What newfangled gadget? 你是个什么**玩意**儿? (Ni^3 shi^4 ge shen^{2}me **wan^{2}yiər^4**?) What the hell are you?
war^3 bu zhuan^4 玩儿 不转	应付不了 (ying^{4}fu bu^{4}liao^3) difficult to deal with the situation	离开了你,他们就**玩**儿得**不太转**了. (Li^{2}kai^1 le ni^3, ta^{1}men jiu^4 **war^3** de **bu^2** tai^4 **zhuan^4** le.) They can hardly get along well without you.
war^3 de zhuan^4 玩儿 得转	应付得了 (ying^{4}fu de liao^3) handle a situation with ease	三个人干的事儿你一个人干,你**玩**儿**得转**吗? (San^1 ge ren^2 gan^4 de shər^4 ni^3 yi^2 ge ren^2 gan^4, ni^3 **war^3 de zhuan^4** ma?) You are doing the job that is supposed to be done by three people. Can you handle it?
wo^1 窝	郁积着 (yue^{1}ji^1 zhe) hold in	你心里老**窝**着这些事,病会好吗? (Ni^2 xin^1 li lao^3 **wo^1** zhe zhe^{4}xie shi^4, bing^4 hui^4 hao^3 ma?) How can you recover with all these feelings held in?
wo^{1}bo^3 窝脖	碰一鼻子灰 (peng^4 yi^4 bi^{2}zi hui^1) meet with a rebuff, get snubbed	她给我来了个大**窝脖**. (Ta^1 gei^2 wo^3 lai^2 le ge da^1 **wo^{1}bo^3**.) She gave a big rebuff to me.
xi^{4}gao^{1}tiaor^3 细高 挑儿	瘦长 (shou^{4}chang^2) tall and slim	他的女朋友是个**细高挑**儿. (Ta^1 de nü^{3}peng^{2}you shi^4 ge **xi^{4}gao^{1}tiaor^3**.) His girlfriend is a tall, slim girl.

253

xiãr³ 响 儿	声音 (sheng¹yin¹) sound	没 响 儿 了. (Mei² **xiãr³** le.) No sound was heard.
xiao¹bai¹ 瞎掰	徒劳 (tu²lao²) futile effort, in vain	你 没 预约 就 跑去, 不 是 **瞎掰** 吗? (Ni³ mei² yu⁴yue¹ jiu⁴ pao² qu⁴, bu²shi⁴ **xiao¹bai¹** ma?) It would be futile to go there without making an appointment first.
xiao¹ting 消停	停息, 安定 (ting²xi¹, an¹ding⁴) stop, come to an end	他 打点 了 好多人, 但 还是 **消停** 不了. (Ta¹ da²dian³ le hao³ duo¹ ren², dan⁴ hai²shi⁴ **xiao¹ting** bu⁴liao³.) Though many people were bribed, still the case cannot be settled.
xiao²jiu²jiu³ 小九九	盘算 (pan²suan⁴) planning, selfish calculation	大伙儿 心中 都 有 个 **小九九**. (Da⁴huor³ xin¹ zhong¹ dou¹ you³ ge **xiao²jiu²jiu³**.) Everyone has his own calculations in mind.
xiao³ 小	将近 (jiang¹jin⁴) nearly, close to	我 住 这儿 快 **小** 十 年 了. (Wo³ zhu⁴ zher⁴ kuai⁴ **xiao³** shi² nian¹le.) I have been living here for almost ten years.
xie¹cai⁴ 歇菜	算了 (suan⁴ le) stop thinking about doing sth.	你 有 六十 了 吧? 反正 扒 边儿 了. 还 想 学 拳击 呢. **歇菜** 吧 你! (Ni³ you³ liu⁴shi le ba? Fan³zheng⁴ ba¹biar le. Hai² xiang³ xue² quan²ji¹ ne, **xie¹cai⁴** ba ni³!) You are sixty? Anyhow, approaching sixty. You still want to learn boxing? Forget about it!
xie²mər² 邪门儿	不正常 (bu² zheng⁴chang²) strange, odd	我 觉得 **邪门**儿 呢. (Wo³ jue²de **xie²mər²** ne.) I feel something strange.
xing¹xu³ 兴许	也许 (ye²xu³) perhaps	问 老张, **兴许** 他 知道. (Wen⁴ Lao³ Zhang¹, **xing¹xu³** ta¹ zhi¹dao.) Ask Lao Zhang. He may know it.
xiu³ 宿	夜 (ye³) night	我 整 宿 没 睡觉. (Wo³ zheng² **xiu³** mei² shui⁴jiao⁴.) I did not sleep the whole night.
ya⁴gər¹ 压根儿	根本 (gen¹ben²) from the start	别 听 她 的. **压根**儿 没 这 档子 事儿. (Bie² ting¹ ta² de. **Ya⁴gər¹** mei² zhe⁴ dang²zi shər⁴.) Don't listen to her. It is sheer fiction

		from the very beginning.
yao^{1}e^{2}zi 幺蛾子	鬼 点 子 (gui^2 dian^{3}zi) wicked idea	她 出 的 **幺蛾子** 真 绝, 把 他 治 得 一 愣 一 愣 的. (Ta^1 chu^1 de **yao^{1}e^{2}zi** zhen^1 jue^2, ba^3 ta^1 zhi^4 de yi^2 leng^4 yi^2 leng^4 de.) The wicked suggestion she gave was wonderfully effective. She rendered him stunned.
yi^{4}gen^{1}jiər^1 一根筋儿	死 心 眼儿 (si^{3}xin^{1}yar^3) one-track mind	你 真 是 **一根筋**儿, 不 知 变 通. (Ni^3 zhen^1 shi^4 **yi^{4}gen^{1}jiər^1**, bu^4 zhi^1 bian^{4}tong.) You are a man of one-track mind. You don't know how to be flexible.
yi^{4}lian^{3}qiər^4 一连气儿	一 口 气 (yi^{4}kou^{3}qi^4) in one breath	她 **一连气**儿 唱 了 五 六 个 歌儿. (Ta^1 **yi^{4}lian^{3}qiər^4** chang^4 le wu^3 liu^4 ge ger^1.) She sang five or six songs in one breath.
yi^{4}sər^3 一死儿	固 执 (gu^{4}zhi^2) stubbornly	不 让 她 去, 她 **一死**儿 要 去. (Bu^2 rang^4 ta^1 qu^4, ta^1 **yi^{4}sər^3** yao^4 qu^4.) Though she is not allowed to go, she persists in going.
yi^{4}shi^{2}ban^{4}huər^4 一时半会儿	短 时 间 (duan^3 shi^{2}jian^1) a little while	这 场 雨 **一时半会**儿 停 不 了. (Zhe^4 chang^2 yu^3 **yi^{4}shi^{2}ban^{4}huər^4** ting^2 bu^{4}liao^3.) The rain won't stop in a little while.
yi^{4}tour^2 一头儿	一 块 (yi^{2}kuai^4) together	我 和 美 美 是 **一头**儿 在 鲜 鱼 胡 同 长 大 的. (Wo^3 he^2 Mei^{2}mei^3 shi **yi^{4}tour^2** zai^4 Xian^{1}yu Hu^{2}tong zhang^3 da^4 de.) Meimei and I were brought up together in Xianyu Hutong.
yi^{4}xiaor^3 一小儿	从 小 (cong^{2}xiao^3) from childhood	他 **一小**儿 就 爱 运 动. (Ta^1 **yi^{4}xiaor^3** jiu^4 ai^4 yun^{4}dong^4.) He has loved sports ever since he was a child.
yi^{4}zhuər^3 一准儿	一 定 (yi^{2}ding^4) surely	王 先 生 还 没 到, **一准**儿 是 塞 车 了. (Wang^2 xian^{1}sheng hai^2 mei^2 dao^4, **yi^{4}zhuər^3** shi sai^{1}che^{1}le.) M r. Wang has not come; he must be stuck in a traffic jam.
yi^{4}zõr^3 一总儿	一 并 (yi^{2}bing^4) in the lump	月 底 我 **一总**儿 给 钱. (Yue^4 di^3 wo^3 **yi^{4}zõr^3** gei^3 qian^2.) I'll pay you a lump sum at the end of the month.

ying²shḗr 营生儿	工作 (gong¹zuo⁴) job	吃喝玩乐就是他的**营生**儿. (Chi¹he¹wan²le⁴ jiu⁴ shi ta¹de **ying²shḗr¹**.) His job consists of eating, drinking, and pleasure seeking.
you¹zhe 悠着	控制点劲 (kong⁴zhi⁴ dian³ jin⁴) take things easy	你**悠着**点儿, 慢慢来. (Ni³ **you¹zhe** diar³, man⁴man lai³.) Take it easy! Take your time.
you²zi 油子	阅历多而油滑的 人 (yue⁴li⁴ duo¹ er² you²hua² de ren²) foxy old hand, person full of craft	要学好京腔, 去找两个京**油子**. (Yao⁴ xue² hao³ jing¹qiang¹, qu⁴ zhao³ liang³ ge jing¹ **you²zi**.) To master Beijing dialect, find a couple of native Beijing foxy old hands for help.
you³ bi²zi you²yar³ 有鼻子有眼儿	说得逼真 (shuo¹ de bi¹zhen¹) describe in detail as if sth. is true	她说得**有鼻子有眼**儿的, 千万别 信他. (Ta¹ shuo¹ de **you³ bi²zi you²yar³** de, qian¹wan⁴ bie² xin⁴ ta.) She described it in such vivid detail that it sounded quite real. Don't believe her.
zai⁴pur³ 在谱儿	在理 (zai¹li³) reasonable	他说的不**在谱**儿. (Ta¹ shuo¹ de bu² **zai⁴pur³**.) What he said is not reasonable.
zao¹gai³ 糟改	用语言戏弄 (yong⁴ yu³yan² xi⁴nong⁴), 挖 苦 (wa¹ku) play tricks on, tease	干吗呀你? 净是绕脖子**糟改**我. (Gan⁴ma² ya ni³? Jing⁴ shi rao⁴ bo²zi **zao¹gai²** wo³.) What are you doing? You are keeping teasing me in a roundabout way.
zen³mezhe 怎么 着	怎么做 (zen³me zuo⁴) how to do, what to do	一个人不能想**怎么着**就**怎么着**. (Yi² ge ren² bu⁴ neng² xiang³ **zen³mezhe** jiu⁴ **zen³mezhe**.) No one can just do as he pleases.
zha¹duir 扎堆儿	聚在一起 (ju² zai⁴ yi⁴qi³) gather together	这些老太太每天吃完晚饭就**扎 堆**儿聊天. (Zhe⁴xie¹ lao³ tai⁴tai mei³tian¹ chi¹ wan² wan³fan⁴ jiu⁴ **zha¹duir** liao²tian¹.) After every supper these old ladies gather together to have a chat.
zha⁴cər⁴ 炸刺儿	吭声 (keng¹sheng¹) utter a sound	只要老板娘一吱声儿, 没有敢**炸 刺**儿的. (Zhi³yao⁴ lao²ban³niang² yi⁴ zi¹shḗr¹, mei²you³ gan³ **zha⁴cər⁴** de.) When the proprietress says something, no one dares to utter a sound.

zhang¹luo 张罗	1. 应酬 (ying⁴chou), 招待 (zhao¹dai⁴) greet and entertain 2. 忙 (mang²) take care, get busy	1. 您别**张罗**了, 我们一会儿就走. (Nin² bie² **zhang¹luo** le, wo³men yi²huər jiu⁴zou³.) Don't bother about anything. We'll only stay for a few minutes. 2. 孩子们的事儿让他们自个儿去**张罗**吧. (Hai²zi men de shər⁴ rang⁴ta¹men zi⁴ger³ qu⁴ **zhang¹luo** ba.) Let the children take care of their own affairs.
zhang²lian³ 长脸	增光 (zeng¹guang¹) do credit to	孙子考上了哈佛, 为奶奶**长脸**. (Sun¹zi kao³ shang⁴ le ha¹fo², wei⁴ nai³nai **zhang²lian³**.) Her grandson was enrolled by Harvard and this adds luster to her face.
zhang³ xin¹yar³ 长心眼儿	开窍 (kai¹qiao⁴), 逐渐懂事 (zhu²jian⁴ dong³shi⁴) grow up and gradually be sensible	孩子**长心眼**儿了. 说话得小心. (Hai²zi **zhang³ xin¹yar³** le. Shuo¹hua⁴ dei³ xiao³xin¹.) The children have smartened up. You'd better talk carefully.
zhao⁴miar⁴ 照面儿	露面 (lou⁴mian⁴), 现身 (xian⁴shen¹) let oneself be seen, make an appearance	他半个月都不**照个面**儿. (Ta¹ ban⁴ ge yue⁴ dou¹ bu² **zhao⁴** ge **miar⁴**.) He hasn't shown his face for half a month.
zhe⁴mezhe 这么着	就这样 (jiu⁴ zhe⁴yang⁴) like this, this way	不**这么着**, 那怎么着? (Bu² **zhe⁴mezhe**, na⁴ zen²mezhe?) If we do not do it like this, what can we do?
zhen¹zhao¹ 真招	清楚 (qing¹chu) clear	那台液晶电视倍儿**真招**. (Na⁴ tai² ye⁴jing¹ dian⁴shi⁴ bər⁴ **zhen¹zhao¹**.) That LCD TV is really clear.
zhi¹zhaor¹ 支招儿	从旁替别人出主意 (cong²pang² ti⁴ bie²ren² chu¹ zhu³yi) make suggestions for others at his side	看棋**支招**儿也可以集思广益啊. (Kan⁴ qi² **zhi¹zhaor¹** ye³ ke²yi³ ji²si¹ guang³yi⁴ a.) To offer advice when watching chess will contribute to brainstorming.
zhu³xin¹gu³ 主心骨	靠山 (kao⁴shan¹) backbone, chief support	我们把他看作是我们的**主心骨**. (Wo³men ba³ ta¹ kan⁴zuo⁴ shi⁴ wo³men de **zhu³xin¹gu³**.) We regard him as our backbone.
zhuan⁴you 转悠	闲溜达 (xian²	我到商场去**转悠**了一下.

	liu¹da) stroll	(Wo³ dao⁴ shang¹chang³ qu⁴ **zhuan⁴you** le yi²xia⁴.) I went for a walk in the mall.
zhur³ 主儿	某种类型的人 (mou² zhong³ lei⁴xing² de ren²) a person of certain type	他是个蛮不讲理的主儿. (Ta¹ shi⁴ ge man¹bu⁴ jiang²li³ de **zhur³**.) This chap is never governed by reason.
zi¹ 滋	喷 (pen¹) gush up	罐子的拉襻一拉开, 可乐就**滋**到 天花板上去了. (Guan⁴zi de la¹pan⁴ yi⁴ la¹ kai¹, ke³le⁴ jiu⁴ **zi¹** dao⁴ tian¹hua¹ban³ shang qu⁴le.) When the tab of the can was lifted, the soda gushed up to the ceiling.
zuo¹bie³zi 喝瘪 子	让人难堪 (rang⁴ ren² nan²kan¹) put sb. in an awkward situation	你是不是想让我**喝瘪子**? (Ni³ shi⁴bushi⁴ xiang³ rang⁴ wo³ **zuo¹bie³zi**?) You intend to embarrass me, don't you?
zuo³bulie¹ 左不 列	左撇子 (zuo²pie³zi) left-handed	克林顿和奥巴马都是**左不列** 吗? (Ke⁴lin²dun⁴ he² Ao⁴ba¹ma³ dou¹ shi⁴ **zuo³ bulie¹** ma?) Are both Clinton and Obama left- handed?